EUROPEAN STUDIES SERIES

General Editors	Colin Jones
	Richard Overy
Series Advisers	Joe Bergin
	John Breuilly
	Ruth Harris

This series marks a major initiative in European history publishing aimed primarily, though not exclusively, at an undergraduate audience. It will encompass a wide variety of books on aspects of European history since 1500, with particular emphasis on France and Germany, although no country will be excluded and a special effort will be made to cover previously neglected areas, such as Scandinavia, Eastern Europe and Southern Europe.

The series will include political accounts and broad thematic treatments, both of a comparative kind and studies of a single country, and will lay particular emphasis on social and cultural history where this opens up fruitful new ways of examining the past. The aim of the series is to make available a wide range of titles in areas where there is now an obvious gap or where the existing historical literature is out of date or narrowly focused. The series will also include translations of important books published elsewhere in Europe.

Interest in European affairs and history has never been greater; *European Studies* will help make that European heritage closer, richer and more comprehensible.

EUROPEAN STUDIES SERIES

Published

Forthcoming

More titles are in preparation

The Birth of Absolutism

A History of France, 1598–1661

YVES-MARIE BERCÉ

Translated by Richard Rex

© Editions du Seuil 1992
English translation © Macmillan Press Ltd 1996

Published 1996 by
MACMILLAN PRESS LTD
Houndmills, Basingstoke, Hampshire RG21 2XS
and London
Companies and representatives
throughout the world

Originally published by Editions du Seuil, Paris, under the title *La naissance
dramatique de l'absolutisme, 1598-1661* (1992)

ISBN 0-333-62756-3 hardcover
ISBN 0-333-62757-1 paperback

10 9 8 7 6 5 4 3 2 1
05 04 03 02 01 00 99 98 97 96

A catalogue record for this book is available
from the British Library.

Typeset by Nick Allen/Longworth Editorial Services
Longworth, Oxfordshire.

Printed in Malaysia

Contents

Foreword

You have in your hands a work which I would certainly never have undertaken of my own accord if the publisher had not approached me to do so. It has turned out to be an incomparable way of discovering a period of history which I reckoned I knew well. I have had to spend time reflecting on whether to include this battle or that edict, whether they deserve a place in a necessarily brief account, or whether they illustrate some general trend, in order to assess the significance of particular events and individuals within their historical context.

The work is a history of France, a genre with a long ancestry, and one which arouses certain almost stereotyped expectations in readers. It must of necessity contain the tale of the fortunes of France, the collective entity and national community embodied in its State structure, the monarchy (the most ancient in Europe), the nursery of all the political developments of the country's future. It seems as though, in the case of France, the State begot the nation, or at least that the two developed in parallel. The French people of the early modern period looked to the Crown and its symbols, and to the person of the king, when they wished to evoke the essence of their communal existence. They had no doubts as to its inherent excellence and its capacity to transform the customs and welfare of its people. They showed no hesitation in extending its institutional structures and laws to each new territory conquered by French arms. The reader's first priority in approaching this book will therefore be to find an account of the ups and downs of the French State between 1598 and 1661. But political history cannot be restricted to the chronicle of central government, a procession of kings and ministers, and a balance-sheet of their successes and failures. It must also cover the political and intellectual alternatives: different opinions; institutions and powers other than those of the central State; the influences of other corporate bodies and social groups, such as churches, families and cities; expectations, dreams and hopes; the thousand and one ways of escaping the grasp of politics, of living outside official history with its conventions and restrictions. Of course I can hardly hope to have fulfilled such a manifesto, but this is where I find the justification for some original and perhaps surprising observations.

The years from 1598 to 1661 were crucial in deciding the political destiny of France. The still changeable and pragmatic will of kings and their ministers, together with the constraints of the Thirty Years War, gave birth to the 'fiscal State' and set the monarchy on the path to centralisation, even absolutism. Yet as late as the death of Mazarin the game was not yet won. History could still have been written differently. The obligation of laying down my pen in 1661, arbitrarily cutting off the chain of events at that point, has at least provided an opportunity for considering potential political alternatives. It seems to me that historians run the risk of economising on reality when, secure in their knowledge of how things turned out, they write history as a sort of one-way ticket to the future. They are more faithful to the period under consideration when they give some thought to the stillborn alternatives, to the other possibilities envisaged by those who actually lived at the time. In other words, we should not look at the story of the Fronde as if it could only have led to the State of Louis XIV. Treating the past in this deterministic way takes the edge off it and diminishes its significance. If one accepts that human history contains its share of accident and contingency, then this approach, albeit imaginative and arbitrary, ought to prove fruitful. These pages, as it happens, were written in the summer of 1991, and the dramatic changes which that year saw in Eastern Europe had the trivial side-effect of strengthening my taste for asking new questions and calling into question the complacency of the *fait accompli*.

If the history of France is no more to be identified with that of its State structure than is the history of any other country, neither can it be limited exclusively to the French viewpoint. It was not written in the stars that Roussillon and Artois would be annexed to the kingdom. The war aims and political views of Spanish ministers, Italian princes and Dutch merchants have as much historical relevance and legitimacy as the presumption that makes the formation of the French 'hexagon' almost a law of nature. A brilliant exercise in comparative history can be found in the magisterial essay by the British historian J. H. Elliott, setting the careers of Olivares and Richelieu in parallel (*Richelieu and Olivares*, Cambridge, 1984; translated into French as *Richelieu et Olivares*, Paris, 1991).

Another taste of mine is for drawing illustrative examples and anecdotes from the provinces, in an attempt to escape the traditional short-sightedness of grand history told from Paris. Finally, the general chapters at the end of the book, which under the constraints of space and time are unable to offer an adequate synthesis, attempt to sketch the life and customs of the people. The history of the silent majority sometimes takes little account of the more easily described course of high politics, as seen from courts and chanceries, but it has the advantage of revealing the slower rhythms of everyday life and, in addition, of adding new material to the familiar contents of historical textbooks.

Yves-Marie Bercé

1 Henri IV and the Years of Peace

1598, The Year of Peace

The peace which came to the kingdom of France towards the end of spring 1598 would prove lasting. More than thirty years were to pass before France once more found itself in open war with the Habsburg powers, while the confessional conflicts which had consumed the realm since 1562 had died down, and would not rekindle in the following decade. The fair prospects for peace are not detectable only with hindsight, but were perceived and felt by contemporaries. The farewell to arms arising from the Edict of Nantes inaugurated a period of pragmatic religious toleration, while the Treaty of Vervins which brought an end to the Franco-Spanish war on the frontiers of Picardy was no fragile outcome of short-term calculation or princely whim. It was imposed on the participants by the logic of events and circumstances. With their resources exhausted and war-weariness everywhere apparent, neither side saw any prospect of victory, and both realised that further military efforts on the scale of the 1590s would not be feasible for many years.

The traditional midsummer bonfires which that year celebrated the feast of St John the Baptist in the Place de Grève outside the Paris Hôtel de Ville saw bundles of weapons and drums ritually consigned to the flames. Municipal authorities across the land had Te Deums sung in the major churches and bonfires lit in the squares. The routines of peace were quickly resumed. Merchants once more took to the roads, and market-stalls and fairground booths went up. Holidays once more rang with youthful dancing and merrymaking. The resumption of pilgrimages to traditional shrines was another sign of the return to normality. The Catholic Jubilee, or Holy Year, of 1600 attracted French pilgrims to Rome in their tens of thousands – far more than from other nations and, according to contemporary accounts, as devout as 'survivors of shipwrecks'.

The wars of religion had in effect come to an end in 1595, thanks to the continued military successes of royal forces against the strongholds of the rebel Catholic League and above all to the grant of absolution made to Henri IV by Pope Clement VIII on 17 November 1595. The young Duke of Guise had made his submission to the king that summer, bringing with him the towns of Champagne. The Duke of Mayenne, giving himself the title of Lieutenant General of the Realm, also came to the negotiating table, and brought with him most of Picardy. The areas which still held out were confined to the periphery. The fortresses of Toul and Verdun, which had been seized in 1589 by the League's ally, Duke Charles III of Lorraine, were restored. The League garrison of Marseille surrendered in March 1596, ensuring peace in Provence. Resistance continued only in Brittany, almost solidly League under its governor, the Duke of Mercoeur, who could not be brought to make terms until March 1598. But even there local truces had already taken effect, and military operations had largely ceased. Radical Catholic opinion, which in 1590 had aligned the greater part of the kingdom with the League and had stood for a moment on the brink of victory, was now not so much defeated as won over to the king, wholeheartedly sharing the general thirst for peace. If there was any shadow on the peaceful horizon, it was cast by the anxieties of the Protestant faction, which viewed with some concern the abjuration of Henri IV and his decisive commitment to the Catholic side. The Protestants had devoted their entire military power to his cause, and had since 1574 equipped themselves with a political organisation consisting of nine provinces, with annual assemblies which were more or less outside royal control. This organisation constituted a political challenge which the king had to face in order to reaffirm the power of the monarchical State.

It was also necessary to bring the war with Spain to a close. Since January 1594, it had suited Henri IV to take on the power of Spain. His sudden decision, taken even though peace was not yet established at home, was intended to allay Protestant fears at home and to satisfy his foreign allies, England and the Netherlands, which had hitherto assisted his cause. However, this counter-intuitive policy had soon turned to the advantage of the enemy. Spain took Cambrai, Doullens, Calais, and even Amiens, the capital of Picardy. Even though the Dukes of Mayenne and Biron (the former head of the League and Henri's most trusted general now, significantly, acting together) retook Amiens thanks to a supreme effort, only a diplomatic settlement could bring peace to the north-eastern frontier.

The two peacemaking processes came to their conclusion at much the same time, with the publication of the Edict of Nantes (13 April 1598) preceding by a few weeks the signature of the treaty with Spain at Vervins (13 May). The locations of these actions reflected the geography of the problems they were addressing. The edict was published at Nantes because the king had taken his forces west in order to overawe both the leaguers of Brittany and the provinces of Touraine and Poitou where the Huguenots were strong. And the treaty with Spain was signed at Vervins, a small town of Vermandois, in the heart of the contested terrain where the plains of Picardy and the rich rolling country of Artois gave onto the Spanish Netherlands.

The Edict of Nantes was a general law laying down the conditions for the practice of the two varieties of Christianity to be permitted in the realm. If people were unable to worship God in the same way, at least their prayers could be offered with similar intentions. The edict provided for the restoration of Catholic worship wherever it had been suppressed, and for the restitution of confiscated property to the Church. It then proceeded to specify in detail the arrangements for the freedom of conscience and worship for the Reformed (that is, the Huguenots), and the individual and collective guarantees which would ensure toleration for the minority. Political, financial, judicial and even military provisions gave the Protestant interest a privileged position within the State. But the edict was not founded on some anachronistic concept of ecumenism. The toleration it established was entirely pragmatic, and its implementation was entirely dependent on royal authority. In the long term it was almost inevitable that difficulties should arise from the profusion of complex provisions and the extent of the privileges accorded to the Protestants. But in the short term, the vast majority of the people saw in the edict the promise of domestic peace.

The negotiations with Spain went on for more than a year under the auspices of a papal legate, Alessandro de Medici, Cardinal of Florence. The pope was playing his traditional role of arbiter among princes, keen to restore peace between the two great Catholic powers. English and Dutch agents did their best to sabotage the talks, but both Paris and Madrid were determined to bring their futile and unsustainable conflict to an end. The frontiers resumed their customary lines as the Spanish handed back Calais, Doullens and other French towns they had seized in the previous three years, but retained Cambrai – unarguably part of Hainault. French propaganda presented the treaty as a defeat for Spain, and the death of the aged Philip II soon after (13 September 1598) could perhaps lend some plausibility to this interpretation. But the truth was that the Spanish had decided to devote their resources to the reconquest of the Netherlands. Over the following decades they were to succeed in binding the southern provinces of the Netherlands (modern Belgium) inextricably to the Spanish cause.

The Fragility of Royal Power in 1598

With long-term peace assured, the ravaged kingdom had to set about the task of reconstruction. Despite the success of Henri IV, State authority remained seriously vulnerable. The king had no children by his wife, Marguerite de Valois (sister of Charles IX and Henri III), from whom he was in effect separated. In a monarchical polity like France, the stability of the regime and the security of the realm depend crucially upon a clear and undisputed succession to the throne. In France, the inheritance custom was clear: the Crown went to the eldest son or, failing that, to the nearest male heir. The 'Wars of Religion' had been, at least in part, a succession conflict. The lack of male heirs to the last generation of the Valois had meant recourse to the Bourbon house of Navarre, whose claim had to be traced back to the thirteenth century, and whose head in 1588, Prince Henri, was a Protestant. The League's inability to produce a convincing Catholic alternative had led to its ultimate collapse and Henri IV's triumph. But there remained the widespread fear that one of the frequent bouts of illness that assailed him would snatch him away, if he did not fall by the hand of one of the assassins for whom he was a regular target. The death of the king had plunged the country into crisis in 1588. Now the heir presumptive was the Prince de Condé, a child and a distant cousin at that. The king was well aware of the problem, and had decided to marry his mistress, Gabrielle d'Estrées (whom he had made Duchess of Beaufort), and to legitimise the three children he had by her. The duchess was pretty and intelligent, and was acceptable not only to the Protestants, who preferred her to the existing matrimonial connection with the old Valois court, but also to the old Leaguers, among whom she had many relatives. However, this plan was not without its own difficulties. The king's first marriage had to be canonically annulled, and the Holy See was unlikely to consent to this under the present circumstances. This would have meant a fresh conflict with the papacy, which would have deepened the scandal at home, where malicious and salacious pamphlets about the king's favourite – 'la duchesse d'Ordure' – were already circulating, blaming her for every ill from heavy taxation to the uncertainty over the succession. The succession of a legitimised bastard would certainly not have gone down well, and might easily have rekindled factional conflict. These views were put to the king by his councillors Rosny and Villeroy, but to little avail, although he did permit discreet enquiries to be made about suitable prospective brides at the princely courts of Europe.

For two years Henri IV treated Gabrielle as queen in all but name, elevating her family to royal rank, lodging her at the Louvre, and decorating the walls of his palaces with the monogram HG. An attack of illness in October 1598 prompted him to decisive action. In February 1599 he announced his forthcoming marriage to Gabrielle around Easter. Formal preparations got under way, but fate intervened. The duchess died suddenly, after a miscarriage, on Holy Saturday, 10 April 1599. Devastated, Henri gave her a magnificent funeral.

The sudden, unexpected, but also, it has to be said, timely death of the Duchess of Beaufort prompted rumours of poison. Yet while it is true that her removal greatly simplified the political scene, it seems that the poor woman really did succumb to a terrible case of eclampsia. In any case, the field was now clear for a more considered solution to the succession crisis.

The first step remained the annulment of Henri's first marriage. Negotiations with Rome were already under way before Gabrielle's death, but Marguerite de Valois, resentful of the favourite's rise, was reluctant to assist it in any way. Now that the king's mistress was out of contention, Marguerite did all she could to smooth Henri's path. The chief negotiator at Rome was the French ambassador there, Cardinal Arnaud d'Ossat (1536–1604). The son of a blacksmith from Magnoac, Ossat, like many intellectuals, had carved out a career for himself in the Church. Coming to Rome in 1577 as secretary to another ambassador, he had never left, and became a staunch defender of French interests at the Curia. His shrewdness was legendary: it was said that he studied character with all the skill of a siege engineer surveying fortifications. Together with Cardinal Du Perron he played a leading role in securing Henri IV's absolution in 1595, and he had even managed to sell the Edict of Nantes to Pope Clement VIII, whose initial reaction was that he had 'received a slap in the face', and who had considered revoking the king's absolution. Ossat had just been admitted to the college of cardinals when he was commissioned to secure the king an annulment, and he was well able not only to marshal suitable arguments from canon law but also to persuade the Curia of the political expediency of the cause. Agreement was reached in August 1599, and the judgement took effect in December. Marguerite de Valois, Queen Margot, retained her royal title notwithstanding the separation, and retired to Nérac in Gascony, where she gathered around her a little court of scholars and writers.

That left Henri's councillors with the matter of finding a suitable foreign princess to be his bride. They drew up a shortlist of candidates from all over Europe, and the choice finally fell on Marie de Medici, the niece of the Grand Duke of Tuscany. The ruling house of Tuscany had enjoyed ties with France since the days of the Valois, when the future Henri II had married Catherine de Medici. Links had been renewed in 1589, when Grand Duke Ferdinand had married Christine de Lorraine, the daughter of Claude de France and sister of the last Valois kings. Moreover, throughout the protracted civil wars, royal finances had depended heavily on the services of the Florentine bankers: the accumulated royal debt to them was in excess of a million *écus*. For the French, the generous dowry of a Florentine princess represented a valuable offset to that huge debt. For the Italians, the connection with the ruling house of France not only lent a welcome lustre to their own parvenu dynasty but also gave them somewhat greater freedom of action in the face of Spanish domination of the peninsula. The Tuscan coast was overshadowed by Spanish strongholds such as Orbetello, Piombino and Elba, while the land route to the north across the Apennines led to Lombardy, another Habsburg territory. Equally, the alliance with Tuscany brought France diplomatic influence on the peninsula for the first time since the disastrous Treaty of Cateau-Cambrésis. Last but not least, it signalled Henri IV's complete commitment to the Catholic cause and improved his understanding with the papacy without making any concessions to Spain. The choice thus proved an excellent one. Marie, a younger daughter of the previous Grand Duke, Francesco, by an Austrian princess, was twenty-seven years old and reckoned pretty. The blossoming of her womanhood boded well for her health and her fertility. Negotiations during 1600, first at Florence and then at Lyon, focused on the vital question of her dowry, which was eventually fixed at 600,000 *écus*. But only 350,000 of these were ever paid over, the rest going to reduce French debt.

1600: War with Savoy and the Royal Wedding

The attention of the French court was being drawn back towards Italy at precisely the moment when a piece of unfinished business from the wars of religion necessitated a major military effort beyond the Alps.

The duchy of Piedmont and Savoy held what was at that time a position of especial strategic importance. The ducal domains straddled the Alps, bordering Burgundy at one end and Lombardy at the other, and were thus caught between the rival powers of France and Spain. So if the dukes allied with one party, they were bound to incur the hostility of the other; and as long as the two kingdoms remained in competition, the dukes could hardly sit on the fence. From 1580 to 1630 the duke was Charles Emmanuel, who opted for a Spanish axis, sealed in 1584 by his marriage to the Infanta Catherine, daughter of Philip II. Charles Emmanuel was a brilliant and accomplished man, ambitious and indomitable, but somewhat rash and unrealistic. His overriding aim was the recovery of the territories lost to the duchy earlier in the century: the marquisate of Saluzzo, where the Alpine pass of the col de Larche opened onto Piedmont, in French hands since 1512; and the city of Geneva, which had broken away in 1536 after a coup by Protestant citizens. Neither objective was easy. At Cateau-Cambrésis the French had insisted on retaining the outpost of Saluzzo, which commanded the Alpine pass and thus ensured them some continuing interest in Italian affairs. As for Geneva, despite its population of a mere 13,000 and its restricted hinterland, it had become over the years a religious capital with a significance out of all proportion to its geographical extent or position. Looking on their home as a new Israel and a holy city, and enjoying international respect, the wealthy citizens of Geneva were well equipped to offer effective resistance to Savoyard aggression.

Taking advantage of the French civil wars, Charles Emmanuel had, with no forewarning, driven the little French garrison out of Saluzzo in autumn 1588. Over the next decade his alliances with Spain and the cities of the League gave him plenty of scope for operations against Geneva, in the Dauphiné and in Provence. Savoy was a party to the Treaty of Vervins, but the question of Saluzzo was left unresolved. In December 1589 Charles Emmanuel made his way of his own free will to the court of Henri IV, and stayed for three months at Paris and Fontainebleau with his glittering entourage. Negotiations were conducted with a view to an exchange. The duke was to retain Saluzzo, but to hand over to Henri IV his possessions on the right bank of the Rhône, notably the territories of Bresse and Bugey.

During the summer of 1600 Henri IV put on a show of force to overcome the duke's hesitation. Several columns entered ducal territories. Marshal Biron entered Bourg-en-Bresse on 12 August, and Savoy was entirely occupied as far as the valleys of Beaufortain, Tarentaise and Maurienne. Duke Charles Emmanuel attempted a counter-attack in November, leading 20,000 troops across the snow-laden passes. His aim was to relieve the citadel of Montmélian, which had held out all through summer, but its commandant, abandoning hope of relief with the first snowfalls, had just surrendered. The duke was obliged to withdraw, and was back across the Little Saint-Bernard just before Christmas.

Papal diplomacy, which had favoured Henri IV's matrimonial policy, now intervened in order to prevent the conflict spreading into Italy. Cardinal Aldobrandini, the nephew of Clement VIII, was at Lyon for the royal wedding in his capacity as legate. The pope commissioned him to preside there over the negotiations which had opened between Jeannin and Sillery representing France, and the lords of Lucinge and d'Arconas on behalf of Savoy. A treaty signed at Lyon on 17 January 1601 left Saluzzo in the duke's hands and in exchange awarded Bresse, Bugey, Valromey and Gex to Henri – in short, the entire right bank of the Rhône from the borders of Geneva down to where it was joined by the Saône.

The provinces thus acquired for the kingdom were worth far more than the little marquisate of Saluzzo, but nevertheless there was resentment at the abandonment of the foothold beyond the Alps, which was deemed derogatory to the honour of French arms and damaging to French prestige in Italy. And it is true that from then on Spanish domination of the peninsula proved well-nigh incontestable. The Duke of Savoy resented in particular the loss of Bresse, which lay at the borders of Burgundy and the gates of Lyon. His French territories were now limited to Savoy proper. But the transfer of the ducal capital from Chambéry to Turin in 1570 had been a harbinger of an irreversible development, the Italianisation of a state whose centre of gravity would henceforth lie firmly in Piedmont. On the French side, the acquisition of new territories was equally important. Lyon was no longer a sort of outlying metropolis, and its hinterland was now exclusively French. And the gains made in 1601 were never to be called into doubt.

Victorious over Savoy, Henri awaited the arrival of his bride. The marriage had been formally celebrated at Florence in October 1600, with an ambassador representing the person of the king. Marie embarked from Livorno on 19 October, and set foot on French soil at Marseille on 3 November. The galley which brought her across had been escorted by sixteen others, supplied by Tuscany, the Papal States, and the Knights of Malta, not only as a sign of honour but as a security precaution against Barbary pirates. The princess and her considerable retinue moved slowly up the Rhône valley by way of Aix and Avignon, finally reaching Lyon on 3 December. Leaving his troops for a while, Henri took up residence with her from 9 December, without waiting for the ceremonies performed on 17 December by Cardinal Aldobrandini. By the time Marie made her state entry to Paris on 7 February 1601 the news that she was pregnant was already abroad, with the hope that the succession crisis would soon, by the grace of God, be solved.

In fine weather, and during the hunting season of autumn, the court resided at Fontainebleau, while at other times of the year the king often left the dark and somewhat tumbledown Louvre for one of his chateaux in the Île-de-France, such as Saint-Germain-en-Laye or Montceaux. It was at Fontainebleau that, on 27 September 1601, Marie de Medici gave birth to a son, the Dauphin of France and heir apparent. The next morning a circular went out announcing the good news to all the governors, cities and royal courts of the kingdom. With five more children born over the following years, the survival of the dynasty was assured. The kingdom would not face another succession crisis for a long time to come. The strength of the French monarchical machinery and the clarity of the rules regarding the succession of the crown made sure of that. Moreover, Henri's regime was now freed from the insecurity which had beset it since the peace of 1598. In order to demonstrate the continuity of the monarchy across the centuries, Henri

chose for his firstborn son the name of Louis, harking back to the
enormous prestige of Saint Louis, Louis IX of France, from whom
Henri IV's claim to the throne derived. No king of France had
borne this name since the death of Louis XII in 1512, and it was
thus a carefully constructed sign of the continuity of the State. The
name was formally conferred upon the Dauphin, who had received emergency baptism at birth, at a subsequent conditional
baptism with the full accompanying ceremonies which took place
on 14 September 1606. The court was at the time once more at
Fontainebleau, because of rumours of plague in Paris. Pope Paul
IV, represented by a legate, was the godfather, and the Duchess of
Mantua, Marie's sister, the godmother. Rarely has a royal birth
been so eagerly awaited and so joyously celebrated. In a certain
sense the Dauphin's birth sealed his father's political triumph, and
the French enjoyed a brief period of royal euphoria.

But all this heartfelt loyalism does not mean that Henri IV's
reign was some kind of golden age. That was a legend which grew
long after the event. For the time being it was a matter of recon-
structing the devastated provinces and ruling from day to day.
This involved putting royal finances back on a sound footing and
restoring taxes, which inevitably provoked disappointment and
discontent.

The Biron Conspiracy

The thirty years of civil war had greatly encouraged social mobility,
with many remarkable rises owed to the fortunes of war – not only
the achievement of nobility, but also the spectacular advancement
of families already possessed of noble rank. Nobility itself, in a
time of troubles and of weakened royal authority, was no longer a
strictly defined social distinction upheld by the sanction of the
State. Rather, it was a way of life, a product of social status no
longer subject to edicts and ordinances, something which had
acquired its own sanctions independent of royal control. Aristocratic behaviour – bold, open, powerful and predatory, secure in
the consciousness of belonging to an élite – transcended the
boundaries of provinces, denominations and even States. In all

States the nobilities were reclaiming a greater role in government, the right to counsel their kings, elect them or even call them to account.

These movements are often misnamed 'feudal', as if they did nothing more than continue medieval baronial traditions. But in fact they were responding to the peculiar conditions of the sixteenth and seventeenth centuries, a period of transition which saw the emergence of new nobilities, more varied and more numerous, less dependent on purely landed wealth, and dedicated instead to the pursuit of profit through office-holding or the fortunes of war. The confusion with medieval feudalism has been facilitated by the casual and uncritical acceptance of Marxist terminology and even by a tendency among historians to underestimate the forces which at one time or another set themselves against the construction of the modern States.

The career of Henri IV himself is almost a case-study in early modern social mobility. From his relatively modest background in the house of Navarre, a poor and marginal kingdom, he rose first to the head of a powerful religious party and ultimately to the throne of France itself. Of course his Capetian ancestry – and that alone – conferred upon him the necessary legitimacy by making him the sole heir to the throne. But set aside that genealogical distinction – as many of his companions in arms and a wide range of popular opinion were only too ready to do – and there is little to distinguish him from many another provincial squire who acquired wealth and honour through courtly intrigue or military success. The peace of 1598 left many ambitions unsatisfied and services unrewarded: frustrations, resentments and impatient yearnings made many nobles avid for another chance. And soon a new generation of nobility would grow up, bored with the blessings of peace and keen in its turn to try its luck in arms.

Many Catholic noblemen had rallied to Henri IV in 1589, whether out of principle or pragmatism. They recognised the validity of his claim to the throne, and accepted him as the lesser of two evils. They served under his banner, but this did not mean that they approved of his political braggadocio or his scandalous – and hardly 'private' – private life. Biron was one such. His father Armand de Gontaud, Baron of Biron (in Agenais), was a loyal follower of the house of Navarre and had fought in every theatre from Italy to Lorraine. Made a Marshal of France in 1577, a Catholic and a trusted friend of Henri III, he had frequently repelled the young Henri of Navarre's advances into Guyenne. In 1589 the call of duty had put him under that same prince's orders, and he fought on Henri's side at Arques and Ivry, meeting his death in the king's service during 1592. He had never had much respect for the person of the new king. His son Charles de Gontaud, born in 1562, had accompanied his father on campaign from an early age, receiving a commission as a colonel in the Swiss regiments in 1583. He enjoyed a glittering career under Henri IV, taking the stronghold of Laon in 1594 and campaigning successfully from 1595 to 1597 in Burgundy, Franche-Comté, Picardy and Artois. He received a marshal's baton, became a duke and was made Governor of Burgundy, yet reckoned all this but poor reward for one who, in his own eyes, had secured Henri his crown.

Biron was not only a man of action. He had also served several times on diplomatic missions, travelling to Brussels in 1598 to ratify the Treaty of Vervins, and to England in 1601 to explain Henri IV's refusal to intervene in the Netherlands. His ambition was sufficiently obvious for Spanish and Savoyard agents to try and draw him into their plans. Discussions were well advanced in 1600 when war with Savoy broke out. It was suggested that Biron should help overthrow the king by local military operations or even by assassination. In return, Biron would marry a daughter of the Duke of Savoy and become the sovereign lord of Burgundy and Franche-Comté, thus resurrecting the State once ruled by Charles the Bold and his ancestors. Negotiations took place at Somma, a little fortified town on the shores of Lake Maggiore, a summer residence of the Dukes of Milan. The Governor of Milan, the Spanish Count of Fuentes, was present in person, and Biron was represented by a gentleman adventurer from the Bourbonnais, Jacques de La Fin, seigneur des Pluviers, a veteran of dubious causes who had served with the Duke of Anjou in the Netherlands, with Don Antonio the pretender to the Portuguese throne, and latterly with Marguerite de Valois. Rumours of the plot soon reached Paris by way of Cardinal d'Ossat and the French party at Rome. In March 1602 La Fin sold his secrets to the King's Council. Biron, who had ventured to court, was arrested there on 16 June by order of the king. His case was promptly dealt with by the Parlement de Paris, and he was executed on 31 July.

The political scandal was immense, for Biron quite understandably enjoyed widespread popularity and esteem. Stringent security precautions had to be taken in Paris, especially around the Bastille where he was imprisoned, as well as in his province of Burgundy. The dukes who were called upon to sit in judgement over him in the Grand-Chambre of the Parlement de Paris refused to have anything to do with the affair. Henri IV was besieged with appeals for clemency, but the unarguable proofs supplied by La Fin combined with considerations of *raison d'état* to force the unpleasant decision upon him. Obviously Biron's execution was a matter of political expediency. Equally guilty conspirators later in the reign were not always treated with the same harshness. But Biron was made an example, to convince public opinion in general, and the greater nobles in particular, of the heinous character of crimes against the Crown and the State.

Contemporaries were quick to spot the parallels between Biron's fate and that of the English Earl of Essex. Robert Devereux, Earl of Essex and favourite of Queen Elizabeth, had been loaded with honours by his sovereign. He had been made Viceroy of Ireland with the task of stamping out the incessant revolts in which its Catholic peasantry indulged with Spanish assistance. On his return to England he had decided to displace the chief minister, Robert Cecil. He tried to raise the London mob and to take possession of the city, but his failure led him the scaffold (June 1601). In each case a favourite, an intimate friend of the sovereign, had engaged in a foolish conspiracy, and the sovereign, head ruling heart, had sacrificed personal affection on the altar of State affairs. The tales pointed two common political morals: the mutability of fortune and the ingratitude of kings. The first lesson, that even great figures of this world were not immune from the ups and downs of earthly existence, represented the ironic vengeance of the lowly, a proverbial source of consolation since Roman times. It also constituted an argument for Christian humility, emphasising the transience of worldly glory. The second lesson could be understood in various ways, depending on whether one took selfishness and severity as a political obligation for princes, or whether one blamed them for pride, contempt and ingratitude for services rendered. This latter view prevailed among the nobility and the people. Laments for the death of a faithful soldier and a friend in hard times spread through Aquitaine, where Biron and his brother-in-law, the Duke of La Force, were major landowners. As for La Fin, he met his end in April 1606 on the Notre-Dame bridge, cut down by an unknown gang of cavaliers for whom no one made any search. In most people's eyes, the Biron affair was not a case of treason: it was on the contrary a tale of devoted service denied its due reward, and of the cold cruelty of a king.

The Conspiracies of the Duke of Bouillon

The investigation of the Biron plot rightly or wrongly implicated many other people who none the less went unpunished and, it seems, continued their dealings with Spanish agents. Henri IV himself had no wish to dig too deep into the affair, for to do so might have compromised his favourite mistress. His second marriage had not changed his character, and he carried on a series of notorious and scandalous affairs. One woman to whom he took a fancy was Henriette d'Entragues, the daughter of Charles IX's mistress Marie Touchet, whom he made Marchioness of Verneuil. In 1599 he made her a rather unwise promise of marriage – in writing – and he cherished the son she bore him. The duchess had a half-brother, the bastard son of Charles IX. Charles de Valois, Count of Auvergne and a companion in arms of Henri IV, was the stalking-horse of Spanish conspiracies.

Moreover, the tentacles of conspiracy extended even among some Protestant nobility who distrusted the king. As the Protestant churches no longer had a Protector (a title which Henri IV himself had formerly borne), the pre-eminent place among the Protestant nobility was now held by Henri de La Tour d'Auvergne, Viscount of Turenne, Duke of Bouillon and Marshal of France. His lands of Turenne, which lay on the border of the Bas-Limousin (the modern Corrèze) and Quercy (the modern Lot), enjoyed liberties and privileges which made them a virtually autonomous province, where royal officials had no jurisdiction. A short-lived marriage to Antoinette de La Marck had brought him the principality of Sedan, a small sovereign territory on the border between Champagne and the territories of the Prince-Bishop of Liège. He was thus possessed of two places outside the kingdom that were in effect sovereign bases where not only the Protestant party but also noble discontent could flourish without interference. Related by marriage to the Prince of Orange and the Elector Palatine, Bouillon was thus a figure who could aspire to an international role.

In November 1602 Bouillon was summoned to court by the king to give an account of himself. But instead of complying, he toured the Reformed communities of Languedoc before heading by way of Geneva and then Heidelberg (his brother-in-law's capital) to the safety of Sedan. From the shelter of his frontier fortress he could co-ordinate the forces of discontent. Among the notable guests there was the pastor Antoine Renaud, who busied himself in stirring up the German Protestant princes against Henri IV.

In November 1604 the king finally realised that he had to take decisive action against the Entragues faction. The Count of Auvergne was thrown into the Bastille, and proceedings against him were commenced in the Parlement de Paris. The sentences handed down by that court in February 1605 were draconian: five death sentences, and an order that the Marchioness of Verneuil be shut up for life in a nunnery. But the sentences were not carried out, and by the end of the year Henri had resumed his affair with the duchess. The Count of Auvergne, however, was not released from the Bastille until 1616. This selective severity was not without political significance: a prince of the blood royal, even a bastard, retained an element of legitimacy which prompted this cynical prudence.

The noble clientages of Bouillon and Biron were spread across the mid-west, from Quercy to Marche. In summer 1605 the King's Council decided to put on a show of force there. So in September Henri, at the head of 7,000 men, made his way to Poitiers and then Limoges, where he made a solemn entry. Returning to Paris, he left behind a commission of justice which proceeded against several local minor gentry with ties to Bouillon. Six of them were executed. Having thus neutralised the threat of rebellion from the

Turenne region, the king let winter pass and then set in motion a military expedition against Sedan. This time he took with him a considerable artillery force, some forty cannon. Bouillon took the hint and opened the gates of Sedan immediately (April 1606). On his return journey Henri made sure that he spent Holy Week at Reims, where he performed the traditional ceremony of touching for the king's evil. This sign of respect for the ancient city of coronations (despite the fact the Henri himself had been crowned at Chartres) forged another link with the ancient traditions of the kings of France. With this symbolic gesture completed, Henri made a triumphal entry on his return to his capital, with the Duke of Bouillon prominently placed in his retinue as a public sign of his submission.

The series of plots and military progresses through the provinces is evidence of the limits of the monarchical State and of the fragility of its still nascent centralisation. Possibilities such as the re-emergence of a powerful Duchy of Burgundy, the creation of a Protestant principality or the secession of a province with the encouragement of Savoy, or of the far more powerful Spain, were ever present. In his dealings with even his most trusted councillors, Henri sometimes manifested an obsession with treason which fuelled the gossip and intrigues of the court. The Duke of Lesdiguières, an old comrade and long-serving Protestant war leader, Governor of Dauphiné and an effective defender of the south-eastern provinces, was accused of seeking to carve out a sovereign principality for himself among the Alps. His attempts to trace his descent from the first Dauphins of the Viennois were delated to the king as evidence of his intentions. Particular attention was given to his authority with the Parlement de Grenoble and among the nobility of the Dauphiné, as well as to the numbers of his guard troops, the scale of his fortifications, and the size of the arsenals he maintained at Vizille and elsewhere, not to mention his connections with powerful Swiss and German families. He too was summoned to give an account of himself. He had to reduce his guard to fifty men, and to explain that his artillery was intended solely for use against incursions from Savoy.

Royal suspicion lighted also upon the young Prince of Condé. A prince of the blood and a potential successor should Henri die without children, Henri de Condé was just twenty years old. Brought up a Catholic, he had left Paris after the birth of the Dauphin. A marriage arranged for him by the king for political reasons had tied him in May 1609 to a daughter of the Duke of Montmorency, Constable of France. As luck would have it, the young duchess was so pretty that the king himself fell for her and wanted to seduce her. On the pretext of a hunting expedition, Condé took his wife away from the court and then, one November night, they set out secretly for the Netherlands with just a few servants. For Condé it was simply a matter of getting out of a ridiculous but awful dilemma. However, for a prince of the blood to flee the country was an inherently political act, and to do so without the king's permission could be construed as treason. The king sent provosts in pursuit of the young couple, who escaped by only a matter of hours. Condé proceeded to Brussels and then to Milan, and was treated with the utmost honour by the Spanish governors of those territories. This story, so petty at first sight, illustrates the romantic and hazardous consequences that of the personalisation of the State and the embodiment of political legitimacy in a single family. These principles, enshrined in the fundamental laws of the kingdom, gave force and durability to the French monarchy, but at the same time made it subject to the hazards of family fortunes, which thus became crucial political issues. Henri IV's whole reign was to be troubled by aristocratic conspiracies and political uncertainties consequent upon dynastic problems. Crown authority and territorial integrity were not greatly in evidence. Only with hindsight, in the dark years of the mid-seventeenth century, did the decade of peace which constituted the real reign of Henri IV assume the character of a golden age. At the time, there seemed no end to intrigues and discontents.

The Restoration of the Finances of the State

In 1598 the kingdom lay in ruins and the Treasury was deep in debt. The demands of war had forced kings (Henri IV in particular) to resort to such fiscal expedients as the alienation of royal desmesne and the extraction of forced loans from the clergy and the major towns. A mass of commercial loans which could be called in at any moment tied the Crown to foreign financiers and to leading Protestant princes such the Queen of England, the Duke of Wurttemberg or the Elector Palatine. The Swiss had provided both money and men, and were owed in the region of 30 million *livres*. And the Tuscan banks of the Medici and the Rucellai had advanced considerable sums: the royal marriage had much to do with this, and the crown jewels were in pawn to the Italians until 1607.

The task of rebuilding the royal finances was entrusted to one of the king's oldest and most loyal supporters, Maximilien de Béthune, Baron of Rosny, who had been in Henri's service since 1576, when he was but seventeen years old. In 1606 he was made Duke of Sully, and it is by this name that he is known to history. A born organiser and a tireless worker, at home with figures and devoted to accuracy, Sully was already one of the king's leading advisers when in 1596 he was first admitted to sessions of the Council concerned with financial affairs. By 1600 he had accumulated a clutch of high offices: *Surintendant des finances*, *Grand Voyer*, Grand Master of the Artillery, *Surintendant des bâtiments*, and *Surintendant des fortifications*. He was a man of war, a haughty nobleman of ancient blood, and a staunch Protestant to the day he died. He prided himself on being different from the magistrates and the rest of the *noblesse de robe*, petty and meddlesome officials, seeing himself as a true nobleman, distinguished by his birth, his upbringing and his taste for action. Never before in the history of France had so many and various offices been concentrated in a single pair of hands. Sully's career was in itself an indication of the centralising tendencies of the age.

By diplomatic action abroad, negotiations over credit instruments, reductions in interest rates and some shrewd dealing, the debt was gradually brought under control. In order to regain alienated domain, the Treasury issued contracts by which companies (*partis*) undertook to repurchase lands, rents or offices for the Crown, with the shareholders (*partisans*) in return enjoying the revenues of the property in question for a number of years. This kind of contract, like all tax-farming, seems to modern eyes to subordinate public interest to private profit. But the royal administration depended on but a few thousand men, and had few officers and agents capable of such work. It was more practical to bring in the human resources of business, and this proved an excellent way of mobilising the ample credit of the richer sections of society in the service of the public debt.

The foundation of royal finance was the *taille*, the only direct annual tax, and one which covered almost all the realm. In the south of the country the *taille* was assessed on the basis of land values recorded in cadastres, whereas in the north it was assessed upon estimates of an individual's total wealth fixed by the consent of the taxpayers as a group. Clergy and nobility were exempt from the *taille*, a privilege which public opinion in general accepted, but so too were the majority of the towns, something which not only greatly aggrieved the peasantry, but represented a considerable loss of revenue. The towns had mostly won their privileges in the course of the political troubles of previous centuries – notably the wars with England – when the Crown was desperate to retain the loyalty and support of the citizens and their walls. Towards the end of the wars of religion, the peasantry rose against the burden of the *taille*, and in particular against its levy in the name of the rival factions which by turns imposed themselves on the country communities. The most serious risings took place in the Limousin and Périgord during 1594–5, where the insurgents calling themselves the 'Tard Avisés' came to be known as the 'Croquants' (i.e. peasants armed with staves or 'crocs').

Henri IV, who was well aware of the parlous state of royal finances, took the advice of an Assembly of Notables which met at Rouen between November 1596 and January 1597. Such assemblies were less cumbersome than the Estates General, and were purely consultative. This one recommended a reduction in the *taille* and savings in military expenditure, especially that on fortifications within the realm, which were very costly and politically risky. In response to the assembly's advice, commissioners were dispatched into all the provinces in August 1598 to investigate fiscal problems. There had already been several similar tours of inspection under Henri III, when Masters of Requests of the Royal Household had been sent into the provinces to make sure that the tax was being levied fairly and lawfully. The Masters of Requests were accompanied on these missions by the Treasurers of France for each *généralité* and by councillors from the various *Cours des aides*, who could contribute their specialised local knowledge. The commissioners were meant in particular to detect unwarranted exemptions and to investigate local grievances about tax distribution. Like all direct taxes at that time, the *taille* was fixed by apportionment: the overall sum, or *brevet*, was fixed at the outset by the King's Council, and this was then divided and subdivided down through the various revenue jurisdictions – *généralités*, *bureaux des finances* and *éléctions*, until it was finally allocated among the parishes. At each level there was a fixed ratio between the units of assessment, known as the *pied*. The *pieds des tailles* were calculated on the basis of what was known about each local community's ability to pay. The commissioners were charged with reassessing and determining these ratios. The findings and recommendations of the commissioners were enshrined in a great edict which was published in March 1600 and served in effect as a fiscal code for many years. Finally, the Council set about reducing not only the proportion of royal revenue raised through the *taille* but also the real burden of the tax itself. The *taille* had risen to 18 million *livres* by 1598, but it had fallen to 13 million by 1602, and stabilised around 16 million by 1609–10.

The Treasury had to find alternative sources of revenue. The Assembly of Notables proposed an indirect tax of 5 per cent on the value of all merchandise entering towns. This tax, known as the *sol per livre* (from its rate) or the *pancarte* (from the placards announcing the tariffs which were posted on the collectors' booths at city gates), was introduced by proclamation in May 1597. But the legal obstacles thrown in its way by the *Cour des aides* prevented it from being effectively levied until early in 1601. Town councils at once started seeking exemption, and some (for example Angers, Caen and Reims) succeeded in escaping this highly unpopular levy at the gates in return for an annual lump sum or 'subvention'. Elsewhere the arrival of the agents who were to introduce the *pancarte* sparked off riots, notably at Poitiers, where the task required the dispatch of a special commissioner – Pierre Damours, a member of the King's Council and former President of the Parlement de Paris – with an armed escort. Damours had been commissioned in 1596 to re-establish royal authority in the former League strongholds of Champagne. In summer 1601 he succeeded in introducing the *pancarte* at Poitiers and throughout western France. A fresh wave of urban protest broke out in early 1602, and *pancarte* agents were expelled from towns such as La Rochelle and Limoges. An official show of strength was put on at Limoges, where another King's Councillor, Le Camus de Jambeville, headed a commission to suppress resistance. The consuls of Limoges were dismissed and the tax was imposed. However, local resistance was too widespread, and in November 1602 Sully resigned himself to abolishing the tax. The mounting violence of fiscal resistance seen in 1602 was reminiscent of the great revolt of the south-western provinces against the extension of the *gabelle* in 1548. Sully now had to find other ways of tapping civic wealth.

The ascent of a family up the social scale had long been sealed by the purchase of royal offices. Public appointments in the judiciary or financial administration had become marketable assets. The purchaser was the proprietor, and could only be removed through forfeiture. It was reckoned at the time that wealth was an index of both competence and fitness to serve the public good, and that the purchaser's position in the local community meant that he would have a useful knowledge of local people and circumstances. With the passage of time, royal edicts had permitted the transmission of office by inheritance, provided that the official resigned his office in favour of his successor at least forty days before his death. Sully proposed to make office heritable on the payment of an annual fee fixed at one-sixtieth of its value. A royal proclamation of December 1604 implemented this scheme. The first financier contracted to collect the fees was Charles Paulet, after whom the fee came to be known as the 'paulette'. Its annual yield stabilised at around a million *livres*, paid into the *Bureau des parties casuelles* (or 'office of uncertain receipts', so called because its revenues depended on chance – *casus* in Latin).

The introduction of the *paulette* was in some respects a success. It answered a genuine social need, it brought in a modest but regular revenue, and it spared the peasants. On the other hand, it could be criticised for curtailing the king's freedom to appoint his officials, and it was on these grounds that the Chancellor Bellièvre strove in vain to block the measure. In the long term it did indeed have serious consequences. The French Crown found itself locked into a system in which recruitment to public office was on the basis of wealth rather than birth, merit, ability or loyalty. There thus arose a bourgeois and noble officialdom which was irremovably entrenched, effectively independent and without any guarantee of competence or fidelity. But these wide ramifications were doubtless inconceivable in 1604.

Sully also led the French Crown down another road which was both long and dangerous: the centralisation of powers within the realm. In fact this was part of a process which had begun arguably as long ago as the reign of Charles VII, and certainly by that of Henri II.

Sully and Henri IV were determined to nibble away at provincial liberties and privileges, especially those of the *pays d'États*, that is of the provinces which had long possessed their own assemblies of the three estates. The annual meetings of these provincial Estates discussed the tax burden, decided on its allocation and collection, and fixed collective expenditure on such things as billeting troops and maintaining bridges and highways. All the provinces of the Midi had their own assemblies, as did Burgundy and Brittany in the north. The privilege ensured that their tax burden was light in comparison with the *pays d'élections*, where the fiscal administration was in the hands of officials of the *Bureaux des finances* at the level of the *généralité* (roughly coterminous with a province, or a modern region) and of the *Cours d'élections* at the level of the *élection* (a fiscal jurisdiction of the order of a modern *arrondissement*).

In 1603 Sully decided to extend the system of *élections* to the *généralité* of Bordeaux, introducing eight new courts. This wealthy province enjoyed widespread exemptions from *gabelles* and *aides*, which it was not feasible to levy there because of the proximity of the salt-pans of Marennes and the power of the wine trade. The reform of the *taille* represented the first encroachment upon its privileges. The Estates of the Agenais and Périgord threw themselves into frantic representations in an attempt to prevent implementation of the edict in 1603. They succeeded in delaying it until 1609, and then obtained its revocation in 1611. Yet a precedent had been set all the same, and similar administrative changes would be attempted in the future.

Henri IV and Sully had frequent recourse, as we have seen, to dispatching special commissioners into the provinces. This too was a time-honoured administrative expedient. There was an element of innovation, however, in the dispatch not of *ad hoc* commissioners but of royal representatives equipped with wide-ranging powers of unlimited duration. Such was the nature of Damours's commission in Champagne during 1596 after the defection of the Duke of Guise to the king's party. These men were not yet entitled *intendants*, but they clearly prefigured the officials who would be seen at work in the next reign. Viçose in Guyenne and Le Camus de Jambeville in Normandy had commissions of this kind. Lyon, the second city of the realm, wealthy and populous, did not preside over a great province, and lay under the jurisdiction of the distant Parlement de Paris. Royal authority was represented there by a single governor. To assist – or else to watch – him, a commissioner or *intendant* was installed there, as in Champagne after the submission of the League (1597). And the commissioners in Lyon, unlike those elsewhere, succeeded each other in an unbroken series, making the post the first example of a permanent *intendant* in a province.

The fiscal administration was the field of one further characteristic innovation. While the auditing of receipts from the levying or farming of taxes was traditionally the task of the *Chambres des comptes*, Sully decided in 1597 to entrust the auditing of accounts from financiers and *partisans* to a special commission entitled the *Chambre de justice*. This innovation was not only a sop to public opinion but also a direct response to a demand made by the Assembly of Notables, namely that financiers and tax farmers who had grown rich out of the wars should be made to cough up. In fact, the *Chambre de justice* met for only a few weeks. Its establishment was simply an inducement to its potential victims to come to terms with the Treasury and thus pre-empt or halt formal proceedings. The measure was thrice renewed: from 1601 to 1604, in 1605, and again in 1607. The tribunals thus sat for a total of six years. It was clearly a political expedient rather than the disinterested pursuit of justice. Indeed, the 1607 tribunal was abruptly dissolved when its over-zealous proctor, Claude Mangot, sought to extend its investigations to a number of senior Treasury officials. The measure would be resurrected in following reigns as the ineffectiveness of the *Chambres des comptes* became ever more apparent.

After some ten years in charge of royal finances, Sully could pride himself on having accumulated in the Bastille, the seat of the *Trésor de l'Épargne*, a reserve of some 12 million *livres*, equivalent to about half a year's revenues. This reserve was in truth rather small and ephemeral, but it was evidence of a more lasting and significant development: the restoration of the credit of the French Crown after half a century of civil war. The speed of the recovery was due not only to the talent of the minister, but also to the extraordinary resilience and dynamism of the monarchical machinery of France and to the enormous potential of the kingdom itself.

2   The Succession Crisis of 1610

The rivalry between France and Spain had long been and would for another century remain the dominant factor in the international relations of Europe. Spain, at the height of its power and the pinnacle of its Golden Age, had not managed to prevent the secession of the United Provinces, and its long war in the Netherlands had come to a temporary halt in April 1609, when a twelve-year truce was signed between the warring parties. The continent of Europe was at peace, except for distant Muscovy and the borders of the Ottoman Empire. But a succession crisis which suddenly emerged at this juncture in a small State in western Germany threatened the delicate religious and political balance in that sensitive area of western Europe.

The War over Cleves

Duke John William of Cleves, Jülich, Marck and Berg died in March 1609 leaving no clear successor to his conglomerate of predominantly Catholic territories, which lay along the borders of the United Provinces and the Spanish Netherlands and occupied a strategic position between the Rhine and the Meuse. Two brothers-in-law claimed the succession: the Duke of Brandenburg and the Count of Neuberg, both of them Protestants. The Emperor Rudolf II intervened to cut the dispute short, sequestering the territories and entrusting their government to imperial repre-

27

sentatives. This caused considerable disquiet in the Protestant camp, among the Dutch and the German princes who since 1608 had made up the Evangelical Union. Henri IV saw in this situation an opportunity to challenge the Habsburgs, and made common cause with the claimants. In summer 1609 he set about making diplomatic and even military preparations with a view to supporting them against the emperor.

France dispatched ambassadors to foreign courts in a quest for allies should it come to blows, but to little avail amidst the general desire for peace. The pope's nuncios and the ambassadors of Philip III of Spain for their part worked vigorously for the preservation of the peace in Europe. The only real success for the French was with Charles Emmanuel of Piedmont and Savoy, who agreed under the Treaty of Bruzolo (April 1610) to send his forces against Milan in the event of war. The alliance was sealed with an agreement for a marriage between one of Henri's daughters and Victor Amadeus, the Piedmontese heir (both parties were still infants). Henri was confident of his material strength and was egged on by advisers whose belligerence was motivated by Protestant conviction in some cases and by hatred of Spain in others. So, despite his relative diplomatic isolation, he decided over winter to put on a show of force, and was perhaps contemplating a more protracted campaign against the Habsburgs of Vienna and Madrid. His decision was confirmed by the news of Condé's flight to the Netherlands. This storm in a teacup, which had blown up out of his private life, was in his eyes not only a political outrage, but also evidence of a Spanish plot. He may even have felt it as a blow to his amorous reputation.

France was called upon to make an exceptional military effort. An army of 32,000 infantry and 5,000 cavalry was assembled in Champagne, at Châlons and Mézières, ready to march towards the Meuse corridor. This well-armed and well-paid force, equipped with ample artillery, was the fruit of Sully's policy. Not since the Italian wars had France considered military action on this scale. Secondary campaigns were also contemplated, with Lesdiguières taking the troops of the Dauphiné into northern Italy, and the Marquis of La Force invading the Spanish Netherlands. The plan could have ignited a European conflagration, but it remained nothing more than an idea. Only the advance towards Cleves was firmly on the agenda, destined for the end of May 1610.

As the forces awaited the campaigning season, it was decided for various reasons to proceed with the coronation of Marie de Medici. This would not only justify the delay but also do something to appease domestic Catholic opinion, which was disturbed at the prospect of a war against Catholic interests, as well as to lend further legitimacy to the regime that would govern in the king's absence. The ceremony was performed in the Basilica of Saint-Denis on Thursday 13 May, and on the following Sunday the queen was to make a solemn entry into Paris.

The coronation of a queen was nothing new in French political ceremonial, but in the context of the war preparations it took on the aspect of a concession to public opinion and of a security precaution. Viewing the rite from a twentieth-century perspective, we see it also as a sign of the power which the monarchy, in its dynastic and family form, exercised in French society. Finally, it illustrates Henri IV's constant desire to speak to the popular imagination, to prove all the time, as he had sought to do ever since his accession, the legitimacy of his rule, and thus to graft his new branch onto the family tree of the kings of France. But all these meanings, explicit or implicit, would be swept into oblivion by the political tragedy which befell the next day.

The Death of Henri IV and the Accession of Louis XIII

On 14 May 1610, at about four in the afternoon, the king was crossing Paris from the Louvre to the Arsenal to survey the preparations for the queen's entry on Sunday. In the rue de la Ferronerie, where the king's carriage was brought to a halt at a bottle-neck in the only east–west through route on the city's right bank, a lunatic leaned in through the door and stabbed the king twice. Henri was dead within minutes. Despite the horror and amazement, the permanence of the State was affirmed at once. In the next few hours the great officers of the Crown and the Parlement de Paris recognised and proclaimed the reign of Louis XIII,

Henri's eldest son, a nine-year-old boy who had suddenly and inevitably become king.

The procedures for the transmission of the Crown had gradually crystallised amid the circumstances and contingencies of preceding centuries. This body of customary law (that is, never formally codified), enforced only by history, denied women the right to the succession by the so-called Salic Law, supposed to have prevailed among the Salian Franks, the people of Clovis, the first king of France. The succession was restricted to male heirs in strict order of birth. The king was deemed to have attained his majority on completing his thirteenth year. Until then he was subject to a Regency Council. Finally, the King of France had to be a Catholic, a point which had been driven home by the conversion of Henri IV. These rules were known as the 'fundamental laws of the realm', the laws of the French State, nation, republic or Crown (terms at that time almost synonymous). These fundamental laws were above even the will of the king. Thus the French monarch, despite being called absolute, had no power to alter the order of the succession as fixed by these rules. His rights in the kingdom were inferior to those of a private person in his property. The kingdom was not a patrimony for the king to dispose of as he wished, but a benefice that he entered at his accession and left only at death. The king was mortal, his person was vulnerable, but the dignity of the Crown was perpetual. The clarity and almost automatic operation of these rules gave considerable strength to the French monarchy, which was spared, for example, the protracted succession conflicts which beset England in the fifteenth century.

These rules were well known among the statesmen and magistrates of early modern France. The king required no formal recognition or proclamation whatsoever, be it by an assembly of princes of the blood, a meeting of the Estates, or a court of law, as was the case in other monarchies. He became king the moment his predecessor died, a fact summed up in common law by the adage 'death seizes the living' (that is, puts the survivor in possession of the dead person's property), and in public law by the analogous phrases, 'the king is dead, long live the king' and 'the king never dies'. In another constitutional context the principle remains with us to this day: it is what we call the continuity of the State.

Chancellor Sillery, who as the head of the king's judiciary was the highest officer of the Crown and the foremost authority in the law, bowed down before the little boy who had so recently been the Dauphin and was now his king. An hour later the Duke of Épernon, Colonel General of the Infantry, presented himself before the Parlement de Paris with a message from the Queen Mother, calling on them to recognise her as regent. This approach was somewhat ambiguous, as the Parlement de Paris was but one sovereign court among many. It had its advantages, of course – it was based in the capital, it was the oldest of the Parlements and its jurisdiction was the most extensive (covering nearly a third of the realm) – but it had never been a council of government, nor was it the sole repository and custodian of the law of the land. Any doubts were cleared away the following day (15 May), when the young king was brought to the Parlement in person to hold a *lit de justice*, that is to express his will according to a political ritual centred around his appearance within the precincts of the court. From his person alone emanated all legitimation and all power. It was for the king himself to declare his intentions regarding the regency. The ceremony saw the Chancellor receive the king's statement, and then take the advice (not on the fact, but on the manner) of the princes of the blood, the dukes and peers, the cardinals and spiritual peers, the Presidents of the Parlement, the members of the King's Council, the Masters of Requests, and finally the Councillors of the Parlement. The Chancellor then proclaimed the outcome of the *lit de justice*, namely that the Queen Mother was the regent. Assigning the regency to the Queen Mother had a long series of precedents in French history, most recently in the case of Catherine de Medici, thrice regent for under-age or temporarily absent sons.

The ceremony of 15 May, apparently unanimous and a mere formality, left some things unsaid. In order to secure the goodwill of the Parlement, Queen Marie had accepted its pretensions to tutelage over the law of the Crown. The princes and the great officers of Crown and Parlement, who might have made some claim to the appointment, gave way before the queen, whose authority would be weightier and more effective in troubled times.

That all this could be done amidst the confusion and panic without any dissension or delay testifies to the institutional maturity of the French Crown, its deep roots in the political structure and its capacity to adapt to the most trying and terrible circumstances.

The Doctrine of Tyrannicide

It is necessary now to return to the murder of the king and decide whether we should see in that event an unforeseeable accident, the work of a lunatic, the fruit of a plot or even the culmination of a deep-rooted crisis of confidence.

We should begin with the almost trivial observation that it is in the nature of monarchy, by attributing all power to a single individual, to expose that individual to the risk of assassination. It must be so in any regime based on the personalisation of authority. But if assassination can befall a regime of this kind in any age, the frequency of and justification for assassination vary according to the particular conventions and political conditions of different historical periods. The closing decades of the sixteenth century had seen assassination employed across much of Europe. Fanatics who were willing to sacrifice their own lives in order to end those of a hated statesman were imitating the classical model of tyrannicide. The religious divisions of the Reformation and outbreak of religious wars led to dramatic situations in which subjects found themselves torn between the obedience which they owed to their sovereign and the obligation to rebel if that sovereign should prove a persecutor or a heretic. If the crimes of a wicked ruler extended to altering the religion of his people and thus putting their eternal salvation in jeopardy, then anyone who was in a position to do so ought to bring his career to an end. The annals of French history are rich in such episodes: the murders of François de Guise, of the Admiral Coligny, and of Henri III himself bulk large in contemporary chronicles. Henri IV was himself the target of many attempts on his life, among them those of the old boatman turned League soldier, Pierre Barrière, in 1593, and of the student of the Jesuits, Jean Chastel, in 1594.

Magistrates and politicians, aware of the terrible and enduring threat of subversion inherent in the moral justification of tyrannicide, sought to erect a bulwark of legal sanctions and moral teachings against it. They enacted and executed draconian penalties against regicide: Barrière and Chastel were quartered alive. As was often the case, the law sought to use exemplary and horrific deterrents to compensate for its inability to plumb society's depths in order to forestall and prevent such attempts.

In pursuing their investigations, magistrates devoted particular attention to the Jesuits, who, of all the Catholics, put forward the most cogent defence of the faith against deviant rulers. The direct dependence of the Jesuits upon the papacy, which put them outside the ambit of local jurisdictions whether ecclesiastical or temporal, made them a standing example of insubordination and of a provocative independence from State control. The Parlement de Paris, which, from the moment the Jesuits arrived within its jurisdiction, left no stone unturned in its attempts to oppose their expansion, used the Chastel affair to secure their expulsion. But Henri IV himself recognised the intellectual calibre and religious dedication of the fathers, and authorised their recall in 1603. But it took several *lettres de jussion* to compel the Parlement to accept the return of the Society of Jesus to the capital, and the reopening of its colleges. The Gallican proclivities of most of the magistrates, and their determination to defend the rights of the State and the French Church against the prerogatives of the Holy See, made them in effect more royalist than the king, more committed than he to the doctrine of absolute monarchy – an ideological position they were to maintain until the Revolution.

In fact, the Jesuits neither preached nor taught differently from any other of the Catholic bodies, such as the Franciscans or the Feuillants, which were thick on the ground in France. And Protestant authors, notably in the 1570s, had likewise inculcated the obligation to resist tyranny by arms and thus, by implicit or explicit extension, to put a tyrant to death. The question of whether tyrannicide was permitted or even binding upon the Christian conscience was one of the commonplaces of the age, normally but a dry discussion topic, yet capable in certain circumstances of becoming a burning question of immense practical importance.

The Ravaillac Affair

The violent polemics of Protestants against Charles IX, and of Catholics against Henri III or (until 1594) Henri IV were by 1610 a thing of the past. Religious peace had returned to the kingdom. It was the planned campaign in Cleves which had reawoken disquiet among some Catholics. The recent jurisdictional conflict between the papacy and the Republic of Venice, and the polemics of James I against the plotting of English Catholics aroused fears of a renewed Protestant propaganda offensive in Europe. That Henri IV should contemplate a war against a small Catholic duchy in defiance of papal policy seemed to lay bare either the insincerity of his conversion or the sheer cynicism of his convictions. A rumour current around Christmas 1609 had it that the Protestants were planning a massacre of Catholics and that the king was going to wage war against the pope himself. Henri IV's assassin had heard it and believed it. Such provocative rumours were symptomatic of the malaise which afflicted hardline Catholic opinion. Political history cannot overlook rumour, false news, prejudice, popular opinions, and commonplaces, however great the evidential difficulties they present. The tragic episode of Henri IV's assassination casts some revealing shafts of light into these usually obscure areas.

The assassin was one François Ravaillac. The personality of the poor wretch who made such a brief but dramatic appearance on the historical stage deserves some attention, to the extent that it casts light upon the significance of his action. He was a little over thirty years old, from a pious and educated background in Angoulême. Like his father he was a solicitor at law, but neither of them had made much of a living at it. The father had been reduced to penury and the son kept a little school. François sought to join the Feuillants, a branch of the Benedictines, but he was rejected because he had visions. In short, he was a needy intellectual, deeply if tormentedly devout. He was driven to regicide by lofty scruples which transmuted his fantasies into conscientious obligations.

The commissioners of the Parlement who examined and tortured him sought tirelessly for information on the accomplices and conspirators who – they supposed – were behind his deed: great magnates, Spanish agents, or even his confessors or spiritual directors. Their efforts were in vain, for it is beyond doubt that Ravaillac acted entirely on his own, and that his action was the result of nothing more than undocumented grievances against the king's foreign policy.

Assassination Fever

It seemed to the magistrates not only implausible but improper in the extreme that so daring a blow should have been struck by such an insignificant figure, and impossible that the crime of a single individual should have such far-reaching consequences. They wanted the result to correspond with their predispositions, and they wanted at least to incriminate their favourite scapegoats, the Spaniards or the Jesuits. Despite all the evidence of their investigations and interrogations, despite Ravaillac's own tragic sincerity, they stayed on the scent of their spurious plot. An investigation pursued in such a manner inevitably takes full advantage of coincidences, ambiguities and vague suspicions. *Raison d'état* can harvest disturbing secrets from the simplest of stories. And the enduring attraction of conspiracy theories resides in the sense they give their adherents of being independent minded souls who are not taken in by appearances. By ascribing the hazards of fate to human agency, conspiracy theories provide targets for the instincts of blame and revenge, and exorcise the feelings of frustration and impotence which such events induce. They run throughout history and can arise in almost any circumstances.

If the enduring and insidious attraction of conspiracy theories played its part in the reactions to Henri IV's death, so too did another psychological impulse of a more limited and culturally specific character: the discovery of portents and omens presaging the assassination. A dream of the queen's, sudden uneasiness on the part of the king, advice from his friends to be cautious – all were told and retold after the event. Proofs of a conspiracy were found in the ravings of lunatics and drunkards uttered days before the event. Omens were identified in changes in the weather or in such trivial accidents as lightning striking a shield blazoned with the fleur-de-lys and a bull falling into the moat around a royal château. Horoscopes and prophecies were also found to have foretold the crisis. Judicial astrology (that is, the reading of the future in and the basing of decisions upon the position of the stars) at that time enjoyed widespread credence at all levels of society, from the most cultivated to the backwoods village. Its vogue rested (like that of conspiracy theories) upon a reluctance to ascribe the vicissitudes of human existence to trivial, or even more to vague and uncertain, causes and circumstances. Presages restored random events to their proper place in the decrees of divine providence, making them worthy to be noted and foretold in the signs of heaven.

Ravaillac was quartered in the place de Grève on 27 May 1610. A vast and frenzied crowd witnessed the slow and barbarous execution and then, pushing through the archers, tore the corpse into pieces which were then taken away and burned in the villages of the suburbs.

The embalmed corpse of the king lay in state in the Louvre until the end of June. His heart was taken to the chapel of the Jesuit college of La Flèche, in accordance with a vow he had made. The funeral took place in Saint-Denis on 1 July.

The widespread unpopularity which had beset the king in 1609–10 gave way on the news of his death to sincere and universal grief. His plans for war and taxation were instantly forgotten, and memory dwelt only upon his solid historical achievements: the establishment of the new dynasty, the restoration of domestic peace and the consolidation of the frontiers. The news of his death rekindled all the old worries as people suddenly came to appreciate how valuable and how vulnerable were the fruits of his reign. In that moment the myth of 'good King Henri' was begotten, a myth that would flower over the years in an abundance of apologetic literature recounting the life and deeds of the dead king. Poetry and history were supplemented by sculptures, paintings and engravings which depicted him in the guise of Jupiter or Hercules, an emperor or a Roman general in triumph, a knight or a prince, armed, equestrian or crowned with laurels, dispensing justice, or at prayer. It was on the 23 August 1614 that an equestrian statue in bronze forever fixed the image of Henri IV in the heart of Paris, at the Pont-Neuf. His wit and wisdom, the glorious feats of arms of his youth and the shrewd policies of his reign were endlessly repeated, embellished or invented. Henri IV belonged henceforth to the enchanted realm of an idyllic golden age.

The Coronation of Louis XIII

The Queen Regent wisely decided to make no changes in the personnel of the late King's Council, and to preserve the balance of personalities and opinions among the Secretaries of State as Henri IV had established it. Two powerful individuals dominated the Council: Sully, the great Protestant aristocrat, committed to alliances with the northern powers and putting his financial wizardry at the service of an aggressive foreign policy; and Villeroy, the Catholic bureaucrat, solicitous above all for peace. Sully's achievement is the better known, not least because he himself devoted his long retirement to the compilation of his penetrating and informative memoirs, the *Mémoires des sages et royales économies d'État* (or *Économies royales* for short), which were an instant and enduring success from the moment they were first published in 1641. Nicolas de Neufville de Villeroy died in 1617 and was soon forgotten. Originally an adherent of the League, he had subsequently played a crucial role in the negotiations which led to the defection of the major League chieftains, and became a close adviser to Henri IV, who entrusted him with the conduct of foreign affairs. An expert in the tangled politics of the Italian peninsula, he enjoyed for that reason the confidence of Marie de Medici, and his advice henceforth prevailed in Council.

One urgent necessity was to reassure Protestant opinion, which was concerned that the assassination of the king was the signal for a Spanish attack. One of the first acts of the regent was therefore to issue a full and solemn confirmation of the Edict of Nantes

(3 June 1610). Under the provisions of the edict, two elected deputies permanently represented the 'R.P.R.' ('Religion Purportedly
Reformed') before the Council. They were appointed for a term of
three years by the national synod, an assembly itself composed of
representatives from the sixteen provinces into which the Protestant Church was organised in France. As the term of office was
nearing its end, the regent authorised the national synod to meet
early in 1611.

The expedition against Cleves was carried through much as
planned. The army, which had been ready to set out from Champagne in May, now advanced along the Meuse valley and passed
peacefully enough through the Spanish Netherlands and the episcopal principality of Liège. The towns of the duchies were
occupied by September, and the imperial commissioners were expelled. The territories were divided between the two Protestant
princes who laid claim to them, on condition that they respected
the Catholic faith of the population. The Spanish made no
attempt to oppose the French advance, and the Empire accepted
the *fait accompli*. The threat to the strategic balance proved
groundless, and the danger of a European conflict receded.

The Council decided to have the young king crowned. Neither
law nor convention specified a particular date for the coronation.
It was purely a matter of political convenience. In this case, the
youth of the king, the regent's lack of prestige, and the division of
the kingdom between religious and princely factions made an
early coronation advisable. The decision had been taken by July,
and foreign ambassadors began to arrive in Paris for the occasion.

The traditional place of coronation was the cathedral of
Notre-Dame in Reims. Henri IV had been unable to follow this
tradition in 1594 because the League still held Champagne. He
had therefore been anointed at Chartres with a holy oil brought
from the Abbey of Marmoutier. It was now essential in most
people's eyes for the French court to find its way back to Reims.
The spirit of place which under the peculiar circumstances of
1594 had seemed a secondary consideration was by 1610 restored to its former importance. The rich and powerful
province of Champagne was jealous of its privilege, and the
power of a time-honoured tradition could reinforce the majesty

of the little Louis XIII. He was therefore crowned in Reims at noon on Sunday 17 October.

The crisis of the later sixteenth century had heightened awareness of monarchical symbolism. The religious and political signification of royal ceremonial were widely known and understood. The ceremonial anointing during the coronation did not make the king. It was not *constitutive*, and added nothing to his rights, which he already enjoyed in full by virtue of his accession. It was *declaratory*, making explicit the king's powers and spiritual dignities. The liturgical and ornamental details of the ritual evolved from reign to reign, but the main words and actions had been fixed in 1365 in the coronation *ordo* of Charles V, and had been broadly followed since. The essential components of the ceremony were the two oaths which the king swore to the bishops and to the people, and the anointing, which was administered by the Archbishop of Reims. In his oaths, the king swore to uphold the laws and liberties of the Church, to maintain peace and dispense justice among his people, and to defend the Christian faith. The anointing which he received upon nine places of his body was carried out with a mixture of holy oil or chrism (as used in baptism) and an ointment contained in the Holy Ampulla, a phial believed to have been brought to St Remy by an angel for the baptism of Clovis.

The coronation was a sign of God's favour for the person of the king. It conferred upon him a clerical status: he was no longer a layman, but was what they called a 'bishop over externals' (in the manner of the Emperor Constantine), with the authority to regulate the temporal life of the Church within his realm. Finally, he was invested by the coronation with a miraculous healing power. The thaumaturgic gift of the French kings was regarded as a proof of the outstanding dignity of their kingdom and their dynasty, and as overwhelming evidence of their legitimacy and of their peculiar mission among their people. The gift was exercised upon those afflicted with scrofula, 'the king's evil' (in technical terms, tuberculosis of the lymph nodes). The symptoms seem to have been widespread, as victims came in their hundreds and thousands when, on the major feasts of the Church's year, the king announced that he would touch for the king's evil. The king would

pass along the ranks of the sick, touching each of them and utter-
ing the sacred formula, 'The king touches you, God heals you.'

As was customary, the king remained at Reims for some days.
On Thursday 21 October he made his way to the village of Cor-
beny, on the border between Champagne and Picardy, where a
shrine held the relics of Saint Marcoul, a holy abbot of bygone
times to whose intercession the kings of France were said to owe
their healing power. According to the testimony of his physician,
Héroard, the boy king touched some nine hundred sick people
that day. Like his father, Louis XIII remained loyal all his life to
that miraculous ritual, the most extraordinary symbol of his royal
dignity.

The Expectation of Reform

Notwithstanding the burden of grief imposed by the old king's
death, the accession of a young king in spring 1610 was seen as a
sign of renewal and hope for the future. A new generation of
young noblemen, bored with a decade of internal and external
peace and envious of the monopoly which veterans of the Wars of
Religion still had upon military honour, was vaguely expectant of
a new order of things. Public opinion had at first welcomed the
retention of Henri IV's old advisers, but they were soon being
called the 'greybeards', because they were seen as belonging to a
bygone age and an outdated fashion which soon grated upon the
new generation rising at court and in the city. The regent's time-
honoured sop to public opinion – repealing various fiscal edicts
and writing off more or less irrecoverable arrears of tax – seemed
to herald the new order. Sully, the *Surintendant des finances*, was
made anxious by the circulation of rumours crediting him with
many years of misappropriation: he had, after all, been in complete control of the country's finances for a dozen years,
accountable to nobody except a king who had total confidence in
him. He made as if to retire to his estates around the time of the
coronation, but the regent subsequently recalled him to court.
However, two months later, in January 1611, realising that his
authority in the Council was both diminished and contested, Sully

resigned as *Surintendant* and also as Captain of the Bastille (a post which had hitherto guaranteed him effective control of the capital). He retired to his Poitou estates. His fortune was already made, and during his long retirement he maintained its level by exchanging royal offices for shares in tax farms. When he died in 1641 he had over 5 million *livres*.

Having thus dealt with the unfinished business of Henri IV's reign, the regency then embarked upon a new style of government, more pragmatic and unsteady, reflecting the inevitable political fragility of a royal minority.

3   The Regency of Marie de Medici

From May 1610 to October 1614, the Queen Mother, Marie de Medici, ran the government of France as regent in the name of her son. And even after Louis XIII had attained his majority, she continued to dominate the Council thanks to his filial compliance until, in April 1617, he suddenly broke his reins and assumed personal control of his affairs. Thereafter the Queen Mother retained a certain but by no means consistent influence over her son and thus over the affairs of the realm. Marie de Medici must therefore be regarded as a person of prime importance in the political history of the time. Historians have tended to judge her rather harshly, concentrating on the petty squabbles between the ageing queen and her son, and above all on her political struggle with the all-conquering Cardinal Richelieu, which brought her at last to a death in exile. Picking up the themes of the pamphleteers who spoke for her powerful enemies, they have taxed her with limited intelligence and a quarrelsome vanity. Yet if we judge the tree by its fruits, the period of her rule was one of the most prosperous and brilliant of the early modern age. The critics of her regime have failed to look beyond its superficial problems, the jockeying for position of princely factions and the court intrigues which seemed so significant for the future of the country.

The Princely Factions and their Struggle for Power

The social and political influence of the great magnates in early seventeenth-century France was enormous. It derived primarily from their landed wealth. As the owners of huge estates scattered over several provinces but concentrated in a few areas where their holdings were especially consolidated, the magnates disposed of vast landed income – the richest and most secure income the age could offer. Hundreds or thousands of peasants, farmers, merchants and lawyers owed their livelihoods to these men. But the prestige of the great magnates was more than a matter of mere money. It also involved the antiquity of their lineage and the degree of their relationship with the royal house.

Among the criteria which more or less explicitly fixed an individual's place in the social hierarchy, pride of place went to the length of the family tree. For certain legal or fiscal purposes, nobility had to be capable of written proof. But more than title-deeds of nobility drawn from illegible charters, what really mattered in confirming a nobleman's position was public opinion, the general recognition that such and such a baron was pre-eminent in a particular locality, the weight that he carried in the provincial Estates, his participation in the feudal levy, and the honour that he achieved though serving the king in peace or war. In an age which idealised stability and continuity, it was accepted that virtue and merit were hereditary, and that the passage of time provided proof of their presence in given families. The most outstanding families had therefore been noted by kings and rewarded with peer-duchies. Admitted by their rank to the king's inner circle, the peer-dukes represented the very pinnacle of nobility.

The princes of the blood belonged to the actual kin-group of the king. They therefore enjoyed a share in his legitimation to the extent that they were nearer or further removed from the succession. When Henri IV inherited the throne in 1589, he traced his claim back to a son of St Louis: he was a ninth cousin once removed of the king he succeeded! Princes of the blood owed their peculiar status neither to landed nor to commercial wealth, but to their potential claim to the throne. The king shrewdly exploited the value of great names in recruiting the officers of the Royal Household, the provincial governors, and the commanders of fortresses and strongholds. The obedience of a local nobility, the loyalty of a province, and the effectiveness of royal legislation and demands could all be guaranteed by the prestige of a princely name.

The commoners of the realm were well aware that a place in the client network of some great family could open doors, secure valuable favours, and offer useful help in finding an advantageous marriage, in pursuing litigation, or in obtaining advancement in a legal or military career. A newcomer desirous of an introduction to the court, or a foreign ambassador anxious for information and connections, would alike make approaches to the entourage of a great magnate. The king for his part had to keep a close eye upon his magnates, to stay abreast of their influence and their relationships, and to know how to retain their loyalty and support by the judicious distribution of friendship, favours, pensions and appointments.

Gathering up scraps of power was clearly one of the means of social climbing. There was already a pretty wide appreciation of the role of the State as an engine of social advancement, as the dispenser of social status and above all as the distributor of tax revenues. Moreover, in the absence of any intellectual equipment for understanding economic forces (notably inflation, which was rampant in the early years of the century), it was assumed that the impoverishment of the nobility and of landholders in receipt of fixed seigneurial rents was simply the result of the despicable ingratitude with which the State rewarded their loyalty. It therefore seemed that in fairness the King's Council should show the utmost generosity to those nobles whose birth and distinction qualified them as of right to serve the king.

Two families in particular compelled recognition at court: those of Condé and Guise. The house of Bourbon-Condé was descended from a younger brother of Antoine de Navarre (Henri IV's father), Louis de Condé. His eldest son, Henri I de Condé (1552–88), had been the military leader of the Protestant faction before Henri de Navarre himself. And his son, Henri II de Condé (1588–1646), born after his father's death, and brought up as a Catholic, was next in line for the throne should Henri de Navarre die without legitimate children. We have already seen how he had found himself obliged to seek refuge abroad in 1609, and how his departure could have been seen as the fruit of some Spanish plot.

His triumphant return to Paris in July 1610 signified that a new leaf had been turned in the annals of France and that a new generation was coming to power.

The house of Guise, a branch of the sovereign ducal house of Lorraine, enjoyed enormous prestige in Catholic France, especially in the eastern provinces which held its territorial base. Charles II (1571–1640), the son of the Duke Henri who had led the League, was won over to Henri IV's cause in 1595 and served it faithfully thereafter. Even in the most difficult days of the regency, he remained a constant supporter of royal authority.

Other great names also figure in the annals of the time. The Duke of Épernon, Colonel General of the Infantry, a friend of Henri III and a companion of Henri IV, was a touchy and uncouth fellow, though attractive enough to judge by the extent and loyalty of his client network. The Duke of Nevers, cousin to the Dukes of Mantua, had been made Governor of Champagne in return for rallying to Henri IV. Fabulously wealthy and fervently Catholic, he had the new town of Charleville built on the frontier.

A numerous and powerful Protestant nobility also had to be taken into account. The Duke of Bouillon, lord of what he maintained were two sovereign fiefs (the viscountcy of Turenne in Quercy, and the principality of Sedan at the edge of the Ardennes), aspired to be recognised as the military leader of the Protestant churches. But this role was snatched from him by a nobleman from the far west, Duke Henri of Rohan (1579–1638), who held extensive lands in Brittany and Bas-Poitou. A relative of Sully, Rohan was Colonel General of the Swiss Guard from 1605, and took part in the Cleves expedition of 1610. His counsels were dominant in the political assemblies of the Huguenot faction.

From winter 1610 it was clear that Condé was seeking a leading role in government. He demanded compensation for the expenses incurred by his father in the service of Henri IV, together with guaranteed tenure of the strongholds in his charge and the command of two companies of light horse. By dint of procrastination and judicious concessions, of pensions and governorships, the Council managed to satisfy the demands of the princes. Villeroy, who fifteen years before had masterminded the negotiations with the magnates and cities of the League, maintained that it was better to spend money than soldiers' blood. Remaining in power until 1616, he adhered faithfully to his principles, negotiating and purchasing agreements as long as the kingdom laboured under the handicap of an under-age king.

The Royal Marriages and the Crisis of 1614

Papal diplomacy was anxious for some confirmation of the peace among the Catholic powers, and there was no better way of achieving this than a marriage alliance between the ruling houses of Spain and France. The papal nuncio Ubaldini, who was in residence at Paris from 1607 to 1616 (an unusually long posting), played a crucial role in the negotiations. He had already urged such an alliance upon Henri IV, and from June 1610 his plan enjoyed the regent's full support. Spain, now disentangled from war in the Netherlands, and France, fresh from victory in Cleves, were both in a strong position, unconstrained by pressing obligations. The tender age of the royal children was no obstacle to the project, and contracts were hammered out for unions which would not take place until many years later. The only difficulties on the French side arose from Protestant unease at an alliance which might prejudice their privileged position within the realm. And there were attempts at obstruction on the part of foreign powers which would themselves have welcomed a marriage alliance with the French dynasty: the Duke of Savoy and the King of England each wanted one of Henri IV's three daughters (Elisabeth, Henrietta Maria and Christine) for their own eldest sons. The most serious problems were with the court of Turin, which was indignant at the French for reneging on obligations undertaken in the Treaty of Bruzolo. The furious Charles Emmanuel reacted by seeking his own understanding with Madrid. Similarly, James I now started angling for a Spanish Infanta for the Prince of Wales. But the court of Madrid reckoned only a French match was fit for the Spanish Crown, and paid no attention to these distractions.

The project for a twofold alliance, with the young King Louis XIII marrying the Infanta Anne of Austria, and Princess Elisabeth of France marrying the future King of Spain, was formally put before the King's Council on 26 January 1612. In March, during a party held in the Louvre to mark the pre-Lenten celebrations of Carnival, the Spanish ambassador delivered a speech to Princess Elisabeth, publicly treating her as the future Queen of Spain. The marriage contracts, having been studied in great detail by both councils, were solemnly and simultaneously signed on 25 August 1612 (the feast of St Louis) in Madrid and Paris by special ambassadors. The princesses renounced their rights to the Crown of their native lands, and the dowries were equal: 500,000 golden *écus* (an *écu* was equivalent to 3 *livres*). The contracts expressed the mutual amity between the two nations, but specified no further treaty obligations. Each country retained complete freedom of action with regard to future events. Yet although the treaties thus gave nothing away, they at least signalled the peaceful intentions of the two governments, heralding perhaps a few years of peace and tranquillity in western Europe.

That the disquiet of the French Protestants had no untoward political consequences was largely thanks to the prudent counsels of the two great magnates of the Reformed faction, the Duke of Bouillon and the Duke of Lesdiguières, both of them firm supporters of royal authority.

Among the higher nobility there was considerable opposition, although the Spanish match was itself little more than a pretext masking more fundamental grievances about the limited role allotted to princes in the Council, the narrowness of the regent's inner circle and the right of the Queen Mother to the regency at all. Condé and his uncle, the Count of Soissons, made themselves spokesmen for this aristocratic discontent, aggrieved because, although the tutelage of the young king belonged to them by right as the nearest princes of the blood, they were only invited to Council sessions in order to rubber-stamp decisions which had already in effect been taken. They protested about the unworthiness of the favourites on whom the regent heaped places and pensions, and contested the legitimacy of the regent's position, which, they maintained, ought to have been confirmed by an assembly of the Estates General.

These grievances and jealousies focused in particular upon the most faithful friends of the regent, Concino Concini and his wife, a Tuscan couple who had come to the French court in 1601 and had since been loaded with rewards and privileges by the Queen Mother. They were targets for the rhetorical commonplaces of the time, upbraided for their Italian origin, their low birth and their meteoric rise. French opinion had long been suspicious of the droves of Italians who had flocked to Paris as a result of the Italian Wars and the Tuscan marriages of the kings, filling the court with Italian noblemen, churchmen, artists, businessmen and adventurers. They were reckoned at best parasites and tricksters, at worst cynical and despicable criminals. Another piece of received wisdom in an age which idealised stability was the impropriety of social mobility. It was therefore common to disparage the birth of those whom one wished to dismiss as upstarts. Concini was a perfect target for such attacks. Although he was son and grandson to secretaries of the Grand Dukes of Tuscany, he was dismissed as of lowly birth. Although he was intelligent and witty, he was dismissed as ignorant. And although he was largely indifferent to the regent's diplomacy, which was inspired by Villeroy, he was taken for a devotee of Spain. His ambitions had been assisted by his marriage in 1601 to Leonora Dori, called Galigaï, a childhood friend of Marie de Medici. In summer 1610 he was admitted to the King's Council and given command of several strongholds in the north. He subsequently became Marquis of Ancre, in Picardy (1611), and then a Marshal of France (1613). These hasty and ill-judged promotions made him the model of that hated figure, the court favourite, insolent and obnoxious.

Princely opposition took on a dangerous form early in 1614. The Duke of Nevers seized the citadel of Mézières in January, and Condé took possession of Sainte-Menehould in May. Masters of two vital frontier fortresses, they were in a position to dictate terms to the Council. Marie de Medici and Villeroy were well aware of the gravity of the situation. They made a show of strength by dispatching the best Swiss regiments to Champagne, but at the same time appointed two leading magistrates of the Parlement de Paris, the President Jeannin and the noted historian Jean-Auguste de Thou (a personal friend of Condé), to open negotiations. These led to the Treaty of Sainte-Menehould, signed on 15 May, by which the princes laid down their arms in return for certain assurances. The Spanish marriages were not called into question, but the Council undertook to convoke the Estates General in the near future. As Louis XIII was soon to reach the age of majority on his thirteenth birthday (27 September), and the regency was thus approaching its natural end, it was necessary in any case to legitimise the new regime. An assembly of the Estates General dovetailed neatly with the plans of the regent and the Council. The prospect of recourse to the traditional means of sounding the collective wisdom and expressing the collective hopes of the nation was welcomed on all sides, and the decision provoked a flood of pamphlets and leaflets expressing both widespread satisfaction and widespread expectations. These publications testify to the intensity of the political debate raging among the nobility, the officials and magistrates, and even the ordinary people of the capital.

In the face of these developments, the regent and Villeroy revived the idea of impressing royal authority upon public opinion by means of a grand royal progress through much of the realm. Catherine de Medici and her Chancellor, Michel de l'Hôpital, had resorted to a similar expedient in a similar situation, when the young King Charles IX found himself facing a kingdom on the brink of civil war. The royal progress through France in 1564–5 had displayed the young king to those provinces most distant from the capital. The occasion for this new progress was provided by the behaviour of the young Duke César of Vendôme (1594–1665), the legitimised son of Henri IV by Gabrielle d'Estrées. Louis XIII's half-brother was Governor of Brittany, and it was feared that he was digging himself in in some far off corner of that province. The king set out from Paris on 5 July and made a rendezvous at Orleans with a force of 20,000 men, an imposing escort. This force made its way slowly westwards, enjoying triumphal welcomes at every city along the way. The objective was kept a secret, for the western provinces contained several strongholds controlled by such princes as Condé and Vendôme, as well as some of the more important Protestant safe-havens. Having called first at Tours and Poitiers (one of Condé's places), the king veered off towards Loudun and Saumur, where Protestant garrisons were made to leave, and then made by way of Angers for Nantes. Arriving on 12

August, Louis presided at an assembly of the Provincial Estates. Vendôme hastened to pay homage to him at the château of Nantes, and the deputies of the Estates gave an unequivocal demonstration both of their loyalty in principle, and of their devotion to Louis in particular. The king's train then returned in short stages to Paris, arriving on 16 September amid scenes of rejoicing. Pamphlet literature reflected the success of the royal stratagem. The baronial literature which had dominated the market in May now gave way before a tide of publications extolling the virtues of domestic peace.

Louis XIII attained his majority on 27 September. On 2 October he held a *lit de justice* in the Parlement de Paris. The Queen Mother, kneeling before her son, relinquished the regency. Louis thanked her for her good government and then declared that, though he was taking the reins, she would still remain the head of his Council and was expected to attend it as before. In reality, therefore, nothing changed. The regime emerged strengthened from the crisis of 1614. The assembly of the Estates General would further confirm the success of the regime of Marie de Medici and Villeroy.

4 The Estates General of 1614

The Estates General was one of the oldest institutions of the French monarchy. Since the fourteenth century the king had had the power to summon representatives from his entire realm to form an assembly which was in theory strictly consultative. Its role was primarily to provide the sovereign, at moments of political crisis which called for difficult decisions, with the support of the social groups which composed the kingdom. It was neither permanent nor even regular, and met entirely at the king's pleasure. He could choose whether or not to convoke it, and even then remained free to follow or to ignore its advice. During the later sixteenth century, the problems engendered by the royal minorities and the Wars of Religion led the Estates General to meet with an unprecedented regularity which in turn gave it an unprecedented political importance. The Estates were convened in 1560, 1576, 1588 and 1593, and many of the recommendations of these assemblies were subsequently embodied in royal ordinances. The assembly which met in 1614 was thus heir to a living tradition.

The king's subjects were, by ancient custom, divided for purposes of consultation into three groups ('orders' or 'estates'): the clergy held pride of place, the second order was that of the nobility, and the remainder constituted the Third Estate. Nobody at that time supposed that the concept of the 'three estates' represented an exhaustive delineation of the social hierarchy: it simply reflected the basic calling or standing of the king's subjects. Early modern social thought saw each individual as a member of various communities or corporate bodies which related or overlapped with each other to form a sort of enormous social mosaic in which each subject had his due place with its appropriate privileges and status.

The Election of Deputies

Letters patent dated 7 June 1614 were sent to all the bailiwicks and seneschalcies of the realm requiring the selection of representatives of the three estates in each jurisdiction, and inviting the compilation of statements of grievances to be debated at the assembly, which would hammer out from them a composite statement for presentation to the king. In order to be carried out, these instructions had to be passed down to the level of the parish, the basic unit of communal life and public administration. Copies of the royal letters were therefore sent to all the rural parishes, to be read from the pulpit by the parish priest during Sunday Mass. In the towns and boroughs, the letters were addressed to the municipal magistrates, to the judges of lower courts, or even directly to the public by means of town-criers, or else by notice pinned to a market cross or church door. The clergy were notified by means of letters sent to each bishop. And the nobility and gentry were convened by the bailiff or seneschal himself. For while the principal units of local jurisdiction (known as bailiwicks in the north and as seneschalcies in the south) were in practice managed by a magistrate (namely the lieutenant-general in the case of the bailiwick) who was by calling a lawyer and an office-holder, the post of bailiff or seneschal itself was always held by a nobleman of the highest rank. The post of bailiff, retained even though it had become largely ceremonial, symbolised the twofold basis of royal justice, which rested on both the prestige of the nobility and the learning of the magistrates. It was for the bailiff and nobody else to communicate the king's orders to the noble families of his jurisdiction. Thus nobody could fail to be aware of the king's decision or of the importance of this enormous and unusual consultation of the community of the realm.

July saw the process of election under way throughout the kingdom. Discreet instructions were sent to provincial governors and the lieutenants general of the various jurisdictions to make sure that the deputies appointed were all faithful servants of the king – that is, to ensure that none were notorious clients of princely patrons. We know that many of those in high places at court and with influence in the provinces exerted themselves to this end: Sully in the west, Lesdiguières in the Dauphiné, the Cardinal de Sourdis in Aquitaine, and Concini in Picardy. We know too that the aldermen of the major towns kept a close eye on elections within their walls, that governors kept control of gatherings of the nobility, and that secret ballots (generally regarded as a sign of faction and disorder) were everywhere forbidden. On the whole, the desired result was achieved. Most of the deputies of the Third Estate were royal officials, almost all hostile to the princely party. They began to arrive in Paris about the beginning of October.

The Business of the Estates

Royal heralds in the livery of the fleur-de-lys traversed the streets of Paris proclaiming that the Estates General would convene on 22 October in the Hôtel de Bourbon, a grand residence near the Louvre. On that day, 140 churchmen, 132 nobles, and 192 deputies of the Third Estate would gather to hear speeches by the king, the chancellor, and a spokesman of each estate. They would go on to hold their separate sessions in the same building in order to facilitate communication between the three orders. In order to propose an issue or a text for discussion, formal delegations would be sent from one order to another to make a presentation. It was agreed that the procedure of the Estates should follow the models laid down in the records of their predecessors. The *Prévot des marchands* of Paris (equivalent to mayor, the capital having no magistrate of that rank), Robert Miron, who was also a President of the Parlement de Paris, managed the preliminary debates in which the deputies of the Third Estate decided on their procedures. It was agreed that they should split into twelve sections, one for each of the governorships of the realm, and that each section should elect a spokesman. Each group would then go through the

Parisian statement of grievances article by article, comparing them carefully with similar articles in the provincial statements. It was explicitly stated that this procedure did not constitute recognition of any pre-eminence for the capital, but was adopted purely for clarity and convenience.

Two issues attracted particular attention from the delegates: royal authority, which was upheld against arguments which tended to limit its exercise; and the sale of offices, which most delegates wanted to see abolished forthwith.

The First Affirmation of Absolutism

In a matter of twenty-five years two French kings had died by the hand of an assassin, thanks to a political climate of civil conflict. The fragile peace which now prevailed depended upon the vulnerable person of a young king. It therefore seemed essential to the servants of the State that the authority of the Crown should be safeguarded against such accidents. The first step was to launch a horrified denunciation of political theories which undermined royal authority or exposed kings to the risk of tyrannicide. The justification in conscience of an act of tyrannicide was diametrically opposed to the principles of *raison d'état*, and had been developed during the religious crises of the previous century, as first the Protestants accused Charles IX of murderous persecution, and then the Catholics denounced Henri III's treachery and Henri IV's heresy. The magistrates who for the most part made up the Third Estate, along with the councillors of the Parlement de Paris, who flattered themselves on guiding and shaping public opinion, called for firm statements of the inviolability of the king's person and of his superiority within his kingdom to any human jurisdiction. This claim of course entailed the independence of the State from papal authority, and thus inevitably brought the royalist magistrates into conflict with the papal nuncio, most French bishops and the Jesuits, who all upheld as sound doctrine the pope's power to authorise subjects to disobey an oppressive or heretical prince. Fierce disputes on the hierarchy of powers could be ignited by a paragraph in a book or by a mere verbal technicality. But they were not trivial – witness the political murders which stain the annals of the time. Nor were they anything new: the hostility of the Parlement de Paris to the Jesuits dated back to 1560, when the Jesuits were first established in the kingdom. The magistrates, committed to the defence of the royal prerogative against the encroachments of the clergy, stood in a long tradition of tension between Church and State, apparent in every Catholic kingdom, England and Spain as much as France. Nineteenth-century historians coined for this tradition the convenient name of 'Gallicanism'. The term did not exist in the seventeenth century: the adjective 'Gallican' simply denoted the Catholic Church in the kingdom of France, and there was no abstract noun denoting a system of thought hostile to papal authority. Such a doctrine was rare among churchmen at the start of the century, but was found rather among the magistrates. In 1610, the syndic of the Faculty of Theology of Paris, Richer, published a Latin treatise which added an ecclesiastical dimension to the 'statist Gallicanism' by upholding the rights of bishops within their dioceses and of general councils within the universal Church against the the rights and powers of the papacy. In consequence, the term 'Richerism' came to be applied to challenges made by the French clergy against decisions from Rome.

The Parlement de Paris had long kept a close eye upon the content of theological publications in order to censure the slightest tendency to exalt papal power above that of kings. This vigilance intensified after 1610, when, at the instigation of the King's Advocate, Servin, the Parlement campaigned vigorously against the writings of the learned curial cardinal, Robert Bellarmine, who was controverting the absolutist claims of King James I of England. The Parlement also condemned the writings of the Spanish Jesuit Francisco Suárez, a professor at the University of Salamanca. The King's Council had to intervene, and in December 1614 issued a decree overruling the Parlement's censures. The Estates, meeting in the midst of this dispute, furnished the magistrates with a further and imposing platform from which to urge the Gallican case.

The Parisian spokesmen in the Third Estate wanted a declaration of the absolute rights of the king to figure at the head of the composite statement of grievances, and the first article read, in proclamatory fashion:

> The king is begged to decree it in the assembly of his Estates as a fundamental law of the land, inviolable and universally acknowledged, that as he is sovereign in his State, holding his Crown from God alone, there is no power on earth, be it spiritual or temporal, which has any authority within his realm, on any ground or pretext whatsoever, either to depose the anointed person of the king, or to dispense or absolve his subjects from the loyalty and obedience they owe him.

The text further demanded that an oath to this effect should henceforth be exacted from all officeholders, preachers and teachers. When the clerical estate were informed of this article, they opposed it on the grounds that it exempted the State from all moral constraint, flouted the universal spiritual authority of the papacy, and implicitly claimed for the Estates General competence in matters of religious doctrine.

The King's Council was embarrassed by the unwelcome zeal of the Third Estate in thus setting monarchy against papacy. Marie de Medici, with her usual skill, managed to persuade the Third Estate not to press the disputed article. Their statement of grievances therefore began with a blank page, followed by the second article: the space for an absolutist manifesto was, as it were, left for the future.

The clergy had their hearts set on a particular objective of their own, one which likewise reflected a certain conception of the State. They wanted the immediate reception and formal integration into the law of the land of the decrees of the Council of Trent, which had concluded its deliberations fifty years before. Neither the Third Estate nor the King's Council were prepared to accept this. The royal response was that this was a spiritual matter for the clergy alone, and that it was up to them to implement the Tridentine decrees as best they could; but that the legislation as such was alien to public law and was therefore incapable of integration into the law of the land.

The Attempt to Abolish the Sale of Offices

It was the noble estate which called for the abolition of the sale of offices, and in particular of the *paulette* which, since 1604, had granted officeholders the right to bequeath their offices upon payment of an annual tax. The demand was presented in the chamber of the nobility on 12 November by the Marquis of Urfé. In this matter it was the nobility, rather than the Third Estate (dominated as it was by officeholders), who reflected popular opinion and indeed popular expectation. The auctioning of public offices and the effective annexation of those offices by wealthy officeholding dynasties was a scandal which, it was felt, should be brought to an end. The *paulette* was a particular grievance, for it had driven up the price of office by making it hereditary, and had thus made achieving office difficult for the gentry and practically impossible for the peasant élite. Moreover, the increased price of offices made their incumbents more likely to seek to recoup their expenditure by taking bribes. Above all, the king had almost no choice at all in the personnel of his administration and was hampered on the ground by entrenched vested interests and by powerful networks of officeholding families. The experiment of the *paulette* was only ten years old, and should be curtailed at once in order to prevent the consolidation of a parasitic officeholding oligarchy and to restore the king's freedom of action.

Those in office, of course, had no desire to give up the obvious advantages of hereditary office, which was the foundation of their fortunes and their future security. But the force of public opinion was too strong, and the grievances from the provinces which they were called upon to answer were explicit. So the Third Estate added its voice to the call for the repeal of the *paulette*. But the deputies shrewdly added a call for a reduction in the pensions received by so many noblemen, a tit-for-tat designed to interfere with the motion regarding the *paulette*. If each of the three estates was thus pursuing an objective of its own at the expense of the other two, there was nevertheless a near unanimity on a call for the reform of financial scandals, be they the unlawful inheritance of office, the misappropriations of tax farmers who advanced money to the king, or the mounting burden of pensions. The

King's Council readily expressed its support on such matters. The closing ceremony of the Estates General took place on 23 February 1615, in the great hall of the Hôtel de Bourbon. After listening to addresses from the spokesmen of each of the three estates, the king formally received their statements of grievances and promised them a quick response.

A large number of the deputies remained in Paris to see what form that response would take. The second article of the Third Estate's grievances was a petition for regular meetings of the Estates General, perhaps every ten years. This was a time-honoured and long-standing petition, and if the French Crown had ever granted it, then the institutional structure, and indeed the entire history, of France would have been very different. That the deputies stayed in Paris until March, with each order holding meetings in the residence of its president, was perhaps a tentative initial step in the direction of the supervision of government by a representative body of the whole realm.

On 24 March the king summoned the leading deputies to the Louvre. There they were told by Chancellor Sillery that the complexity of their grievances ruled out an immediate and wholesale solution, but that he was able to give undertakings in the king's name on the main points raised. In particular, he announced that the king had decided to abolish the sale of offices, to reduce pensions and to establish as in the past an extraordinary tribunal to investigate financial irregularities. He concluded by declaring that the Estates should be satisfied with this. The deputies returned to the provinces feeling pretty pleased with themselves. Political pamphlets over the next few weeks spoke of the 'fall of the *paulette*', reflecting popular expectations. It seemed as if the regime was contemplating a major reform, for even if financial investigations and pension reductions were customary fiscal expedients, the abolition of the sale of office presupposed a fundamental reordering of the machinery of government, which would henceforth be more in line with popular, and for that matter noble, opinion. But for all the play of imagination, the promise of reform was never to be put into effect.

Once the deputies had departed for their constituencies, the Parlement de Paris set about reminding the Council of its own role in the State, a role which had been greatly reinforced by the events of May 1610. The Estates General had shown the potential of widely based public opinion and had revealed the extent to which it ran counter to the ideology and interests of the officeholders. The Parlement was therefore keen to consign the whole episode to oblivion and make good its own pretensions to be the sole mediator between Crown and people. It had behaved similarly in the wake of the Estates of 1588, and had succeeded in preventing the Estates from meeting during the effective reign of Henri IV. But this time the Parlement had been unable to prevent the Estates being summoned or to keep it from voting against the sale of offices.

The First President of the Parlement, Savaron, took pains to point out that curtailing the *paulette* and the sale of offices would not only mean a loss of revenue for the Treasury but would also constitute an injury to many notable families, with the consequent risk of serious political discontent. The Prince of Condé supported this case, and encouraged some of the younger councillors to press the issue. The princes, like the Parlement, represented a source of counsel in the State which had been overshadowed by the prestige of the Estates General. On 28 March 1615 the Parlement de Paris, in a plenary session of all its chambers, went so far as to convoke on its own authority the princes and great officers of the Crown for a general discussion of the state of the nation, with particular respect to the statements of grievances presented to the king by the three estates. The Parlement de Paris was in effect claiming superiority over the Estates General, a preeminence in government as the natural and foremost council of the king. It might even have been aspiring to supervise the royal power itself, as it claimed the right to summon the great officers of the Crown, and thus in effect credited itself with universal political competence. But the king forbade the meeting the following day, and the Parlement obeyed. Nevertheless, the King's Council appreciated the significance of this parliamentary initiative, which expressed the anxiety and annoyance of the officeholding class. It appreciated equally its own inability to embark on fundamental political reform in a period of monarchical weakness. Instead of setting about this implausible reform, the Council took refuge in procrastination. It was announced on 13 May 1615 that the *paulette* would be provisionally extended until 1 January 1618. In fact, the project was buried, and the hopes and dreams of early 1615 were buried with it.

The wrangling between the three orders, the oblivion into which the grievances they presented were soon consigned, and the disrepute into which the Parlement de Paris successfully cast the assembly itself, thanks to its control of the means of propaganda, have led historians to give little attention to the Estates General of 1614. It is true that their demands – for the abolition of the sale of offices, financial accountability, sumptuary legislation aimed at luxury expenditure and social mobility, and the regular convocation of the Estates – were traditional to the point of commonplace. But while they had often been demanded by the assemblies which had met since 1561, the remonstrances drafted in 1614–15 were perhaps the most coherent and came closest to success. An edict of 1618 embodied several of the proposals, but the Parlement, significantly enough, refused to register it, while the King's Council, equally significantly, did not think it worth the trouble of a *lit de justice* and let it go at that. But the assembly's ideas remained among the received wisdom of its generation, resurfacing in the programme of the assembly of notables which met in 1626, and in an even better known text, the *Testament politique*, said to have been written by Richelieu.

The lost article of the Third Estate, which set royal power above all other human authority, making it absolute, was to have its own part in the political developments of the following decades. Its text was printed by the Parlement de Paris and widely distributed, and the day would dawn when an assembly of the clergy of France itself would adopt it as the norm for relations between the spiritual and the temporal power (the so-called Declaration of Four Articles of May 1682). The absolutism of Louis XIV was thus already formulated. It was a modern creation, the fruit of the political crisis of the later sixteenth century, not a legacy of the Middle Ages. The generation which came to maturity during the peaceful reign of Henri IV rejected with horror the civil discord and disorder of recent memory. The State appeared to them as the only reliable guardian of the peace and prosperity of the kingdom's subjects. Because it was overburdened with disappointed hopes or with texts sketching the distant future, the Estates General of 1614–15 is not a landmark in institutional history. But it is revealing about the state of France itself, as the king's minority drew to a close. It outlines the conflicting hopes and opinions of the French people, and reveals embryonic political possibilities which suggested the promise of a future which was never in fact to be realised.

5   The Government of Concini

After the deputies of the Estates had returned home, the King's Council found itself once again faced with the related political ambitions of the Parlement de Paris and the princes. On 22 May 1615 this opposition returned to the attack. A delegation of forty councillors of the Parlement appeared before the King's Council to remonstrate forcibly against the regime's alleged dissipation of the late king's treasure and reversal of his policies – in effect, to complain about Concini's place at court and the projected marriage alliance with Spain.

During June, Condé withdrew from the court and retired to his estates at Clermont-en-Beauvaisis, where he was joined by the Dukes of Longueville, Mayenne and Bouillon. A published manifesto announced a number of serious grievances: that the elections of deputies to the Estates had been rigged; that the resolution of the Third Estate and the Parlement on the absolute character of royal power had been ignored; that the Council was sacrificing the kingdom to Spanish interests; and that the princes should resort to force to prevent the Spanish match.

The behaviour of the princes was eloquent in terms of the political grammar of the time. For a great nobleman to withdraw from court, to make a show of leaving the king's entourage, was a spectacular political gesture. It signified breaking off relations, defiance, an appeal to public opinion, and was often followed by a call to arms. The next steps were the rallying of the magnate's noble friends and relations, the publication of a seditious manifesto, and the seizure of fortified places. It does not seem likely that Condé was committed at any stage of his career to any fixed political principles. His interest in the parliamentary remonstrance was nothing more than an attempt to win over Parisian opinion, and his opposition to the Spanish match was likewise designed to appeal to the Protestant faction.

It is worth noting that the noble calls to arms of Henri IV's and Louis XIII's reigns brought great magnates together irrespective of their confessional allegiance, with Catholics like Mayenne and Condé standing alongside Protestants like Bouillon and Rohan. And in the same way, magnates who were as far apart in their religious views as Guise and Lesdiguières rallied to the support of royal authority. In the summer of 1615, a political assembly of the Huguenots was permitted to convene at Grenoble. The moderate delegates, who were in the majority, wished to remain at peace with the King's Council, but more extreme elements had managed to establish more or less permanent but completely unauthorised bodies, known as *abrégés* or *cercles*, which fostered armed agitation in various Protestant strongholds, such as the Cévennes, the Montauban region and the Charentais region.

It must be remembered that these local calls to arms, although lacking royal authorisation, never saw themselves as rebellions or envisaged the subversion of the State. They were intended simply to influence Council decisions and to demonstrate the determination of their leaders, the extent of their client networks, the number of their followers and their general strength within the kingdom. The call to arms was thus a risky and rather too frequent means of vindicating one's social ascendancy, one's ability to mobilise and one's role in government. In every age and political system, groups seeking a share of power stake their claim with conventionalised displays of strength: the noble call to arms of early seventeenth-century France was just such a demonstration.

In the face of this new challenge from Condé, Marie de Medici, realising that the policy of negotiation and concession which she and Villeroy had pursued since 1610 had been worn out, sent out letters on 30 July instructing all governors to be on their guard and stand up to the rebels. August saw preparations afoot for a progress to the far south-west to conclude the royal marriages. The court left Paris on 17 August, and, after a lengthy stop at Poitiers because of the sudden illness of Princess Elisabeth, finally reached Bordeaux on 7 October. The troops of the Royal Household, under the command of the Duke of Guise, provided an escort, as there were real fears of a noble coup along the way. French and Swiss regiments stayed behind in Paris and the Île-de-France to protect the capital against possible rebel attack, while a third force under Concini, strengthened with mercenaries recruited from the principality of Liège, gathered in Picardy. But the princely faction had its own strongholds and made its own dispositions. Condé and Bouillon stood on the borders of Champagne and the Île-de-France, Vendôme was mobilised in Poitou and Brittany, and the Duke of Rohan held the Garonne region with a small Protestant army based between Montauban and Lectoure. Yet though the princes were putting on a show of strength, none of them had any desire to provoke a confrontation or make an irrevocable break.

The Royal Weddings

The royal marriages passed off peacefully enough in the course of the autumn, amid the rejoicings of the towns and provinces through which the court made its progress. But it is worth lingering over them because, as we have said, power was focused upon the single person of the king, and the legitimacy and security of the regime hung upon the joys and sorrows of his family life. Every event within that family circle took on a historical dimension, and simple family occasions were invested with the rites and ceremonies of political tradition, rich in significance and would-be eternal symbols.

It had been agreed that the two weddings should take place simultaneously in the two kingdoms, at Burgos and Bordeaux on 18 October. The Infanta Ana, daughter of Philip III of Spain and Queen Margaret of Austria, a pretty young blonde of fourteen, was married to Louis XIII (represented by the person of the Duke of Lerma, the Spanish king's chief minister) in St Augustine's Cathedral, Burgos; while in St Andrew's Cathedral, Bordeaux, Princess Elisabeth of France was married to the Prince of Asturias, heir to the Spanish crowns (represented by the person of the Duke of Guise). Elisabeth was the oldest and favourite sister of Louis XIII, and they parted tearfully on 21 October. Such was the fate of princesses, to leave family and country at a tender age, never again to return. Philip III for his part accompanied his daughter Ana to the banks of the Bidassoa, which traditionally marked the border between France and Spain. The princesses were exchanged on 9 November on the little island of Faisans, in the middle of the river, at the precise conjunction of the two kingdoms. A pavilion was erected at the centre of the island, and the formal ceremonies of the exchange were performed with scrupulous exactitude by the appointed agents. From that moment Ana became Queen Anne of France, and Elisabeth became Isabella, future Queen of Spain. The new Queen of France was escorted by the Duke of Guise to Saint-Jean-de-Luz, and then through the Landes, keeping clear of the rebel troops of the Garonne valley. She reached Bordeaux on 21 November, and was ceremoniously greeted by Louis XIII. The wedding ceremony was repeated in the cathedral on 25 November, and it was announced the next day that the union between the fourteen-year-old queen and the fifteen-year-old king had been consummated. The news was of political importance because it guaranteed the validity of the marriage and thus the solidarity of the *entente* between the two realms. But in fact the couple did not begin to live together for another four years. The court of France left Bordeaux on 17 December, but remained in the provinces for several more months, as the dissident princes had not yet been pacified.

The Peace of Loudun

During October, Condé, at the head of some 3,000 or 4,000 men, managed to cross the Orleanais to Berry, thus threatening to rendezvous with the Protestant forces in the west and cut off the court's route back to Paris. But the royal forces were superior in both numbers and quality. Concini kept Condé in check with his force of 10,000 men from the north, and even took possession of Condé's estates around Clermont-en-Beauvaisis. And Guise had little difficulty in dispersing a force of Protestant gentlemen from the west on 6 January 1616. A few weeks later negotiations got under way at Loudun, a little Catholic centre near the Protestant strongholds of the Saumur and lower Poitou regions. The talks were protracted because of the large number of parties and the vast range of the princely and Protestant demands. The 'confederates' had drawn up long lists of demands for the royal representatives, led by Villeroy, to consider. The treaty signed on 3 May was essentially a lengthy catalogue of pensions and appointments distributed to the leading malcontents, Condé and Rohan, and their various allies and connections (including even Sully and his son). It was reckoned that the price of peace was anything up to 20 million *livres*. The policy of appeasement which characterised the regime of Marie de Medici and Villeroy was once more to the fore. According to the political conventions of the time, the power of the State and the fortune of the magnates and their client networks were mutually dependent: the magnates were expected to put their social muscle at the disposal of the State, and in return they expected their due reward in pensions and privileges.

In summer 1616 the King's Council found itself divided along factional lines. The rivalries of Villeroy, Condé and Concini had their echoes in incidents on the streets of Paris, and even in the backwoods of Picardy, where there were constant clashes between Concini's men and princely clients. Concini was adept at placing trusted friends in key government posts. The Secretary of State for Foreign Affairs was Claude Mangot, a young advocate from Loudun who thanks to Concini patronage had been made first a President in the Parlement de Bordeaux and then a Master of Requests. Another Concini protégé, Claude Barbin, was put in charge of financial affairs. Like Mangot, Barbin was of modest origin, a mere district official who had moved via the service of the Tuscan banker Gondi into the clientage of the Concini. But, also like Mangot, he had the reputation of an honest and talented man.

In the eyes of public opinion, however, it seemed as though the Crown had fallen into the toils of a foreign adventurer and his low-born lackeys. Concini was at the height of his unpopularity in Paris. Condé, in contrast, was seen as the defender of Crown and people, and his every public appearance, whether at the hôtel of some great magnate or the residence of a foreign ambassador, was an occasion for noisy popular rejoicing.

The Queen Mother and Concini, apprehensive at the strength of feeling in the capital, decided on a coup. This was no unfamiliar expedient in the annals of a century in which the sovereign frequently found himself compelled to engineer a plot in his own court, even to resort to force, in order to regain the full and free exercise of his own power. The discretion of his closest friends and the loyalty of his guards were often the only assistance available to a king with his back to the wall.

The Queen Mother let the Marquis of Thémines (an old servant of Henri IV) into the secret, along with the officers of the Swiss and French Guards. On the morning of 1 September 1616, as Condé left the Council chamber, he was arrested by Thémines on the king's orders and then confined in the Bastille. His family and clients tried to foment a riot in the capital, and one of his household dependents, a cobbler named Picart, led a mob 10,000 strong to sack Concini's hôtel near the Luxembourg. But the uproar ended there, making no impact in the provinces, where the peace of Loudun had borne its fruits. Condé remained in confinement until October 1619.

The Royal Coup of 24 April 1617

In September 1616 Concini seemed master of the kingdom. He reshaped the Council in his own image, paying scant attention to 'greybeards' and princely clients alike. He was able to call on 'new men' who owed their political careers entirely to their place in his clientage. Barbin remained in control of finances, but Mangot became Keeper of the Seals. His position in charge of foreign affairs was entrusted from November 1616 to a gifted young cleric who had been spokesman for the clergy in the recent Estates General: Armand Du Plessis de Richelieu, Bishop of Luçon in lower Poitou. The immediate task which faced this able and well-knit team was to deal with recurrent noble agitation in the sensitive regions of Picardy, Champagne and the west.

Concini himself never had any particular political programme.

His personal fortune was entirely dependent on the Crown, and he saw the necessity of upholding royal authority at a difficult time in the face of princely and Protestant discontent. He had favoured the Spanish match for the sake of peace, but he had no particular interest in alliance with Spain as such, and had not accompanied the court on its progress to Bordeaux. He did not bother attending the Council and had no intention of intervening in major policy decisions. His sole interests were the augmentation of his own fortune and the advancement of his relatives and clients. From 1610 to 1616 he had laboured to establish himself in Picardy, where he accumulated estates and military commands which gave him control of a rich province in a strategically crucial position. But in spring 1616 he changed his objective, giving up the governorship of Amiens for that of Caen, and investing heavily in land and position in lower Normandy. Arrogant, ostentatious and foolhardy, he was the focus of popular resentment of upstarts and earned the contempt of almost the entire nobility, especially the family of Condé, whose lands in the Beauvaisis he had seized and against whose very person he had masterminded a coup. Nor was he attentive enough to the young king who, having now reached his sixteenth year, was beginning to resent being kept away from real power by his mother and her insolent favourite. Louis XIII had already learned a lot: he had been a part of the coup against Condé, and the history of the French Crown offered many other examples of royal coups. He knew that he could count on only a handful of close friends and associates, foremost among whom was Charles d'Albert de Luynes, a twenty-year-old Provençale gentleman who was in charge of the royal falconry and had enjoyed the king's trust and affection for several years.

After the arrest of Condé, the Dukes of Mayenne and Nevers had expressed the resentment of the nobles. Royal troops were in a state of readiness from early 1617, fearing a noble call to arms, and in March they were deployed in Berry, Champagne and the Île-de-France. The focus of activity was the stronghold of Soissons, under Mayenne's command. A royal force under the Count of Auvergne laid siege to it. The outcome was still uncertain when, on Monday 24 April 1617, Concini, making his way to the Louvre, was momentarily separated from the strong escort with which he usually surrounded himself, and was challenged in the name of the king by the Marquis of Vitry, Captain of the King's Bodyguard, who then shot him several times. On hearing the news which he had been anxiously awaiting, Louis XIII exclaimed 'Many thanks to you. From this moment I am king!'

The royal coup was almost a repeat of the assassination of the Duke of Guise on the orders of Henri III in December 1588. As the king was the supreme justice, a murder carried out on his orders took on the aspect of a death sentence, which was how it was seen by the magistrates of the Parlement de Paris who hastened to the Louvre that same day to offer their congratulations. They dismissed as a waste of time the idea of a posthumous treason trial: 'The king himself caused him to die, and the mere will of His Majesty makes up for any deficiency in due process.' The legal analogy between 1588 and 1617 was very clear, but the historical circumstances were very different. Guise had been enormously popular, and his murder threw the country into civil war. Concini was universally hated, and in the eyes of the public his death was a guarantee of reform. Louis XIII's deed aroused widespread enthusiasm. In the capital the workshops closed and crowds filled the streets crying 'Long live the king'. At the besieged town of Soissons, the gates were thrown open and the opposing forces greeted each other warmly. The princely faction rallied to the king amidst this general rejoicing.

Concini became the scapegoat for the general ills. The day after his murder, a rioting mob dug up his corpse in the church of Saint-Germain-l'Auxerrois, hanged it on the Pont-Neuf, and then tore it to pieces. They then roamed the streets and looted his houses without anyone lifting a finger to stop them. In the view of the rioters, the travesty of judicial process to which Concini's corpse was subjected rounded off the royal condemnation, as if the raging mob was possessed of rights which gave it a proper part to play in the designs of the king. The massacres perpetrated in Paris during the Wars of Religion, and the popular revolts which were to proliferate through the seventeenth century, provide plentiful examples of similar beliefs and behaviour.

Hundreds of ephemeral pamphlets and leaflets, often in verse, marked this event. This rich polemical harvest put a scholarly gloss on the popular outburst, sanctioning the judicial and censorial role which was almost explicitly assumed in the horrific rituals of the mob. These texts harped on Concini's fundamental crime, the usurpation of royal power. His path to the penalty of treason had been paved with gross indignities: a wretched foreign adventurer on the make, he had sought to take advantage of the feminine frailties of the Queen Mother and to deprive the French people of their freedom and their State. Central political themes were thus interlaced with the social passions, presumptions and prejudices of the age. The assassination of Concini was presented as an act of purgation and a new beginning.

All of the marshal's offices and goods were confiscated. His widow, Leonora Galigaï, the childhood friend of the Queen Mother, was tried by the Parlement de Paris, which, having sought to convict her of witchcraft, condemned her to death for treason. She was executed on 8 July. The clients who had risen on Concini's coat-tails got off more or less lightly. Barbin was the most harshly dealt with, gaoled until 1618 and then exiled to Franche-Comté. Mangot was forced to resign, while Richelieu, having retired to his diocese, was then exiled to the papal enclave of Avignon. The Queen Mother herself had to withdraw from court, and she retired to virtual house arrest at the château of Blois.

Luynes and Vitry, together with the other triumphant conspirators, were heaped with honours. The young king entrusted the business of government to his father's old councillors: Villeroy, Sillery, Jeannin and a number of other septuagenarians made a final come-back at the Council table.

The kingdom found itself suddenly at peace, with no immediate threats of revolts or conspiracies on the horizon. The substitution of one favourite for another at the head of the Council seemed enough to guarantee the common weal. Or, at least, public opinion was as ready then as in most other ages to convince itself that such was the case.

6   The Regime of the Young Louis XIII

1617 heralded a period of stability in government. Whereas since the death of the late king, each year had brought its crop of shocks and crises to a country which none the less remained fundamentally peaceful and prosperous, the assumption of power by the young king henceforth guaranteed a certain continuity in the conduct of public affairs. Europe too was at peace. The truce concluded in 1609 between the United Provinces and Spain was still holding, and nobody could foresee that political problems in Bohemia would bring down a horrific conflict upon a Germany which at that moment seemed to have a prosperous future. The warlike powers of Sweden and Muscovy seemed far enough away, Venetian trade with the Balkan ports was flourishing without hindrance, and the unsatisfied ambitions of the Duke of Piedmont were unable to disturb the plains of northern Italy.

The Estates General of 1614 had identified and denounced the main problems which tended to weaken the French State and to diminish its resources: the sale of offices was a fiscal expedient which deprived the king of control over his own agents; and the distribution of pensions and privileges to princely clients and Protestant communities in order to keep the peace deprived him of control over vast areas. The King's Council was well aware of stakes. After the death of Villeroy in December 1617, Chancellor Sillery and his son the Marquis of Puisieux (Secretary of State for Foreign Affairs) dominated the Council, with the trust and support of Luynes who, either from prudence or lack of talent, never concerned himself with the minutiae of business.

There was no reason why the reforms demanded by the Estates should not now be put into effect. The king was young, the kingdom was at peace, and a fresh start seemed at hand.

The Assembly of Notables, 1617

To consider concrete proposals, recourse was had to another traditional consultative body, an Assembly of Notables, a sort of enlargement of the King's Council which brought in a wide range of persons of high standing or special expertise. Henri IV had convoked such an Assembly in 1596 in order to secure the necessary financial resources to bring the civil wars to an end. An Assembly of Notables was a far more flexible instrument than the Estates General, consisting of a few dozen individuals chosen by the king rather than elected, and expected to present not general statements of grievances but specific advice on precise issues following an agenda fixed by the king. The Assembly of 1617 was held at Rouen, partly following the precedent of 1596, and partly because Luynes was Lieutenant General of Normandy. The king opened proceedings in person on 4 December in the great hall of the archbishop's palace. He addressed a gathering of fifty-two persons, all of them nobles, comprising eleven bishops, fifteen magnates and twenty-six magistrates. The body was reasonably representative of the diversity of the kingdom. Only a handful of those present were Parisians, and almost all provinces were represented by either a magistrate or a prelate. A clerk noted the outcome of the discussions, and the conclusions were summed up in proposals presented to the king at the closing session, held in Paris on 29 January 1618. The Assembly had considered the principal demands of the Estates General and sought means for putting them into effect. On 15 January a Council decree abolished the *paulette*: the suppression of venality remained the order of the day but its implementation had to be postponed until adequate revenues could be found to make good the loss to the Treasury. A lengthy edict embodying the reforms in officeholding and a host of other administrative measures was drawn up in July by the secretaries of the Council, but institutional inertia or the ill-will of the Parlement de Paris meant that it never went beyond this initial stage. In July 1620, at a moment when the Wars of Religion were set to resume, the *paulette* was provisionally reinstated in order to mollify the magistrates. The reinstatement was meant to be temporary, and the idea that some radical institutional reform was necessary remained widespread. Everyone still thought that the sale of offices was an abuse and that it would be necessary sooner or later to recast the administrative structures of the realm.

The Wars Between Mother and Son

The virtual house arrest of the Queen Mother in her château at Blois was a political scandal that profoundly shocked a public with a high regard for crowns. The situation was still more unsatisfactory in that it seemed clear that the estrangement within the royal family had been fuelled by the Duke of Luynes, who, taking Concini's place at the head of the Council, had set about persecuting all those who had had any kind of connection with the old ruling clique. His behaviour was not without a certain risk, as sooner or later public opinion would be tempted to blame the difficulties of the moment on the new favourite, and thus find a new scapegoat. One discontented magnate, the Duke of Épernon, had already withdrawn ostentatiously from court in May 1618, retiring to one of his provincial governorships, the powerful frontier fortress of Metz.

The Duke of Épernon was one of the most illustrious public figures of the day. As Colonel General of the Infantry he had responsibility for and command over all the king's footsoldiers, with the result that a large number of gentlemen depended on him for advancement in the army. He had been a personal friend of Henri III, and as a great Catholic magnate his rallying to the cause of Henri IV had played an important part in the latter's reconquest of the realm. A veteran of the wars, advanced in years and heaped with honours, he was in effect the military conscience of France.

He had been offended by the regime's refusal of support at the Roman Curia for a cardinal's hat for one of his sons who had embarked on a clerical career. By withdrawing to Metz he seemed to be putting himself at the head of a new faction of malcontents.

The last straw for Marie de Medici was the conclusion of a marriage, over which she was not consulted and to which she was not even invited, between her younger daughter Christine and Prince Victor Amadeus, heir to the duchy of Piedmont and Savoy. The wedding was celebrated at Paris on 10 February 1619. On 22 February the Queen Mother, with the assistance of agents of Épernon, escaped from Blois and joined the duke, who was waiting for her at Loches with a sizeable force to escort her to the stronghold of Angoulême. This easily defensible château, in the safety of another province of which Épernon was governor and had the trust of the local gentry, made Marie and her cause safe from immediate reprisals.

Louis XIII and Luynes had to take prompt action. The standing regiments, some 20,000 men, were deployed at the usual key points in Champagne and the south-west, with the largest unit dispatched towards the Angoumois under Schomberg. In fact, negotiations were soon under way between representatives of the Queen Mother and the king, and on 30 April an agreement signed at Angoulême marked the reconciliation of mother and son. Marie's case had been ably pleaded by her right-hand man, Richelieu, the Bishop of Luçon, who had returned from his Avignon exile. The Queen Mother was entrusted with the governorship of Anjou, and on 3 September the family truce was sealed by an affectionate reunion in Touraine, amid the applause of the court.

But the Queen Mother had not regained her former ascendancy. She was still excluded from the capital and from her son's Council, and had to remain in the background at the château of Angers. A fresh misunderstanding arose in October 1619, after the release of Condé from the Bastille, where he had been detained since 1616. A royal proclamation pronounced him innocent and placed all the blame for what had occurred on Concini, a political subterfuge which reflected badly on Marie de Medici. Luynes then secured from Louis XIII the creation of some sixty

Knights of the Holy Spirit. Thus this rare and precious honour, in the personal gift of the sovereign, seemed to be reserved for Luynes and his kin. Finally, Marie's maternal dignity was affronted as it had been the previous year: the education of her second son, Gaston, still a youth, was altered without consulting her. Richelieu had no difficulty in orchestrating the chorus of grievances provoked by the blunders of Luynes, and several great nobles withdrew from court into retirement in Poitou or Anjou, close to the Queen Mother.

In July 1620 Louis XIII felt obliged to make another military progress through his more troubled provinces, a move sometimes described as the 'second war between mother and son'. At the head of a small army the king first toured Normandy, where the Duke of Longueville had taken up arms, and then, passing without trouble via Rouen and Caen (17 July), marched on Anjou. The Queen Mother's supporters were in possession of the château of Ponts-de-Cé, which commanded the principal crossing of the Loire, near Angers itself. On 7 August the royal force, a mere 4,000 men with only two pieces of artillery, broke up the rebels, leaving hundreds dead, in an engagement known as the 'farce of Ponts-de-Cé'.

The Government of the Realm from Luynes to Richelieu

On 10 August 1620 a treaty signed at the château of Angers once more restored peace between the king and his mother. Marie de Medici was readmitted to the capital, and installed herself in the Palais du Luxembourg. She had acquired this residence in 1612, and had employed Salomon de Brosse to restore it. Rubens was later to decorate it with enormous pictures telling her life story.

The Duke of Luynes, loaded with honours, having even been created Constable of France (a post vacant since 1614 which was revived especially for the king's favourite), died by chance on 15 December 1621 of a fever caught while he was with royal troops on campaign against the Huguenots in the Midi. Next month Marie de Medici was once more admitted to the King's Council, and harmony once more seemed to prevail within the royal family. This serene image was welcome to public opinion, and seemed to guarantee the stability of the regime and the strength of the State. This guarantee was essential, as it was to the State with its growing power that the new generations of the early seventeenth century looked for solutions to the tensions and quarrels which racked French society.

After the death of Luynes, chief responsibility in the conduct of affairs passed to the old Chancellor Brulart de Sillery, whose career had begun in 1589 as a Secretary of State under Henri III. His son, Nicolas de Puisieux, managed foreign affairs. Approaching the end of his long life, Sillery strove above all to keep France out of the European conflict which had begun to unfurl in Germany in 1617. A court faction accused Sillery and his son of misappropriation, a perennial and unanswerable charge which often accompanied the disgrace of councillors, and they were thus hounded out. Management of the Council passed to the Marquis of La Vieuville, the *Surintendant des finances*. But he did not stay long either, victim in his turn of the intrigues of another faction, which orchestrated a sudden and powerful pamphlet campaign to impugn his competence and his integrity.

La Vieuville, unable to brazen it out or to convince the young king, was dismissed and imprisoned in August 1624. It seemed as if anyone who monopolised the confidence of the young king was bound to end up sooner or later as a criminal. Disgrace and the loss of office were inevitably accompanied by a charge of fraud and a presumption of political crime. As legitimation was located in the prince alone, the chief minister was inevitably both extremely powerful and extremely vulnerable: powerful because he was the servant of an absolute master; but vulnerable because he lacked the privileges which accompanied high birth. The typical minister of the early modern period was an educated man, a magistrate or churchman, but without the prestige and protection conferred by high nobility. His position depended entirely on the fragile and all too human friendship of the prince. This change in the style of government occurred at the same time as the emergence of the force of public opinion – or rather of new expressions of opinion such as pamphlets, broadsheets and newspapers. The ability to manipulate this new force was henceforth an integral part of political competence.

The ups and downs of the successive leaders of the King's Council turned out to the benefit of an extraordinary person who would make a profound impact on his age: Cardinal Richelieu.

Richelieu and Louis XIII

Armand-Jean Du Plessis de Richelieu was born in 1585 into an established noble family of Poitou. His father, François, had been part of the entourage of Henri Duke of Anjou during his brief career as King of Poland. When Anjou became Henri III, he rewarded his faithful friend with the post of Grand Provost of France. François de Richelieu had thus been responsible for security and the administration of justice within the king's household. After his father's premature death, Armand was entrusted to the care of his maternal uncle, Amador de La Porte, a Knight of Malta. Under his guidance, Richelieu received a sound training in maritime and naval matters. He was destined for a military career, and his education was directed towards this. But one of his brothers, who had been destined for preferment in the Church and for whom the family had reserved the bishopric of Luçon, decided to join the Carthusians. To safeguard the family's interests Armand therefore adopted the clerical state and, after a brilliant student career, was consecrated bishop at Easter 1607, aged twenty-three.

The young prelate, whose exceptional abilities had already been noted at the Roman Curia, set about reforming his diocese in accordance with the decrees of Trent by means of sermons, parochial visitations and diocesan synods. Elected to the Estates General of 1614, he was a spokesman for the clergy. His talent was noted by Marie de Medici and Concini, and they recruited him, young as he was, to the King's Council, with responsibility for foreign affairs. Concini's fall in April 1617 brought Richelieu down as well, but did not prevent him putting his tact and advice at the disposal of the Queen Mother. It was Richelieu who negotiated the two reconciliations between her and her son in 1619 and 1620. His exceptional intelligence was already obvious to his contemporaries, and nobody doubted that he had a brilliant future ahead of him.

But his attachment to the Queen Mother and his rhetorical ability alike rendered him suspect to Louis XIII, while the Duke of Luynes was no well-wisher either. They had no intention of supporting his aspirations to a cardinal's hat. The custom was that the pope never nominated a man to the College of Cardinals without his sovereign's consent, and Marie de Medici wanted her son to signify his approval to the pope as a reward for Richelieu's services in restoring harmony within the royal family. The death of the Duke of Luynes removed the main obstacle in Richelieu's path, and the cardinal's hat was forthcoming in September 1622. This extraordinary honour, comparatively rare among French prelates, gave him not only enormous spiritual prestige within the Catholic world but also, as a Prince of the Church, a certain political autonomy which even princes of the blood might envy. Marie de Medici campaigned for his return to the Council, which came in April 1624. The astonishing campaign of vilification which brought down La Vieuville was masterminded by Richelieu, and the *Surintendant*'s fall in effect sealed the cardinal's arrival as the king's chief minister and head of the Council (August 1624).

The cardinal's character was already well known at court. Quick-witted, brilliant and assured, Richelieu was as much a man of thought as a man of action. A master of intrigue and a born leader, he could manipulate both personal relations and public opinion. He had a perfect understanding of the political machinery of the age. He understood the importance of patronage and loyalty, the necessity on the one hand of belonging to the entourage of a great patron, an opportunity which had been extended to him by the Queen Mother, and on the other of maintaining a network of devoted and dependent followers who could provide information on and support in their various provincial, social or professional circles. His admission to the King's Council in 1616, his peace brokering between the Queen Mother and her son, his appointment as cardinal and his destruction of La Vieuville were the tell-tale signs of an astonishingly effective political operator.

Richelieu had a particular concern with the impression that his actions made upon his contemporaries, and also with the image that he would leave for posterity. So he always took care to leave clear and reasoned statements of his principles and his policies. Sometimes writing himself, or else employing secretaries and hired scribblers, he left in addition a political testament, apparently made up from his ministerial papers, and some memoirs which were attributed to Harlay de Sancy, Bishop of Saint-Malo. Over the centuries, historians and scholars have set great store by the cardinal's written output. An eight-volume compilation of his papers (*Lettres, instructions diplomatiques et papiers d'État*) was commenced in 1857 by Georges d'Avenel, but it was far from exhaustive, and a more complete edition is now in progress. And in a national historiography already rich in studies of great men, Richelieu is one of the most common subjects of biography. His personality and his achievement are among the most thoroughly explored themes of seventeenth-century history.

In 1624 Richelieu was not yet in possession of any settled design, though he had given evidence of his great ability to seize opportunities and his flexibility in the face of rapidly changing situations. His clearest objective was to uphold the French monarchy and to give faithful service to Louis XIII, the man who embodied the monarchy at that precise moment. The fact that these two men were in such close political harmony from 1624 until the cardinal's death in 1642 explains both their enormous impact on their age and the extraordinary difficulty of attributing to one or other of them in particular the responsibility for the successes, or indeed the failures, of their policies. Although Louis XIII was sixteen years younger than his minister, he had appreciated the force of the cardinal's personality from the outset, and had seen and seized his chance to recruit an adviser whose loyalty and resolution he could depend upon.

Louis XIII has also been a favourite of the biographers, not least because we know more about his life and character than about any other king of France. We have access to an almost unique source, a medical journal meticulously kept by the king's physician, Jean Héroard, from the boy's birth in 1601 through to Héroard's death in 1628. We can therefore follow the young prince's progress day by day, sometimes hour by hour. And the text is of more than the merely historical interest of a record of the life of one of the most eminent men of his time. It is also of an anthropological cast, a minute record of twenty-seven years in the life a human being, following his acquisition of language as an infant, his diet, his sleeping habits, the most trivial physiological changes and details, his moral views and his intellectual capacities. It is therefore possible to maintain, without the usual licence of historical portraiture, that Louis was indeed a remarkably gifted man, a talented musician and artist, a dextrous swordsman, and a keen horseman and huntsman. Cultivated, acute and familiarised from an early age with the daily workings of government, he was well equipped for his royal trade. Pious and scrupulous, he gave it his undivided attention. His character – secretive, sensitive, timid yet irascible, capable of vengefulness and even cruelty – was taken by his contemporaries as the necessary concomitant of ambitious designs. His taste for secrecy and his high, even awesome, conception of the State seemed essential qualities of the ideal ruler.

Louis XIII's personal part in crucial policy decisions should not be underestimated. The importance of the sovereign's role depended firstly on the strength of the monarchical principle as such, and secondly on the remarkable harmony which prevailed between king and minister. The abilities and potential of the minister troubled and even awed the king, while for his part the minister was apprehensive of his master's impulsiveness. The stability and continuity of government depended on Louis XIII's ability to understand and support Richelieu's plans, and on the entire subordination of Richelieu's great talents to the service of his king.

7 The Protestant Churches and the Last Wars of Religion

The Edict of Nantes had given legal recognition to the religious, political and military organisation of the Reformed communities which were scattered unevenly across the land. The R.P.R. (or 'Religion Purportedly Reformed', as it was called) was established as an order within society, a particular type of community with its own liberties and privileges – in other words, subject to a particular body of law in addition to the various other social and regional distinctions which could define the status of an individual with respect to royal authority.

The Structure of the Reformed Churches

The edict recognised the right of the Reformed churches, as worshipping communities ruled by the pastor and elders who formed the local consistory, to govern themselves, to regulate their common life, and to organise themselves collectively into colloquies or, at a higher level, provincial synods (of which there were sixteen). The consistory regulated the spiritual and material life of the local church, censuring the misconduct of sinners and assisting the faithful in their difficulties. Each local church nominated a pastor and an elder to the regional colloquy, and each colloquy in turn sent representatives to the provincial synod. National synods, held with royal permission and in the presence of a royal representative, took place every three years. From 1601 the national synod appointed representatives to reside at the royal court in order to defend and promote the interests of their co-religionists. From 1610 limitations on the frequency of synods began to be ignored, as were the requirements of royal authorisation and of the presence of a royal representative at assemblies at any level. Some provincial synods, known as *abregés* or *cercles*, came to consist only of hardline deputies because more moderate churches either preferred to stay aloof or else followed the advice of a noble patron at court to do so. The debates and decisions of these assemblies came to be dominated by representatives from the Haut-Languedoc, Haute-Guyenne, Aunis and Saintonge.

The political organisation of the R.P.R. was buttressed by its military structure, which in 1610 comprised some two hundred strongholds with governors and garrisons. The appointment of governors depended on the king and also on the local consistory, but in practice commanders obeyed none but the great Protestant magnates. With the garrisons, noble retinues and the urban militias of their towns, the Huguenots were able to put some 25,000 men in the field at short notice – a force far larger than that of the Crown's standing regiments.

The Protestants of France represented some 3–4 per cent of the population, but their distribution was far from even. Some of the notorious towns, like Privas, Nîmes, Castres, Montauban, Bergerac and La Rochelle stood in almost entirely Huguenot hinterlands. And the strength of the Huguenots in Languedoc, Aunis and Saintonge made those areas comparable to the northern provinces of the Netherlands, where Calvinist dominance had led first to political division and then to full secession from Spanish rule. Nor is the comparison an empty one. During the Wars of Religion the French Calvinists might have been impelled by the violence of events to proceed to secession, though they never in fact made this their aim. On the other hand, these concentrations were relative. In several areas the countryside remained decisively Catholic, and rival towns in the vicinity often made themselves strongholds of the League or of militant Catholic royalism. Toulouse and Auch barred the route to Béarn, while Cahors, Agen, Périgueux, Bordeaux and Blaye dominated the waterways of Aquitaine. These local tensions ensured that each town kept itself ready for defence and was able to launch raids into the hinterland should the necessity arise.

Relations between neighbours divided by religion were sometimes friendly and familiar, sometimes tense and violent. To take a few examples, the Huguenot townsfolk of Montpellier in Languedoc or of Saint-Jean-d'Angely in Saintonge dealt on a daily basis with the sharecroppers and peasants of the surrounding countryside, Catholics to a man. In the towns of the middle Garonne relationships were even closer, extending as far as (though no further than) games of skittles and gossip in taverns. Mixed marriages (pejoratively called *bigarrés*, that is variegated) were rare, and were universally execrated. In the great Catholic cities, the inflexibility of youth – scholars of the Catholic colleges on the one hand, and candidates for the Reformed ministry from Protestant academies on the other – led now and then to violent clashes. In Protestant cities the Edict of Nantes had provided for the restoration of Catholic worship, and the cycle of liturgical feasts provided many occasions for strife and confrontation. To cope with the tensions that were ever ready to burst out, the edict set up *chambres de l'édit*, tribunals within the local parlements which heard cases involving parties from different faiths. But while these were quite effective in private disputes, they were impotent in the face of riots. The regime established by the edict was never more than an uneasy compromise, an unstable equilibrium.

The distinctive beliefs and way of life of the Calvinist communities had engendered a liveliness in political debate which is perhaps characteristic of social or ethnic minorities, and which was never found to the same degree in Catholic towns and villages. This is not to say that the French Protestants had distinctive views on political life or the way of the world, or different images of social order and conventions. Noblemen and lawyers dominated their churches and assemblies much as their Catholic counterparts predominated in society as a whole. But their situation left more scope for radicalism and for opening religious perspectives on political questions. Thus humble pastors or even tradesmen might rub shoulders with the Duke of Rohan in times of crisis, supporting him as the most resolute of their leaders and denigrating such other gentlemen or notables as shied away from a recourse to arms. Huguenot communities were thus divided into municipal factions which could come to blows when faced with dramatic choices which might lead to civil war.

The fact that the Edict of Nantes left a large proportion of royal offices open only to Catholics had a long-term effect on the social profile of French Protestantism. Excluded from the market in lucrative public office, the better off were obliged to invest in trade and commerce, especially in tax-farming and in the financial syndicates which advanced loans to the Treasury. The army, however, remained open to Protestants. This only tended to increase religious indifference or licentiousness among a body of young men largely free from moral conventions, and free to associate with German and Swiss soldiers, who were mostly Lutherans.

Disquiet During the Royal Minority

Many Protestants feared for the future of their faith. In the early seventeenth century the Catholic Church was enjoying a tremendous revival, thanks largely to the implementation of the reforms demanded by the Council of Trent. Due to the spiritual insight and social forbearance of the Jesuits and other new religious orders, a Catholic *reconquista* was under way in central and eastern Europe. Missionaries were already crossing the oceans to bring the gospel to peoples hitherto unknown. In France itself, the peace which followed the Edict of Nantes permitted the Catholic clergy to launch preaching missions into rural backwaters and even Calvinist strongholds. In an age which believed in the power of rhetoric and delighted in verbal jousts, the staging of disputations between theologians of the rival faiths could attract huge audiences. The Catholic orators who threw themselves into these contests of polemical eloquence saw that they usually had the upper hand. Their success testified partly to the intellectual calibre of the new orders, and partly to the rising standards demanded of candidates for the priesthood. Conversion from one faith to the other had never been rare, but it was increasingly becoming one-way traffic, and each year saw more, and more illustrious, conversions to Catholicism.

Protestant disquiet was exacerbated by the policy of amity with Spain. This disquiet was evident from the time of the Peace of Vervins, and lasted throughout the reign of Henri IV. It strengthened during the regency of Marie de Medici, and peaked in 1611 at the first national synod of that period. The assembly which met at Saumur showed in microcosm the tendencies which divided Calvinist opinion throughout the realm. Faithful servants of the late king, like Lesdiguières and Sully, advised conciliation, obedience to the king and patience in the face of the difficulties the government made for them. Others argued for opposition and for a show of strength to demonstrate that their religion was still a power within the land. This hardline option was supported by the great noble dynasties – the Dukes of Bouillon, the Viscounts of Turenne and the Princes of Rohan – which had been bulwarks of the Reformed churches during the Wars of Religion, and which in the military sphere had rivalled even the prestige of the House of Navarre. The ambitious and talented Henri de Rohan (1575–1638) was inevitably a man of this stamp. The head of a powerful family with extensive possessions in Brittany Poitou, he could trace his lengthy or legendary ancestry to the royal stock of Brittany and Cyprus. With his younger brother the Baron of Soubise, he had received a good education which had run to travels around Europe and visits to the Prince of Orange and King James. In 1605 he married Marguerite de Rosny, Sully's eldest daughter, and was given command of the Swiss infantry by Henri IV. During the troubled minority of Louis XIII, he was almost always found at Condé's side when the princes took arms, and became in effect the protector of the Reformed churches of France. His standing was as high in the west from which he came as in the southern bastions of French Protestantism. Rohan set about creating an extensive client network among the Protestant nobility, clergy and bourgeoisie. Many of the communities of Languedoc were divided between supporters of Rohan, always ready to take up arms, and the civic worthies, often consuls, who preferred more prudent courses. Those who sought to mediate between the two camps were known by the amusing and evocative name *escambarlats* (the

Occitan word for those who spread their legs in order to walk with one foot on either side of a ditch). Events were to put them rather rudely to the test.

The Béarn Affair

In 1617 a serious dispute arose over the implementation of the Edict of Nantes. The Viscountcy of Béarn, part of the Bourbon patrimony, had long since been dragged by its sovereigns into the Reformed camp. And in 1599 Henri IV, in accordance with the terms of the edict, had caused Catholic worship to be restored for the benefit of those who so wished. But other provisions of the edict, relating to the restitution of confiscated church property, were not implemented in the territory. Then, in 1616, the Council and Estates of Béarn were rather unwisely implicated in the princely troubles. The King's Council therefore thought it timely to proclaim the reunion of Béarn to the Crown (the union had hitherto been purely personal) and to put the provisions of the edict into full effect there. The sovereign Council of the Viscountcy of Béarn, composed of Huguenot magistrates, believed that it could refuse to register the royal legislation, and there matters still stood in 1620, at the time of the second war between mother and son.

After the easy victory over the Queen Mother's supporters at Ponts-du-Cé, the king found himself in early summer at the head of an army in the field (July 1620). He decided to extend the armed progress into the south-west. The people of Béarn opened the gates of their towns, and the king entered the capital, Pau, peacefully on 20 October. He swore solemnly to respect the local privileges of the country, the *fors* as they were known in the south. The only real change was the transformation of the sovereign council into a Parlement, in which only Catholic magistrates were to sit. But this was a change that alarmed Protestant opinion nationwide.

A national assembly of the churches was summoned, to meet at La Rochelle in December 1620. It claimed legitimacy under royal permission granted the previous year. Some seventy-five deputies gathered, mostly pastors or merchants, and all bound more or less closely by ties of clientage or service to the leading noble families. Proceeding despite the lack of royal authorisation, the deputies arranged for the raising of troops and taxes and thus openly prepared for a recourse to arms. Having appealed to the King of England for protection, the assembly remained in session for month after month and took on the appearance of a secessionist government. Of course it never avowed any such break, protesting that it remained loyal to the king and sought only to maintain the liberty of the Reformed churches. Many congregations controlled by Bouillon, Lesdiguières and Sully stayed aloof from such extreme proceedings, refusing to send deputies. Thus the deputies gathered at La Rochelle represented the more hardline sector of Protestant opinion. They decided to organise the Protestant churches into eight military 'circles', each under the command of a governor belonging to the military nobility.

In spring 1621 civil war thus appeared inevitable, and the political stakes were all the higher in that the previous princely agitations had never brought together so many men, in so many places, or showed such clear determination to revolt.

The First War of Religion

On 18 April 1621 Louis XIII and Luynes, in his capacity as Constable, set out southwards from Fontainebleau at the head of the standing regiments. The Huguenot towns of Saumur and Thouars offered no resistance and threw open their gates. For the king it was a matter of striking at a few strongholds of the Protestant faction in order to bring its leaders to the negotiation table. As La Rochelle was reckoned impregnable, the royal army was obliged to make its way through the countryside of Saintonge and Gascony, where the Protestant forces were significant but were scattered across vast Catholic areas. The first resistance was met at the major stronghold of Saint-Jean-d'Angely, commanded by Benjamin de Rohan, Baron of Soubise (and younger brother to the Duke of Rohan). Besieged by the royal army under the king in person, Soubise held out from 11 June to 25 June, and then surrendered with the honours of war. The town alone was punished: its walls were razed and it lost its privileges. The army then headed for Montauban. This wealthy town, the Huguenot capital of Haute-Guyenne, barred the middle Garonne and was well fortified with a powerful garrison under the Baron of La Force.

The minor Protestant centres of Périgord, Agenais and Quercy soon opened their gates, with the exception of Clairac, at the confluence of the Lot and the Garonne, which was taken after a siege lasting from 23 July to 4 August. Montauban then came under siege from 17 August. A siege was always a major military enterprise, and the royal forces, which amounted to no more than 30,000 men, were not equal to the siege of a large, well provisioned, well fortified and well garrisoned town situated in open country and fed by a river. They could not close off all approaches at once and still stand ready to face possible assaults from Aunis to the north or Languedoc to the south. The royal cannon could not get close enough to the walls, and the cavalry could not prevent several hundred soldiers sent by Rohan from entering the city. After several weeks the besiegers were overwhelmed by disease (presumably typhus, the perennial concomitant of large and unfortunate concentrations of people, together with an epidemic of scarlatina). The mortality was terrifying. The Chancellor, Du Vair, succumbed, along with Luynes himself. The siege was abandoned on 10 November, and Louis XIII headed back for Paris, leaving behind him an enfeebled army of some 12,000 men to control the south-west. The set-back was both serious and spectacular.

The Protestant faction had shown the extent of its military capabilities. Soubise had excellent troops at his disposal around La Rochelle, and Rohan had effective control of Languedoc from Castres to Montpellier. The royal forces had in the meantime suffered another reverse at sea. A flotilla of thirteen vessels from Brittany had attacked La Rochelle on 7 October, only to be driven back by the seamen of the port under Captain Jean Guiton. The defending force had only six vessels over 150 tonnes, but these were supported by about forty ships of around 50–80 tonnes, manoeuvrable and armed with light cannon, besides a host of boats suitable for use as fireships. The maritime supremacy of La Rochelle ensured that the port would long retain control of

France's Atlantic coast. The forces of La Rochelle controlled sea traffic and could at will blockade other ports and interdict their trade. The Protestant faction was thus more than capable of holding its own by land or sea against the rudimentary royal army.

Louis XIII stayed no more than four months at Paris. Negotiations were in sight. On the king's side Lesdiguières offered himself as a mediator. Rohan himself wanted nothing more, and had already made several approaches during the long siege of Montauban. But the option of war to the knife also had its attractions. Royalists hoped to overcome the temporary setbacks and to overthrow at long last the military might of the Huguenots. On the Protestant side, it seemed worth trying to press home their advantage. Even the ageing Sully backed the war party. Soubise had already sallied from La Rochelle at the head of 7,000 men with the intention of tightening the Protestant grip on the coasts of Poitou and Brittany. In February 1622 he made raids against various Catholic towns in Poitou, taking Sables-d'Olonne, sacking it and confiscating its ships. He even considered digging in on one of the islands off the Poitou coast.

Louis XIII, his hand forced by events, answered the call of the Breton Estates for help by marching westwards as fast as possible, making his way via Blois (6 April) and Nantes (10 April) to Challans on the edge of the Poitou marshes, which he reached on 15 April. Soubise had just established himself at Saint-Gilles-Croix-de-Vie, the main harbour on the isle of Rié. This 'island' was a sandy spit separated from the mainland by channels which were filled at high tide. The Catholics of the area guided the king's troops along the causeways left by the retreating tide, and they took the Protestant force by surprise at low water, when escape by sea was impossible. Several thousand were killed or taken prisoner, though Soubise himself eluded justice by escaping across the marshes. The battle of the marshes of Rié enjoyed extraordinary press coverage. Some twenty flysheets celebrated the victory which made up for the recent setbacks and cast Louis himself in the role of victorious warlord.

Pressing home their advantage, the king's forces took possession of Royan, at the mouth of the Gironde, and then occupied the Protestant strongholds of Guyenne, thanks to the submission of the Baron of La Force. Bypassing Montauban, the army then successfully assaulted the nearby towns of Nègrepelisse and Saint-Antonin before advancing into lower Languedoc and laying siege to Montpellier.

As in the preceding year, Rohan had kept his forces in the open country, contenting himself with rapid forays, sometimes around Castres and sometimes around Nîmes. The experience of 1621 had moderated royalist expectations, and they now recognised that it was impossible to bring the city to surrender before winter. Both sides therefore looked on the prospect of a truce with some relief.

In the meantime, a naval offensive had been organised with a view to exacting revenge on the fleet of La Rochelle. During the summer, the Duke of Guise had been empowered to bring together a fleet of exceptional size. He had called on all available vessels from Rouen to Saint-Jean-de-Luz, and had even brought round from the Mediterranean six galleys which could face the ocean without too much difficulty. In total, the royal fleet consisted of around forty ships, two of them over 1,200 tonnes. Guiton, the naval commander at La Rochelle, had about fifty vessels, including those captured during the campaigns in Brittany and Poitou. The two fleets engaged in the Breton Straits on 27 October, but a sudden storm cut short the battle and news of the cessation of hostilities soon arrived.

Peace talks had been under way since early October, and Louis XIII came to an agreement with his Huguenot subjects beneath the walls of Montpellier. The main provisions of the Edict of Nantes were confirmed, and an amnesty was granted for all acts of war in 1621-2. The Huguenots were obliged to dismantle a number of their fortifications and to give up their right to maintain garrisons in eighty of the two hundred safe havens originally granted them in 1599. Louis XIII entered Montpellier on 18 October, amid the townsfolk's cries of 'Long live the king' and 'Long live mercy'. The Huguenot assembly at La Rochelle considered the peace terms, accepted them in November, and then dispersed. Thus ended the secessionist policy which had begun in December 1620. The king lingered in the Midi, taking the opportunity to make a solemn entry into Marseille, and then returned by short stages to Paris.

The religious wars, though limited in extent and duration, had been fiercely fought, leaving numerous towns and villages across Guyenne and Languedoc in ruins. In provinces like Rouergue and Vivarais, where the religious map was complex and confused, the little village wars of thirty years before had resumed. Nevertheless, the political stakes were different. The legitimacy of the sovereign and his government had not been called into question. The Protestant rebels had maintained that they were only demonstrating their strength and determination. For his part, the king had wielded both carrot and stick, now executing the strict justice due to political crimes, hanging the captains and magistrates of captured towns, and now showing the mercy which was necessary to foster the prospect of peace. Thus the prisoners taken at Rié, at first condemned to the galleys, were graciously freed some months later.

The course of events revealed not only the limitations of royal resources, but also the traditional character of the war that was waged. The royal forces proved inferior in ships and barely superior in artillery, while their effective manpower rarely exceeded 20,000, and they needed more than a week to reduce flimsy outposts held by mere handfuls of men. The laws of war (that is, the unwritten customs accepted by all armies of the age) were characterised by extremes of savagery and generosity. Prisoners, especially the wealthy, were handed back in return for private ransoms, and the king himself devoted whole sessions of his council of war to sorting out disputes which arose out of such practices. It was also accepted that part of a soldier's remuneration came from plundering the enemy's baggage or pillaging towns taken by assault. Rape, ransom and massacre were viewed as the regrettable but almost inevitable concomitants of war. At the taking of Saint-Jean-d'Angely, Louis XIII bought out his soldiers' rights to plunder at the price of four *sous* each. At Saint-Gilles-Croix-de-Vie he went so far as to ransom one by one the Protestant prisoners who were on the point of having their throats cut. On the other hand, he gave his soldiers free rein when they took the little town of Nègrepelisse, near Montauban, on 10 June 1621. Soubise did likewise when his men took Sables-d'Olonne. The massacre at Nègrepelisse aroused horror because of its scale rather than of its nature, as armed resistance was reckoned treason deserving of the death penalty according to the military conventions of the day. The modern reader would certainly be mistaken to regard such practices as either outdated or unusual. They were generally hushed up or overlooked, but they stand out in the wars of 1621 partly against the background of years of peace and partly because a host of witnesses accompanied the armies.

The Second War of Religion

Despite the triumphant interpretation which the regime sought to impose on the peace of Montpellier, it could never really be more than a fragile truce. The tough negotiations between a king and his subjects, the enormous prestige of the Duke of Rohan, the naval supremacy of La Rochelle, and the ability of the Huguenot communities of Languedoc to mobilise, all promised dangerous times to come. The Protestant faction became restless once more during the winter of 1624, partly because of the commercial ambitions of La Rochelle, and partly because of the intrigues of Soubise, whose rash belligerence often clashed with the more conciliatory policies of his brother, Rohan. The merchants of La Rochelle had done well out of the economic boom experienced by the ports of north-western Europe in the closing decades of the sixteenth century. Commercial, political and family ties linked the traders of La Rochelle with their Dutch counterparts. The growth of the Dutch ports had paralleled that of the French Calvinist citadel, and there was a firm solidarity between them. The merchants of La Rochelle played a crucial part in the marketing of the wines and spirits that came down the Charente and the Gironde – and traffic in those products along those waterways was growing fast. La Rochelle itself was a city of over 25,000 souls, further augmented by the transient sea-faring population. This extraordinarily well fortified city had withstood a major siege in 1572, and had subsequently improved its defences still more, so that it was reckoned impregnable by land or sea. Its shipping exceeded that of all the other ocean ports of France put together, and its naval forces were supplemented by flotillas from other Protestant harbours on the Charente and the Seudre, or from the islands of

Oléron and Ré. Manned by the best seamen, these vessels engaged in trade, fishing and even piracy. From 1617 they carried out raids against rival ports, closing the Blavet or the Gironde at will, and attacking Les Sables, Brouage and Royan. The war of 1621 had been sparked off by Soubise's raid against Les Sables. In 1624, hostilities commenced with a surprise attack on Blavet, in which Soubise seized all the vessels found there. In January and February 1625 he consolidated his control of the harbours along the shores of the Charente, and at the same time he sent agents into the towns of Languedoc to muster support for the new call to arms.

Thus, early in 1625, the King's Council found itself once more obliged to wage war on several fronts in order to deal with the Protestant threat. The royal strategy had three elements. The Marshal de Thémines was dispatched to the Castres region to wage a devastating war against the rural areas which customarily provided a haven for Rohan. Another experienced general, the Seigneur de Toiras, who enjoyed the close confidence of the king, landed on the isle of Ré with an élite force. And finally, a powerful naval force was put together at enormous expense. Due to a lack of sufficient ships in Normandy and Brittany, a score or so Dutch and English ships were hired and entrusted to the command of the Duke of Montmorency. This great magnate was Governor of Languedoc, and had been Admiral of France since 1612, in which role he had worked for years to reorganise the royal naval forces. For the second time a major royal fleet was brought together (the first had been gathered by Guise in 1621). Taking advantage of the fact that many ships from La Rochelle were out buccaneering, Montmorency launched a surprise attack. He blockaded the harbour to prevent a relief force from sailing, while the bulk of his fleet engaged with the ships of Admiral Guiton off the isle of Ré. The Protestant fleet suffered a serious defeat on 18 September 1625. Guiton and Soubise escaped only with difficulty, by taking to the long-boats, and Soubise then sought refuge in England.

Rohan, who had never wanted this conflict, negotiated tirelessly at court, and the path of reconciliation was smoothed by the good offices of the English ambassador. The regimes in Paris and London were in perfect harmony. Louis XIII's third and youngest sister, Henrietta Maria, was sixteen years old and still to be married. With her elder sisters married respectively to Spanish and Piedmontese princes, it was almost inevitable that she would find a husband in northern Europe. The London court had begun making approaches in 1624, and Charles, the Prince of Wales, was a most eligible prospect. The only obstacles were the profound anti-Catholicism of English opinion, and the French determination to safeguard Henrietta Maria's right to worship as a Catholic and if possible secure some relaxation of the persecution faced by English Catholics. The marriage was agreed in November 1624, and celebrated by proxy at Paris on 11 May 1625. The young queen left the Louvre on 2 June, escorted by the Duke of Buckingham, the chief minister of England, and accompanied as far as Dieppe by the Queen and Queen Mother of France.

This was the background against which the English, themselves engaged in a short naval conflict with Spain, agreed to put some of their ships at the disposal of the French. English operations against the Spanish coast had been a complete failure. As a result Buckingham was anxious for some respite, and hoped to gain credit for diplomatic success through brokering religious peace in France. English envoys therefore urged the Huguenots to accept Louis XIII's terms, essentially the confirmation of the privileges granted under the Edict of Nantes, mitigated by the presence in La Rochelle of a resident royal commissioner to supervise the city council. For his part, Louis lacked the resources for further campaigning, and a peace was therefore concluded in February 1626.

The Third War of Religion

English goodwill towards France did not last. The alliance against Spain brought nothing but disappointment, while the Habsburg armies were triumphantly driving back the forces of the Lutheran princes and the King of Denmark. Public opinion in London was quick to denounce the papistry of Henrietta Maria's household, and by August 1626 the Puritan faction had in effect succeeded in having her French attendants sent home. Buckingham was anxious to find some sop for the radical preachers, and assisting the Calvinists of La Rochelle against tyrannical papist persecution seemed a promising option. In summer that same year, Cardinal Richelieu had assumed the specially created office of Grand Master of Shipping ('grand maître de navigation'), and his new naval projects aroused disquiet in London, providing a pretext for breaking off the alliance. The English fleets which dominated the Channel resumed their piracy against French merchant shipping. The French responded by impounding two hundred English ships in the port of Bordeaux when they came over for the new wine in January 1627. War was thus inevitable.

From March 1627, Buckingham set about preparing an expedition to sail from Portsmouth against the French. The fleet, some eighty ships carrying 10,000 men, raised anchor on 30 June. Buckingham took command in person, assisted by Soubise. The force entered the roads of La Rochelle on 10 July. But the adherence of La Rochelle to this open revolt against the king did not come easily. The loyalty of the French Protestants to the ruling house was no empty boast. When Buckingham and Soubise presented themselves at the gates of the city, the aldermen refused to let them in, beseeching them not to drag the city into a revolt from which there could be no turning back. But the dowager Duchess of Rohan was in town at the time, and she, at the head of a mob of the city's lower orders, opened the gates despite the magistrates and led her son to the town hall in the midst of a cheering crowd. A week later, the English disembarked on the isle of Ré. The loyal Marshal Toiras, with 3,000 infantry, shut himself in the citadel of Saint-Martin. War had broken out.

Once more Louis XIII marched west at the head of his army, this time accompanied by Richelieu. On 12 October, they reached La Rochelle, which had already been under siege for a month. The besieging force numbered some 30,000 men, but it was of little effect as the English fleet controlled the sea approaches. But Buckingham was facing similar difficulties, for the citadel of Saint-Martin on the isle of Ré had itself been kept provisioned thanks to the pinnaces of Les Sables-d'Olonne, which had twice breached the English naval blockade by night. A final English assault on 6 November had met with disaster. Toiras made a sortie to rendez-vous with a relief force which landed under Stromberg, and together they inflicted heavy casualties on the English, who were forced to retreat across the causeways through the marshes in the middle of the island. On 8 November the English fleet hoisted sail, although the departing Buckingham promised to send further aid to the city. The outcome remained uncertain. Rohan had mobilised all his forces in Languedoc, rallying the little Huguenot townships one by one, and now had some 5,000 men in the field, a highly mobile force which Condé and Montmorency were unable to contain.

If they were to make any progress, the royal forces had to mount a blockade by sea. They thus evolved the plan of constructing an embankment 1.5 kilometres long to cut off the port completely. Thousands of masons and peasants from Poitou, Limousin and the west were press-ganged into this enormous task under the direction of the architect Métezeau. Old ships weighed down with stone were scuttled along the projected line of the embankment in order to speed the work, but bombardments and sorties from La Rochelle combined with the winter weather to prevent rapid completion. Such stratagems had been seen before in the annals of military history – the English had tried something similar before Saint-Martin – but the sheer scale of the enterprise was unprecedented and its audacity exercised enormous fascination on contemporaries.

La Rochelle's will to resist was revitalised when Admiral Jean Guiton was elected mayor during the siege. A royal assault mounted in March 1628 was victoriously repulsed, and popular confidence in Buckingham's promise of prompt relief remained high.

The fleet promised by Buckingham and anxiously awaited by the besieged hove into view on 15 May. It cruised within view of the embankment for five days, but did not risk coming within artillery range. Abandoning the idea of breaking the blockade, it sailed away without joining battle. A third fleet of a hundred ships was on the point of sailing from Portsmouth when the Duke of Buckingham was assassinated by a Puritan fanatic. Charles I proceeded with the plan anyway, and the fleet, now under the command of Admiral Lindsay, appeared off La Rochelle on 30 September. It bombarded the French positions with little apparent effect until 3 October, and then sailed away north.

Famine and disease had been ravaging the besieged population since June, and their last hopes evaporated with Lindsay's withdrawal. Rohan, though master of Haut-Languedoc, was himself effectively besieged in the Cévennes, and was unable to help. On 28 October 1628, spokesmen emerged from the city to offer unconditional surrender. The next morning saw the city gates thrown open to the royal troops, first a well disciplined body of guards, and then a convoy of supplies to relieve the misery of the city inhabitants. Richelieu celebrated mass in the town on the morning of 1 November, and in the afternoon the king made his entry. There were fewer than 6,000 survivors of the siege. The king granted amnesty to the rebels and upheld their freedom of worship within the city. But the city's ample privileges, which dated back to the thirteenth century, were utterly annulled, and its fortifications were to be completely demolished.

The Huguenot republic of the Atlantic, or at least its potential for revolt and secession, disappeared. The jurisdictional privileges and fiscal exemptions which the port had enjoyed had assured it a supremacy that it would now never regain. But the physical scars of the siege would soon heal, thanks to the geographical advantages of the port and its strong trading links with the nations around the North Sea. Later in the century La Rochelle would benefit, like all the French ocean ports, from the expansion of trade with the Antilles.

Richelieu had throughout remained in personal control of the siege operations. He had committed the State to a massive, and massively expensive, enterprise which for many months showed no returns at all, while English attacks seemed irresistible. The eventual success of his strategy earned him enormous political credit. He had won the wholehearted confidence of the king, and his power and authority in the land were henceforth unquestioned.

In Languedoc, meanwhile, Rohan remained undefeated. It was not until after the royal army had gained some rapid victories in the Alps that Louis XIII and Richelieu set about reducing this last Huguenot military stronghold.

From September 1628, as the prospect of English assistance faded, Rohan looked to Spain for support. His agent was a Huguenot colonel and friend of Soubise, Louis Clausel. An agreement was effectively signed at Madrid in May 1629. But the promised Spanish assistance never had time to arrive, as the royal forces, returning from Italy, had launched an offensive in the Vivarais. The strong city of Privas was put under a tight siege, and fell on 26 May. This small and predominantly Protestant town, which was occupied chiefly in working cloth and leather, numbered some 3,000 souls. The entire population was massacred or put to flight, and civic life did not resume there until the 1640s. The terrible news of the sack of Privas induced the other rebel strongholds of Languedoc to surrender. The Duke of Rohan himself made his submission. He was given the option of exile, and set off with his followers for Venice.

At that moment Louis XIII was at Alès. From there he issued an edict on 28 June, the so-called Edict of Grace, which showed the royal desire to bring an end to a decade of civil war which, though intermittent and localised, had nevertheless been bitter. The Edict of Alès renewed the religious and judicial provisions of the Edict of Nantes, but entirely suppressed the political and military clauses which had granted regular national assemblies, strongholds, garrisons and governors.

The Huguenots remained a separate order within the realm. They retained their churches, their synods and their representatives, but they lost the means to influence political developments and to defy royal authority by recourse to arms as they had done so often over the preceding twenty years. The cycle of religious wars came to an end in 1629. The Edict of Nantes would, for thirty years or more, generally be implemented peacefully. A kind of pragmatic toleration which had never before prevailed would now at last be accepted. Co-existence would, after a fashion, become the norm for the divided communities of Languedoc, Guyenne and Saintonge.

Through political crisis, through tax revolts and finally through the Fronde, the Protestants would demonstrate their prudence, docility and loyalty. Wholeheartedly legalist, they would on every occasion side with the court and with the principles of statist absolutism. Nobody could have foreseen the repressive and restrictive turn that the government would take in the 1660s, or the years of persecution that would follow.

8   The Good Times End: 1624–31

Historians, always alive to the destiny of great men, have been accustomed to linger over the year 1624 because it marked the inauguration of Cardinal Richelieu's ministry. But if we deprive ourselves of the privilege of hindsight, we can recognise that neither the duration of Richelieu's pre-eminence nor the eventual directions of his policy could have been foreseen by his contemporaries. What preoccupied public opinion at the time was first the future of the royal succession, for the king's marriage was as yet childless; and secondly the reform of institutions, which seemed once more within reach now that the problems of a royal minority and of a youthful king were past.

The Political Crisis of 1626

The royal couple, Louis XIII and Anne of Austria, married since 1614, had begun to live together as man and wife in 1619. Unfortunately, the successive pregnancies of the queen had never yet come to term, and the passing of the years brought only increasing misunderstanding between the touchy and jealous king and his inexperienced and unappreciated wife. Despite his youth and a taste for hunting and riding, the king did not enjoy robust health. As a result, ministers and courtiers speculated on what might happen to the throne in the event of his death. The Crown would of course revert to his brother Gaston, Duke of Anjou, a young, happy-go-lucky and outgoing man, lazy and without a mind of his own, albeit more cultivated and enquiring than Louis. The character of the heir presumptive was so different from that of the king that enormous changes in the style of government could be reasonably expected if he were to come to the throne. Even if this outcome remained hypothetical, the marriage of a French prince was in itself a delicate and weighty matter of State, and the marriage of Gaston was therefore high on the political agenda.

Richelieu agreed with Louis XIII and the Queen Mother that the eighteen-year-old Gaston should marry Marie de Bourbon-Montpensier, a princess of the blood royal who would bring a handsome dowry. Gaston himself, advised by his governor, Jean-Baptiste d'Ornano, Colonel General of the Corsican troops, would have preferred a marriage with a foreign princess, which would have given him greater freedom of action and raised his prestige with foreign courts. Anne of Austria, advised by her confidante the Duchess of Chevreuse (widow of the Duke of Luynes), was of yet another opinion. She was entirely opposed to any marriage. She was nervous of Gaston's brilliance, and feared that he would have children. Although unable to acknowledge it, she was also afraid that the king, who already neglected her, or Richelieu, who shared the common opinion that blamed her for the lack of children, might decide to repudiate her. The beautiful and scheming Marie de Chevreuse, genuinely devoted to the queen's cause, managed to rally a fair number of great magnates behind the no-marriage policy.

The cardinal minister took charge of the affair and exploited it determinedly. It enabled him first to get rid of the surviving clients of Luynes, who might otherwise have stood in his way, and then to cast himself as the defender of the king's person by presenting the matrimonial intrigues as not only imprudent and impudent but even treasonable. Gaston's youth and unstable temperament left him an easy prey to such insinuations. There was already a faction which looked to the possibility that Gaston would succeed to the crown. This remained a possibility as long as the royal couple remained without a son. Depending on whether one's perspective was short term or long term, entertaining this possibility was either potential treason or mere prudence.

Firmly convinced of the threat to his own position, Richelieu managed to convince the king that he too was in danger, and had Marshal Ornano and his family imprisoned early in May 1626. In June Louis XIII ordered the arrest of his two half-brothers, César and Alexandre de Vendôme (Henri IV's sons by Gabrielle d'Estrées). The Chancellor, Étienne d'Aligre, disapproved of these arbitrary proceedings and found himself disgraced. He was obliged to hand over the seals, the badge of office, to a loyal follower of Richelieu, Michel de Marillac, and was forced to retire to a château in Perche. Louis XIII went to Nantes to preside over the Estates of Brittany and inform them that the Duke of Vendôme's governorship was at an end. There, on 6 August 1626, the king's brother Gaston, Duke of Anjou, married Marie de Montpensier. He received the Duchy of Orleans as his apanage, and Orleans was the title by which he was henceforth known. During the court's residence at Nantes, a young gentleman who had been caught up in the intrigues of the Duchess of Chevreuse was condemned to death by an extraordinary tribunal and executed on 19 August. His name was Henri de Talleyrand, Count of Chalais, a grandson of Marshal de Monluc. His noble birth and his youth, the cardinal's relentlessness in his pursuit, the king's refusal of clemency and the tragic circumstances of his death, combined to earn him universal pity, and made him one of the first and most sinister victims of the implacable style of politics practised by Louis XIII and his minister.

The clampdown did not stop there. The Duchess of Chevreuse was driven into exile in Lorraine. Marshal Ornano was due to face an extraordinary tribunal when he met a sudden and premature death in prison. Queen Anne herself was subjected to restrictions and reproaches which further aggravated her isolation from the court and her alienation from her husband. And this spectacular crisis consolidated for Richelieu himself a draconian reputation which he was careful never to lose.

As a result of this affair, Richelieu was able to bring into the King's Council two men to whose care he entrusted the administration of the provinces and the reform of institutions. One was the Marquis of Effiat, who became *Surintendant des finances*. A relative of one of Henri IV's Secretaries of State, Effiat had been

Surintendant des mines since 1613, and had carried out various diplomatic missions. A meticulous fellow who was open to change, as *Surintendant des finances* he set his staff to statistical investigations resulting in an accurate map of the kingdom's resources and population which could have laid the foundation for a major reconstruction of the fiscal system. As it happened, he died of fever in the course of a military campaign during 1632.

The custody of the seals was entrusted to Michel de Marillac (1563–1632). It is worth spending some time on him because his intellectual grasp earned him exceptional moral authority in his own time, and because historians have chosen to see in him the embodiment of a particular policy option: reformism at home and caution abroad. Michel de Marillac belonged to a magistrate dynasty: his father Guillaume had been *Surintendant des finances* under Henri IV. Michel had been a councillor in the Parlement de Paris since 1586. Originally a Leaguer, he had been one of the first to rally to Henri IV and had played a crucial role in the reconciliation of Paris in 1594. Learned and devout, he made his household in the parish of Saint-Germain a beacon of piety and charity. Thanks to his young half-brother Louis, commander of Marie de Medici's guards, he was numbered among the most trusted advisers of the Queen Mother. A friend of Richelieu, he had, like the cardinal, been a key figure in reconciling the Queen Mother to her son in 1621. The cardinal did not forget him when he returned to the Council in 1624, and secured for him the office of *Surintendant des finances*. In accordance with the petition of the Estates General of 1614, Marillac immediately established a tribunal to investigate the accounts of the financiers who dealt with the king in the business of tax and customs farming. The fruits of the settlements arising from this helped cover the costs of Richelieu's first intervention in the Valtellina.

The Achievement of Michel de Marillac

Put in charge of French justice in 1626, Marillac acted in complete compliance with the plans of the cardinal minister. His first task was to open the Estates of Brittany which were to ratify the fall of

Vendôme, and then to carry out the prosecution of Chalais at Nantes. Next he had to arrange a new Assembly of Notables in order to refine and implement the reforming policies proposed by the Estates General of 1614 and the Assembly of Notables of 1617.

This time, the notables summoned by the king gathered at the Tuileries. Their sessions took place between 10 November 1626 and 24 February 1627. The assembly comprised fifty-five individuals: about thirty magistrates, thirteen prelates, and ten magnates. Paris and the robe were thus better represented than at the assembly of 1617. The notables deliberated together as a single body, irrespective of rank. In order to deal with more technical issues, they demanded access to documents, which the King's Council made available to them. They divided themselves into three committees which dealt respectively with finance, security and fortifications. Among the economies suggested by preceding assemblies were not only reductions in pensions and in high court offices, but also the elimination of redundant fortifications.

The civil wars had led to a considerable increase in the number and variety of fortified sites: town and village walls, battlements on houses and rural churches, fortified manor houses, city defences, and finally well-nigh impregnable citadels within major cities. These stone obstacles, which dotted the landscape, barring roads and rivers, had real military value. They could often be held by a handful of men against substantial forces because artillery was needed in order to overcome even minor fortifications. Rebels, malcontents and local trouble-makers could easily use them as bases from which to threaten the security and freedom of trade. The maintenance of walls was a heavy drain on municipal budgets, representing by far the greatest single expenditure. Moreover, the military importance of cities gave rise to local disputes over control of the city gates, the organisation of patrols and sentries, and the responsibility for the arsenals of town-houses, setting captains and governors at loggerheads with municipal magistrates, aldermen or consuls. The dismantling of fortifications was therefore a widely endorsed political objective. The recent revolts and civil wars had convinced central government of the threat that such fortifications posed. Only frontier fortresses deserved to be maintained and developed. *Raison d'état* was thus at one with urban and rural opinion in seeing walls as a source of danger and a needless expense. Governors, vice-bailiffs and vice-seneschals – the military officers responsible for the safety of the countryside and the highways – received over the months and years ahead lists of sites which were to be scaled down or razed. The task of demolition was carried out by forced labour levied from local residents. The neighbouring towns and villages were only too happy to comply. Some hundreds or even thousands of sites were dealt with. The effort of 1626 was just the start of what was to prove an enduring policy of domestic disarmament pursued by the monarchy. That year therefore proved a turning-point in the history of daily life and in the development of the French landscape.

The dismantling of fortifications was not the only fruit of the Assembly of Notables. On the basis of the statements of grievances presented to the king in February 1627, which summed up the deliberations of the assembly, the Masters of Requests, under Marillac's guidance, put together a lengthy ordinance (comprising 430 articles) which presented itself as a response to 'the complaints and grievances of the Estates General . . . and the advice tendered by the Assembly of Notables'. It was published by royal declaration on 16 June 1627, and touched on every aspect of government as it was conceived at that time: the administration of justice, the organisation of the Church, the fiscal machinery, the discipline of troops, the maintenance of highways and bridges, the management of hospitals, the conduct of trade, and so on. For example, article 383 laid down the 'direct universal' jurisdiction of the king over his whole territory, anticipating the sovereignty of contemporary States over their territory and all its resources. This new conception clashed with the principle of 'no lordship without title' which prevailed throughout the southern provinces, which were governed according to Roman Law. The Parlements of the Midi were vocal in their opposition to it. In the majority of areas, the ordinance merely codified existing legislation and made existing regulations more logical and effective.

The Parlement de Paris was unhappy to see itself losing not so much the initiative in legislation – which belonged indisputably to the king – as the authority to enact it. It showed the same hostility to the labours of the Assembly of Notables as it had shown to the deliberations of the Estates General. The sovereign courts reckoned that they were being deprived of that privileged position of legislative council which they claimed was theirs by right. Nor was the attack upon the powers of the Parlements purely imaginary: the ordinance in effect limited the traditional power of remonstrance to a period of two months. The Parlement de Paris did not resign itself to registering this ordinance until a *lit de justice* held on 15 January 1629. A further proof of parliamentary discontent appears in the nickname 'code Michaud' (a derisory allusion to Marillac's forename) by which they referred to the ordinance. After Marillac's death, however, nobody – least of all the Parlements – cared to propose any further administrative reforms. As a result, the great project of legislative codification and rationalisation remained unfinished. Efforts like those of 1627, though an important stage in the long process of building a modern State, would not be seen again for another thirty years, with the great reforming ordinances of the Colbert era.

The administration of customs and taxes was covered in about sixty articles. Civil wars and the various transalpine expeditions required considerable resources. It was said that the well-nigh interminable siege of La Rochelle cost in excess of 40 million *livres*, and it is certain that the outgoings of the Treasury for 1629 reached a peak of 54 million *livres*, while the average figure for the preceding decade was 42 million *livres* a year. It was therefore necessary to undertake a complete overhaul of the fiscal system handed down from previous reigns, as well as a search for unexploited resources.

In order to cope with unprecedented financial demands, the *Surintendants* could choose from four highly inequitable expedients. First, they could further exploit the sale of offices by creating new offices or at least new jurisdictions. Second, they could increase taxes on consumption (the *gabelle* on salt, the various *aides* levied on wine and inns, and the levies on the circulation of goods). Third, they could increase the *taille*, the main direct tax, which weighed heaviest on the peasantry. Finally, they could sell off the lands or the local revenues which formed part of the royal desmesne.

The increases in the *taille* imposed during the Wars of Religion had sparked off numerous peasant revolts between 1593 and 1598. There was no possibility of further increasing the crushing burden of this tax, which already amounted to about 57 per cent of the royal revenues. As for taxes on consumption, the complete failure of Sully's attempt to impose a tax of one *sou* in the *livre* showed that there were limits here too. During Louis XIII's early years, *Surintendant* Jeannin resorted to massive alienations of the royal desmesne. But a practice which came down to spending capital or else mortgaging future income could not be continued indefinitely. Breaking with precedent, *Surintendant* Effiat sought to revalue levies on the consumption of various goods whose market was expanding. He succeeded in increasing receipts from the *gabelle* to over 8 million livres, and those from *aides* to about 3 million livres, the latter by concentrating especially on the trade in 'vins brulés' – distilled spirits such as cognac, produced in Angoumois and sold mainly to the Netherlands. But he did not dare go very far along this path: his collectors in the ports were already exposed to regular mob violence at the hands of wine-growers and seafarers.

In 1627 saw the doubling of the target for the *taillon*, a levy introduced under Henri II and assigned to military expenditure. Its tax-base was broader than that of the regular *taille*, as it extended to the major towns which were exempt from the *taille* itself. But this was another failure: after six years, the target had still not been met.

Rather than an increase in the *taille*, what was needed was a better distribution of its burden. At the top level, the burden was shared highly unevenly by the provinces. It fell chiefly on those governed directly by officials of the *bureaux d'élections*, commonly known as *élus*. Provinces where the *taille* was implemented by means of the provincial Estates made but a feeble, often a negligible, contribution. Thus provinces like Normandy and Poitou paid considerable sums, while Brittany, Provence and Languedoc paid hardly anything. It was therefore necessary to advance a little further down the long path towards a uniform fiscal regime for the whole realm. Sully in his time had tried to install the *élection* regime in Haute-Guyenne, but had had to abandon the scheme after representations were made by the areas concerned. The project was resumed in 1622 and implemented in 1624, but the *élections* were only installed at the price of a bloody peasant revolt in Haute-Quercy. In 1628, further edicts established *élections* in Dauphiné, Provence and Languedoc. In Dauphiné in particular, where the reform drove a wedge between the various orders of the Estates, the *élections* took root. Direct royal government was successfully introduced, and the Estates of Dauphiné lapsed into silence and obscurity without ever being formally abolished. In Provence and Languedoc, however, the provincial Estates lobbied at court and succeeded in securing the withdrawal of the edicts in return for an immediate grant.

The patchy fiscal reforms undertaken by Effiat and Marillac were certainly not undertaken in favourable circumstances. From 1628 the kingdom found itself in one of the most terrible crises of a terrible century.

The Crisis of 1630

The traditional agrarian economy was a fragile system. Many parts of the countryside survived on a minimal cereal monoculture, accompanied perhaps by some animal husbandry on waste or common land, and by some market-gardening by women on patches of ground near the house. But the slightest accident – crop disease, spring frosts or summer storms – could reduce or even destroy the harvest. The records of market prices in towns show that the price of grain climbed steadily during the long months which separated one harvest from the next. But at least townsfolk could benefit from purchases of grain ordered by far-sighted magistrates. The great cities would buy six months in advance from distant markets such as the Baltic ports. These great cargos came by sea and were then distributed inland by waterways and highways. The peasants, though, were perforce self-sufficient, and stood virtually outside the monetary economy. In times of extreme dearth they had no option but to abandon their land and go begging at the gates of nearby towns, or those further away. It is true that shortages were often just a consequence of local bad weather, so that one could hope to survive by going begging some distance away. But the effects of this random distribution of dearth would not be relieved until much later, with the improved roads of the eighteenth century, or even more with the railways of the nineteenth.

There had been no serious grain shortage in France as a whole since the 1590s. The harvest of 1627 was poor in several provinces of southern and central France, and in the autumn towns began counting their inhabitants in order to arrange for the purchase of adequate provisions. The harvest of 1629 was once again insufficient, and the crisis assumed the proportions of famine in some parts of the south in spring 1630. Municipal institutions and charitable organisations opened granaries and arranged for doles to satisfy the hundreds, even thousands, of poor and hungry people. In the worst-affected areas, at least a quarter of the population were plunged into poverty, that is, were rendered incapable of surviving on their own resources. More productive areas, where the shortfall was only slight, saw mob riots as people's fears for the future led them to protest about the departure of grain shipments. Bakeries and granaries were often pillaged by mobs of women, always the first to cause disturbances when times became hard. As the northern provinces and the Parisian basin were spared by this crisis, the historical record has not paid it the attention lavished upon the crises of 1662, 1693 or 1709. But in truth this harvest crisis only turned into a catastrophe because it coincided with one of the last and most disastrous visitations of the plague, which had broken out in 1626.

The terrible effects of the interaction of plague and famine cannot be explained, as was long believed, in terms of the debilitation of people through hunger leaving them vulnerable to infection. What really happened was that the interruption of trade by the plague aggravated the food shortages, which themselves made paupers of thousands of people, who were thrown onto the streets as beggars and became carriers of infection. The highly contagious disease known as the plague had first appeared in Europe during the fourteenth century, and had been virtually endemic throughout the continent since 1348, returning in any given region on something like an eleven-year cycle. Arriving from the east, the plague struck first along the Mediterranean littoral, and then spread throughout the west along chance routes of infection. We know now that the carriers of the bacterium were rats and their fleas, but according to the medical theories prevalent in the seventeenth century, contagious diseases spread through the inhalation of polluted or corrupt air, of which offensive odours were the most obvious form. Troop movements in Germany had helped spread the infection since 1624, and two other military operations contributed to its diffusion throughout western Europe: the siege of La Rochelle, especially after the dispersal of the besiegers in autumn 1629, and the siege of Mantua (February 1629–July 1630), whence imperial troops spread the disease throughout northern Italy.

The provinces of southern France were ravaged by the plague between spring 1627 and winter 1631, with the precise chronology varying from place to place. Some cities were spared, but others were afflicted for more than two years, with outbreaks in summer and autumn of both 1630 and 1631. The effectiveness of the isolation measures used to cope with the disease (the complete suspension of trade, watches on the gates, quarantine for suspected victims, the enclosure of the afflicted in lazar houses, and the burning of their furniture and clothing) could no doubt explain the apparently random distribution of the epidemic. The provinces north of the Loire were less severely struck, or at least the epidemic was confined to narrow areas such as the Cotentin, the towns of Champagne or the Breton ports. The worst-affected cities lost as much as half of their population. In one terrible instance, the city of Digne, which had a population of 10,000 in 1628, was down to 1,500 a year later. Chambéry and Aurillac lost half their people, and even great cities like Lyon and Bordeaux lost between a quarter and a third. Figures can hardly be precise, though, as on the one hand registers of deaths could not be maintained in the worst months, while on the other a town's population might be reduced as much by flight as by mortality.

The anatomy of a plague epidemic was fairly consistent throughout western Europe from the fourteenth to the late seventeenth century. The arrival of the disease was heralded by rumour before official notification was published by ruling authorities. Precautions were then taken in the fairs and markets: great fairs were called off, and travellers were required to show a bill of health. Next, after some soldier or merchant had passed through, suspicious deaths were reported in a suburb or an inn, and the physician retained by the town authorities would recognise the telltale black swellings of bubonic plague. The authorities confined victims to shacks outside the walls. They were shut up with the plague doctor and a few men known as 'crows' who were paid to tend the sick, bury the dead and clean (or 'perfume') their houses. At the first news of an outbreak, those who could fled the towns and retired to country houses. Everything stopped: the administration of justice, the levying of customs and the conduct of trade; troops were disbanded and prisons opened; all the notables fled, and the people left trapped in the town had recourse only to a few bold priests and magistrates. The authority of the absent corporation was vested in an extraordinary commission known as the 'council of health'. It was supported by a captain and archers responsible for keeping out strangers, locking up plague victims and preventing the looting of empty houses. Things could go on like this for months or even years, until the abatement of the plague permitted a return to normal life. In towns which were finally free from plague, the survivors would perform an act of thanksgiving, fulfilling a vow made to the Virgin, St Roch or St Sebastian. Fervent processions would wind through the streets to celebrate deliverance from the terrible scourge. It is reckoned the epidemic of 1628–31 carried off between 1.5 and 2 million victims out of a total population of between 17 and 20 million in the area occupied by France today. But the markedly uneven distribution of the epidemic meant that, in the worst-affected cities and regions, the crisis took on the dimensions of an apocalypse.

The crisis of 1630 made an impact on almost everyone's life, and it took a long time for the scars to heal. Not only was there appalling loss of life, but the survivors found that many things had changed considerably. During the months of hardship, the high cost of food and the destitution consequent upon the interruption of trade forced many of the middling sort to sell their lands at rock-bottom prices. Almshouses and urban corporations, faced with a rising tide of poverty, were also forced to sell off assets and incur debts. Patterns of landholding were thus altered as crises provided opportunities for purchase to those who had the means – above all the wealthy townsfolk. These changes were especially apparent in the immediate vicinity of towns, and tightened the grip of urban proprietors over the hinterland.

The finances of the *hôtels de ville* were not among the beneficiaries of these processes, as they had to cope with the heavy expenses of aid and provisioning. Communities incurred massive debts which took many years to pay off. In fact, communities and institutions throughout western Europe found themselves staggering beneath the burden of debt in this period. This not only led to the erosion of their traditional powers but also left them vulnerable to the rising powers of the age – in the case of France, to the domination of the State, whose expansion was in full swing. Moreover, in the following years the expense of lodging and maintaining troops in time of war was systematically shifted onto municipal finances, further increasing an already crushing burden. Meanwhile, the Crown denounced the dishonesty or negligence (which was, so to speak, structural) of civic magistrates. Chronic civic indebtedness became a pretext for ever more vigorous State intervention in local institutions, with control of the administration, confiscation of income, and abolition of often ancient communal powers and privileges. This centralising trend extended over half a century, with the result that it can be missed in the absence of extended local studies. The crisis of 1630 represented its commencement.

If one leafs through the sources for the history of private life – the diaries, memoirs and account-books of the provinces – or if one wishes to chart the development of some particular town, or of some popular celebration or ritual, one sees soon enough that somewhere near 1630 things always take a turn for the worse. Moreover the mortality crisis coincided with the beginnings of significant French engagement in the European conflicts of the period. The military intervention of Louis XIII and Richelieu first in northern Italy and then in Lorraine heralded greater efforts to come. The age of peace which had prevailed since 1598 was drawing to a close. The last of the good times, when people still greeted the summer with dances, and musicians travelled from village to village when the singing and dancing season was at its height, and when autumn fairs attracted hordes of traders, coincided with the period of the siege of La Rochelle. Then began the years of trial and misery and death, followed by a period of unprecedented taxation necessitated by the policy of war. The last of the good times, the later 1620s, lived on in memory as a little golden age whose passing would long be regretted. At the institutional level, this was the age of reforms begun, of plans for national refurbishment, of missed opportunities and of peaceful government. The country would not see its like again for thirty years, until the reformist era of Colbert dawned, and with it the revival of several of the forgotten projects of the age of Marillac.

9 Richelieu and the Beginnings of an Interventionist Foreign Policy

The diplomatic scene of seventeenth-century Europe was dominated by the rivalry between the two great Catholic sovereigns: the king of Spain and the king of France. This rivalry was a geopolitical reality obvious to all the diplomatic players. The diverse and dispersed nature of the Spanish king's territories stood in marked contrast to the compact territory of his French counterpart, densely populated, already strongly centralised and capable of prodigious military efforts. The possibility of a new and terrible confrontation between the two major western powers was made to seem rather remote by the impotence of France during the Wars of Religion, and by the option for peace which characterised the reign of Henri IV and even more the regime of Marie de Medici. But the statesmen of Spain and France knew how unstable the equilibrium really was, and how powerful were the currents of patriotism in the public opinion of the respective realms. Governors of border provinces, and ambassadors in Paris and Madrid (and for that matter in the other capitals of European diplomacy – Rome, Venice, Turin and Vienna), were ever alert to developments, to the building of fortifications here or there, to the raising of troops, and to the aristocratic or popular agitations which could so easily overturn the apple-cart.

The Duke of Lesdiguières, governor of the Dauphiné, a great Protestant magnate, former companion of Henri IV, and a brave military leader, kept himself informed about developments in northern Italy and the Swiss cantons. His role was, so to speak, that of the king's watchman on the Alps. Since 1605 he had been warning against what he saw as the threat posed by the strengthening of the Spanish presence in the duchy of Milan. This rich and powerful possession enabled the Spaniards to intervene effectively in the affairs of the Italian princes, to exert influence over the Catholic cantons of Switzerland, and to control the Alpine passes which gave them access to Germany and formed a vital stage of the 'Spanish Road' by which troops from the Iberian peninsula made their way to the Netherlands. One particular little valley, strategically placed to the north of Milan, was to dominate the attention of politicians for about two decades.

The Affair of the Valtellina

The high valley of the Adda makes its way from the head of Lake Como south of the massif of the Grisons, linking Lombardy to the Tyrol. This route, known as the Valtellina, was negotiable from spring onwards, connecting the domains of the Spanish Habsburgs to those of their imperial cousins. Since the early sixteenth century it had been in the hands of the Grisons League, an ally of the Swiss Cantons. The conversion of the majority of the Grisons League to the Reformation had not fostered a happy relationship with their predominantly Catholic subjects in the Valtellina. In July 1620 the people of the valley had risen and expelled their Grisons rulers. The Spanish governor of Milan had supported their cause, helping them repel the Swiss punitive expedition. The French and the Venetians were uneasy at the territorial gain thus made by the Spaniards in this little corner of the Alps. But as nobody was yet prepared to go to war, an agreement was reached at Milan in 1622 by which the valley remained under the protection of papal troops who guaranteed a kind of peaceful neutrality.

When he returned to the King's Council in 1624, Richelieu reopened the file. In summer that same year, French agents were active in the Grisons, Switzerland, Savoy and Venice – all traditionally pro-French – with a view to military action. A force of some 4,000 men, recruited in Switzerland and commanded by the

Marquis de Coeuvres, expelled the papal troops and occupied the valley in November.

If the French were launching their forces beyond the Alps for the first time since the reign of Henri II, it was because they reckoned they held a strong hand in an alliance which united them not only with Venice but also, and more importantly, with the duchy of Piedmont and Savoy. This sovereign duchy, whose territories straddled the Alps, was master of the passes. Its duke, Charles Emmanuel (1580–1630), was eager for territorial expansion and maintained claims on a variety of towns and lordships in the hands of Genoa, Milan and Mantua. Through his alliance with France in October 1624, he hoped to gain military support which would enable him to dispossess Genoa of a chunk of the western Riviera.

The occupation of the Valtellina in 1624 was due to be complemented in summer 1625 by a joint Franco-Piedmontese expedition against Genoa, the customary landing-place for Spanish troops. A small force led by Charles Emmanuel and the Duke of Créquy (a relative of Lesdiguières, and his Lieutenant General in the Dauphiné) met not easy victory but fierce resistance from the militia of the Genoese Apennines, supported by Spanish forces from Milan. The invaders were forced to retreat, and returned across the Alps in November. The brief success against papal troops was now compromised. And in the north the armies of Spain had just gained an enormous advantage with the 'surrender of Breda' (celebrated in Velásquez's famous painting, also known as *The Lances*) in June 1625. France had no choice but to sue for peace, and the Treaty of Monzon was duly concluded in March 1626 by the French ambassador at Madrid, Charles Du Fargis. This restored the status quo, with the French remaining beyond the Alps, and the Grisons recovering their rights over the Valtellina.

Displaying his customary mastery of propaganda, Richelieu transformed this rather ambiguous result into a triumph. The retreat from the Apennines was attributed to the indecent haste of one small place, Gavi, to surrender. Its captain, an old nobleman from the Dauphiné, was tried by the Parlement of Aix and sentenced to death for contumacy. The rush to negotiate without the consent of Charles Emmanuel was blamed on Du Fargis, who was in effect disowned. Finally, the affair of the Valtellina itself was presented for French consumption as turning out favourably for the national interest. Historians have somewhat uncritically endorsed this interpretation of events ever since. In fact, the Grisons could not risk alienating its powerful neighbours in Milan, with the result that the Habsburg armies enjoyed free passage through the valley, as for example when imperial troops went to besiege Casale in 1629, or when Spanish forces marched to reinforce the Imperialists on the eve of the Battle of Nördlingen in 1634.

In the immediate term, the Duke of Piedmont and Savoy, wounded by the setback and the French desertion, switched sides once again and threw in his lot with the Spaniards in northern Italy. But the events of 1624–5 had at least seen the return of the French to the Italian chessboard. They showed also that Louis XIII and his minister were determined to play their part on the European stage, and were not prepared to allow the Habsburgs a free hand. Serious hostilities had started to tear Germany apart in 1618. Emperor Ferdinand II had triumphed over the forces of the Lutheran princes in Bohemia, Saxony and the Palatinate, and his victorious troops had fought their way to the shores of the Baltic. At the same time, the Spaniards seemed to have the upper hand in their interminable and recently renewed conflict with the United Provinces. The cautious distance which France initially kept from these conflicts was seen as mere poltroonery not only by young bloods of the court avid for military glory, but also by the traditional allies and clients of France – the German and Italian princes who were profoundly uneasy at the apparent European hegemony of the twin branches of the Habsburgs based at Madrid and Vienna. But the neutrality enforced first by Louis XIII's youth and then by the years of internal troubles was no longer inevitable. Richelieu was to be the powerful instrument of a new, self-determined and aggressive policy.

The Mantuan Succession

Another Italian episode gave Paris the chance to demonstrate its new diplomatic and military assertiveness. As luck would have it, the Duke of Mantua died in 1627 leaving no immediate heir. His territories in northern Italy were of a strategic importance greater even than that of the Valtellina. They were divided into two blocks – the Duchy of Mantua itself, and the Marquisate of Monferrato – each of them dominated by a fortified city of exceptional strength. The fortress of Mantua, almost entirely surrounded by the marshes of Mincio, and dominating them with its ramparts and bastions, controlled the route from the north which permitted passage from Germany to Italy by way of the Brenner Pass, down the valley of the Adige, past Lake Garda. The fortress of Casale Monferrato, a little to the west, commanded the Po and thus the natural axis which led from the French Alpine passes towards Venice and the Adriatic.

The nearest heir to these lands came from that branch of the house of Gonzaga which had settled in France during the reign of Henri II: Charles de Gonzague (1580–1637), Duke of Nevers and Governor of Champagne. He was a bold and generous soul who had founded a new city, Charleville, on the border between France and the ecclesiastical principality of Liège. The first stones had been laid in 1606, and by 1627 the project, planned by the architect Clément Métezeau, was nearing completion. In 1619 the Duke had attempted to raise a Christian army, a private volunteer force to go to the aid of the Christian princes confronted by the Ottomans. He set off to claim his Italian inheritance in January 1628, with the blessing not only of France (predictably enough), but also of Pope Urban VIII, who recognised the validity of his claim and saw the value of a French counterweight to Spanish supremacy on the peninsula.

Charles Emmanuel of Piedmont and Savoy, however, contested the inheritance in the name of his daughter Marguerite, widow of a former Duke of Mantua. He claimed for her the lands of Monferrato, whose fertile slopes, rich in vineyards, cornfields, strongholds and strategic sites, would have made a valuable territorial gain for Piedmont. The Spanish Governor of Milan egged on Madrid, or to be precise the Count-Duke Olivares, hoping to reopen the conflict that had broken out in 1625, this time with the support of Piedmont. Olivares, judging that France was too bogged down in the siege of La Rochelle to offer real support to their Mantuan claimant, expected a quick and easy campaign. So in April 1628 a joint Piedmontese and Milanese force laid siege to Casale. With few troops at his disposal, the Duke of Mantua could not hold out long. In summer a small mercenary force set out from France under the Marquis of Huxelles, but it was broken up by the Savoyards soon after reaching the Alps. No further assistance seemed to be at hand, and it looked as though Casale would soon have to open its gates and accept the triumph of Charles Emmanuel.

The conclusion of the siege of La Rochelle did not immediately bring the Protestant revolts to an end, and the Duke of Rohan was continuing his campaigns in Languedoc, and even opening negotiations with Spain. So Richelieu decided to put together a fresh army on the Rhône, leaving himself free until the last minute to decide whether to advance into Languedoc or Piedmont. In February 1629, this force of 35,000 men, led by the king in person, set off east, crossing the Mont-Genèvre Pass on 28th of that month. Italy had not seen such a huge force for many years. On 6 March the troops of the royal household clashed victoriously with a handful of Spanish troops who had advanced up the valley of the Doria Riparia River as far as Susa. The French lost barely a dozen men in the skirmish, less than were lost to avalanches. Charles Emmanuel kept out of the way and retreated. He hastened to negotiate, and offered the French free passage across his domains. The garrison of Casale was relieved, and a strong French force remained behind under Marshal Toiras to ensure its security.

That the Susa campaign has entered the history books is a tribute to the French propaganda machine, to the publicists who wrote up the events at Richelieu's behest. The episode was milked for all it was worth because Louis XIII had led his troops in person, and the easy victory seemed to augur well for Richelieu's interventionist policy. Other successes, equally trivial in military terms but of equal political significance, enjoyed similar publicity: for example, the Battle of the Marshes of Rié in 1621, the first victory over the rebel Protestants; or the crossing of the Rhine by Louis XIV in 1672, the first action of the war with Holland. In truth, the Italian expedition of early 1629 demonstrated France's ability to mobilise. In a mere six months Louis XIII and Richelieu had extinguished the revolt in the west and apparently imposed their solution to the crisis of the Mantuan succession, while their forces stood ready once again to march into the Vivarais and set about the remaining Protestant strongholds.

The success of March 1629 was, however, far from secure. The imperialists in their turn intervened in the war of the Mantuan succession. An initial contingent of 5,000 Germans descended from the Valtellina into the Po Valley on 29 May. During the summer a combined Spanish–imperial force of some 50,000 men was brought together under the command of two eminent Italian generals who had entered Habsburg service: the Genoese Spinola, the victor of Breda; and the Venetian Collalto. Casale and Mantua were besieged, and the Mantuan territories were laid waste by marauding troops. The successes of the imperial armies under Wallenstein against the Protestant forces of the King of Denmark in the north enabled considerable resources to be diverted south of the Alps. The cause of the Duke of Mantua once more seemed lost.

Over the winter of 1629–30, Richelieu amassed another army in the foothills of the Alps. In February 1630 the first contingents made their way through the passes. As they descended into Piedmont, surprise attacks on Pinerolo and Saluzzo, fortresses which controlled access to the plain, won two valuable bases along the route to Monferrato. The Piedmontese put up some resistance at Montmélian and the Little Saint Bernard Pass, but were massively outnumbered and had to fall back. On 18 July the bulk of the Piedmontese army was smashed at Avigliana.

July 1630 brought decisive and tragic developments for both sides. As the French were taking control of Piedmont, the unfortunate Duke Charles Emmanuel, holed up in the north of his lands, died of exhaustion (26 July). But the imperialists were gaining the upper hand at Mantua. The town had been cut off since November 1629, and held barely 6,000 troops under the Duke of Nevers and his general, Marshal d'Estrées, Marquis of Coeuvres. The epidemic which had been sweeping through Europe reached northern Italy in February, striking besiegers and besieged alike. Half of the 40,000 inhabitants of Mantua died, and the decimated garrison could not even provide enough sentries. The city was taken by storm on the very same day (18 July) that the French achieved their victory in Piedmont. The consequent sack of

Mantua, the ancient seat of the Gonzagas, home of one of the most brilliant courts of the Renaissance, and rich in palaces and art treasures, horrified Europe. The Luxembourg mercenary leader Aldringen allowed his men a free hand for three days. For months afterwards, convoys of wagons continued to disperse the booty through Italy and southern Germany.

The news of the fall of Mantua was a terrible blow to Louis and his Council, based for the moment at Lyon, but in the following weeks fresh turns of fortune's wheel would bring some consolations to the French cause. Words like 'fate' and 'fortune' might seem out of place in a narrative which aims to give a clear account and a rational explanation of the course of events. But it must be realised that the warring parties, operating a scanty State apparatus under the pressures of war, found themselves stretched to the limit by a continental conflict whose scale nobody fully appreciated. Under these conditions, the fortunes of war could turn on the slightest thing: the presence or absence of some prince or general, bad weather interfering with the supplying of troops, or changes of opinion, whether among peasants rising against the depredations of soldiers, or among gentlemen indignant at the demands of ministers.

In truth, the vicissitudes of human existence such as the personal involvement of some dignitary in the service of the Crown, the skill or incompetence of a general, the sickness or death of a sovereign seemed much more important in seventeenth-century eyes than even the most overwhelming natural disasters. One cannot fail to observe the utter indifference of politicians to the outbreak of the most terrible epidemic of modern times. Following their lead, most historians have recounted the tale of these years without regard for the hundreds of thousands of people dying of plague in the cities of south-western Europe. But one comes away with an unmistakable impression of the sheer unpreparedness and reliance on improvisation of the opposing camps, of the dramatic fluctuations in the fortunes of war, and of the consequent elements of chance and wager in the decision-making processes of any government of that time. And perhaps also of all times, if we dare for a moment abandon the historian's professional myopia.

Fortune continued to smile upon the French through the summer of 1630, as death removed first Charles Emmanuel (26 July), and then Spinola (23 September) while he was directing the siege of Casale. A truce was arranged at Casale, doubtless because of the impact of the epidemic in both camps, and the ducal throne of Piedmont-Savoy came into the hands of a Francophile prince. Victor Amadeus, eldest son of the late duke, had married Louis XIII's young sister Christine in 1619, and was ready to make the best of the sometimes unequal relationship with his powerful western neighbour.

The truce at Casale expired on 15 October, and Spanish assaults were about to resume when a papal diplomat, Giulio Mazzarino, arrived with news of a general peace concluded at Regensburg by the representatives gathered there for the Imperial Diet, the assembly of the princes and sovereigns of Germany. By bringing hostilities in Monferrato to an end just as the French forces were beginning to run out of steam, Mazzarino had done Louis XIII an enormous favour. The French king would often speak of him in years to come.

The peace of Regensburg resulted from the military disarray of both sides. The imperialists, conquerors of Mantua, and the French, victorious in Piedmont, were alike uncertain of the future in Germany, where the Protestant cause had just found a new champion in the person of Gustavus Adolphus of Sweden. A Swedish army had landed in Pomerania in July 1630. The peace provided for the full restitution of Piedmont and Mantua to their respective dukes. Both the French and the Imperialists were to withdraw beyond the Alps and abstain in future from intervening in Italian affairs. This restoration of the status quo did not satisfy the interventionist Richelieu, who advised Louis XIII to repudiate the treaty. This difficult choice raised a storm in the King's Council which culminated in a major political watershed after which the field was clear for the cardinal's most ambitious projects.

The Political Drama of the Winter of 1630

So far, Richelieu had done no more than sketch out his grand design for foreign policy. His six years of government had seen the first interventions in Italy and the elimination of the military potential of Protestantism at home. His experiences during this time had allowed him to consolidate his world-view and develop a political doctrine. The peace of Regensburg might have nipped the whole thing in the bud. Richelieu affected to see in the recent history of Spain an aspiration towards universal dominion. He made it his task to forestall this ambition and establish instead a balance of power in which France would be the arbiter of Europe. All the resources of France were to be mobilised to achieve this end. As a result, he saw all calls for reform, for the relief of the people, or for the liberty of the nobility or of other orders within the kingdom as obstacles in his path. In the advice he drafted for the king in the course of 1629, a frequently cited text, he made his purpose clear: 'Our overriding objective must always remain to impede the progress of Spain' (January 1629) and again, 'We must put side all thoughts of rest, economy, or reform within the realm' (November 1629).

The Queen Mother, Marie de Medici, who had always been Richelieu's patron, and the Keeper of the Seals, Marillac, his faithful collaborator, had sometimes questioned his decisions, but at the end of the day had always followed his lead and supported his plans, even when these took French troops across the frontiers. But the disasters of 1630 – the epidemic disseminated by troop movements, the fall and sack of Mantua, the mass desertions of troops, and the financial exhaustion – were for them warning signals suggesting a change of course. To reject the peace of Regensburg seemed to them the height of folly. On top of all this, the king suddenly fell ill on 20 September, while still at Lyon. For several days they feared for his life. Gaston's accession and a complete reversal of policy seemed imminent. The Marshals Bassompierre and Marillac and the Duke of Guise gathered to prepare for the future, but the king recovered. The course of events abroad remained unclear, though, and the king continued to hesitate between the rival courses of action: a distant dream of glory against the obvious advantages of instant peace. A Council session at the Queen Mother's Palais du Luxembourg on 10 November seemed to incline Louis decisively towards the peace party. Richelieu thought that he had lost, and hoped to save his life by fleeing to Le Havre, of which he was governor. But on the following day the king summoned the cardinal to his country residence at Versailles, where he liked to go hunting, and assured him of his complete confidence. That same day Louis gave orders for Michel de Marillac to be excluded from the Council and put under surveillance.

This sudden change of heart by the king came to be called the 'Day of the Dupes', as expectations of the court had been reversed in a matter of hours. In fact, nothing changed, for politics continued along the course which Richelieu had plotted in 1625 and underlined in 1629. But public opinion and historians alike love to reduce policies to personalities, to pick out turning-points, and to turn history into a piece of carefully staged theatre. It is thus that this day has gone down to posterity.

Richelieu promptly set about isolating the king and systematically persecuting those who seemed to oppose his policy. Michel de Marillac, the Keeper of the Seals, and his brother Louis, a Marshal, were the first victims of the cardinal's vengeance. They were the embodiment of what has been called the *dévot* (or 'devout') party, that is, those who regarded war between Catholic rulers as not only dangerous but scandalous, and who reckoned peace in Europe and the fair administration of justice preferable to military efforts which the realm could ill afford to sustain. Setting aside the caricatures put about by Richelieu's propagandists and repeated by generations of historians, we must recall that Michel de Marillac, a strong and respected figure, was the only credible alternative to Richelieu as chief minister. In Richelieu's own words, the Marillac brothers 'were the most dangerous figures at the head of the plot hatched against me'.

Michel de Marillac was locked away in the château of Châteaudun, where he died in May 1632. His brother Louis, arrested on campaign in Italy, was hauled before an extraordinary tribunal, found guilty of various misappropriations and improprieties, and executed. Marshal Bassompierre was thrown into the Bastille, never to be released until Louis XIII was dead. And the Duke of Guise had to flee to Italy to avoid a similar fate. The Queen Mother was packed off to Compiègne, where she was kept under armed guard like a criminal. All her friends and relations, along with those of the Marillacs, were forced to choose either exile or retirement into the country. Gaston of Orleans, enraged by the persecution, was utterly unable to weaken his brother's cold determination. The prince came to fear even for his own freedom, and in March 1631, accompanied by several dozen supporters who cheered him with cries of 'Long live Monsieur and the liberty of the people', he fled by way of Franche-Comté to Lorraine, where Duke Charles IV gave him asylum at his court.

Opposition to the Rule of the Cardinal

The events of 1631 seemed to justify the cardinal's gambles. The Treaty of Cherasco (in Piedmont, March 1631), which reconciled the combatants in northern Italy, confirmed the provisions of the peace of Regensburg and brought additional advantages in Piedmont, where the French were able to establish a permanent garrison at Pinerolo, which guaranteed them freedom of access across the Piedmontese plain. This little transalpine territory remained in French hands until 1696.

In Germany, the King of Sweden, who had become a formal ally of France by the Treaty of Bärwald (May 1631), was inflicting a series of defeats upon the imperialists. But Richelieu still faced obstacles at home. Henceforth, hardly a year would pass without plots, revolts, repressions, or persecutions. This was the price which king and minister paid for their policy.

Gaston of Orleans, heir presumptive to the throne of France, published a manifesto on 31 May 1631 in justification of his actions. It was the first in a long series of appeals urging revolt against the tyranny of the king's ministers, appeals which, stretching over three decades, invariably coincided with a noble plot or a popular revolt. Foreign policy was not the issue. Gaston's manifesto accused Richelieu of usurping royal authority for his personal benefit and of making his already legendary fortune out of public funds. To achieve his ends, Richelieu had oppressed the royal family, deprived the Parlements of their role as a constitutional check and a channel for grievances, and reduced the people to a condition which the manifesto summed up as death, dearth and beggary.

In July 1631 Marie de Medici managed to slip her guard at the Château de Compiègne and flee to the Spanish Netherlands. The Duke of Orleans joined her there and managed to scrape together a small force of loyal supporters bolstered by mercenaries recruited locally and in Lorraine. He thought that he could rely on the support of the French provinces because several hundred young provincial nobles had rallied to him. On 23 June 1632 he entered Champagne at the head of his troops, calling on the people to join him, and marched southwards. Dijon refused him admittance, but he found support among the gentry of Provence and the Auvergne. He turned towards Languedoc, whose governor, Duke Henry of Montmorency, had just declared for his cause. The Estates of Languedoc, worried that they might have *élus* (royal tax officials) imposed on them, stood behind their governor, as did several bishops and towns. But the majority of the nobility and gentry held aloof. As a result, the rebel force remained far inferior to the 20,000 men whom Louis XIII was leading southwards in person. Marshal Schomberg needed only 3,000 crack troops to smash the rebels in an engagement at Castelnaudary on 1 September. Gaston and several close friends managed to escape, but Montmorency was wounded and taken prisoner. Shortly afterwards he was arraigned before a special tribunal of the Parlement de Toulouse, sentenced to death and executed (30 October). The king stubbornly refused all appeals for mercy. The putting to death of a peer-duke, scion of one the noblest houses of France, stood out among the numerous executions, impressing upon public opinion the image of a terrible and implacable *raison d'état*.

Richelieu had long been aware that control of public opinion, the control and even the manufacture of news, and the selection of just which facts to set before contemporaries and even posterity, were indispensable parts of the art of governance. He maintained a staff of publicists to disseminate his philosophy and defend his policy. When necessary, he himself took a hand in the work of propaganda, sketching outlines which his secretaries and scriblers were paid to fill out and colour in. The most gifted among his writers of occasional pamphlets were Fancan, Jean de Silhon and Jean Sirmond. At a more intellectual level, lawyers and scholars expounded such themes as *raison d'état*, the absolute character of royal authority, sovereignty and legitimacy. Cardin Le Bret and Daniel de Priézac took up the ideas introduced by Jean Bodin fifty years previously, fitting them to the recent course of events. The historian Scipion Dupleix, author of the *Histoire de Louis le Juste* (1635), fixed for posterity the construction which Richelieu wished to put upon events.

In Richelieu's day the rudiments of the press were already in place. Venice and Amsterdam had since the late sixteenth century housed printer-booksellers who specialised in writing and printing newsletters, gazettes, fly-sheets and periodicals. Since 1605 Paris had had the *Mercure français*, a compilation of news from the court, the city and the world. 1631 saw the birth of the regular weekly news-sheet, the *Gazette de France*. Its editor was a physician from Loudun, a convert from Protestantism named Théophraste Renaudot. This talented man was a client of the cardinal, and each week put on sale for four *sous* a newsletter of a dozen pages, in print runs of between 12,000 and 15,000. Richelieu's secretaries often provided him with ready copy on major events – seen, of course, from the cardinal's point of view.

Richelieu presided over a network of informers, supporters and clients which gave him a power within the land quite independent of his ministerial position, a power tied to his person and family. After the Chalais conspiracy of 1626, the king had furnished him with a company of musketeers to wear his livery and protect his person. And the cardinal knew that he could rely unhesitatingly on an army of magistrates – from State and parliamentary councillors down to modest local officials – and of military officers of high and low rank. From the ranks of these loyal supporters he recruited the special tribunals and commissions with which he would root out opponents.

In contrast to this government apparatus, allied as it was with the forces of propaganda and repression, an alternative political discourse can be found in the memoirs of provincial gentlemen like Normand Henri de Campion, or the account-books of modest merchants, or the papers of country clergy, in any of which the turn of a page can reveal a sudden outburst of hatred for the cardinal. And alternative views could of course also be found in the writings of Marie de Medici's supporters, the most productive and incisive of whom was Mathieu de Morgues, who poured out polemic against the publicists of Paris from the safety of his refuge in Brussels.

The Occupation of Lorraine

The duchy of Lorraine and the duchy of Bar made up a sovereign state on the borders of Champagne and Burgundy, a buffer-state between France and the Empire. Lorraine was a mosaic of territories, dotted with enclaves and bounded by complex and ill-defined frontiers. French influence there had been marked since the acquisition of the three bishoprics (Metz, Toul and Verdun) in 1552. A Parlement was established at Metz in 1633. The people and the prince of the duchy were staunch Catholics. During the Wars of Religion, the League had looked to Lorraine for men and money; and when war broke out in Germany, Duke Charles IV swore loyalty to the emperor. The Duke of Orleans received a warm welcome there when he fled the wrath of Richelieu, and a little later he married Marguerite de Lorraine, his host's sister (January 1632).

The strategic position of Lorraine was rather like that of Piedmont-Savoy. Both were buffer-states between Habsburg and Bourbon domains, uniformly Catholic, partly French-speaking, open to French influence, yet fiercely jealous of their autonomy. For the French, the two duchies were essential means of access in the event of war to the east. Ducal sovereignty counted for little when strategic necessity required that it be breached, and French armies yearned to annex these territories and treat them in effect as extensions of the kingdom's own line of communications. Duke Charles IV's support first of the Emperor and then of French rebels exposed him to the risk of retaliation as military force increasingly displaced considerations of sovereign rights. The growing ferocity of the conflict in Germany, together with the Swedish intervention, led the French to be more watchful of their eastern front. So, for all these reasons, Lorraine became the object of diplomatic and military harassment, which culminated after three years in total occupation.

From the winter of 1631-2, the bulk of the French army took up position on the eastern frontier, and La Force staged manoeuvres clearly aimed at intimidating the Duke of Lorraine. The duke was obliged to ratify two unfavourable treaties (signed at Vic and Liverdun in January and June 1632), guaranteeing French access across his territories and putting at their disposal two vital bridges across the Meuse, at Stenay and Dun, which controlled the route to the Ardennes.

The options for French diplomacy in Germany were earnestly debated at the Council sessions which Louis XIII held during the period of these activities on the frontier. The brilliant successes of the King of Sweden's campaigns in 1631 had disturbed even his allies. The French wanted to prevent him from invading Bavaria, whose duke, Maximilian, like the princes of the German Catholic League, was himself an ally of France and a recipient of French subsidies. Richelieu's hope now was to create a third force which could protect 'German liberties' against not only the centralising ambitions of the Emperor, but also the ravages of the Nordic invader. Two French agents, Charnacé and Feuquières, took to the road in Germany, armed with money, promises and a commission to win the support of the various princes and generals who were in the field between the Baltic and the Alps.

After the defeat of Orleans and his supporters in 1632, French threats against Lorraine intensified. La Force laid siege to Nancy and forced the duke to cede his capital by the Treaty of Charmes (September 1633). Charles IV then abdicated, placing himself and those troops who remained loyal to him at the disposal of the Emperor. The ducal crown passed to his brother Nicolas-François; Lorraine was in effect henceforth a French possession, constantly traversed by royal troops.

Louis XIII imposed an oath of loyalty on the people of Lorraine in 1634, and introduced French administrative institutions: an *intendant* and a governor at Nancy. The depredations of French troops reached their peak, and were accompanied by an epidemic of the plague in the cities of Lorraine, between 1636 and 1640. It was during this tragic decade, in 1632 to be precise, that the

Lorraine engraver Jacques Callot cut his famous series of scenes entitled the 'Great' and the 'Little miseries of war'. Everyone with an interest in the seventeenth century will know these images, with their unforgettable evocations of the horrors and destruction undergone by the lands of Germany in the course of the Thirty Years War. The French occupation of Lorraine lasted until the Treaty of the Pyrenees, in 1659.

The need to protect the eastern front took French troops even further afield. In 1632 Louis XIII sent a force as far as Trier, whose Prince-Bishop had requested French protection. The death of Gustavus Adolphus at the Battle of Lützen (November 1632) was met with relief, even at Paris, but the Swedish army continued on its triumphant path under General Horn even after the king's death. In Alsace, local lords and town-councils called on the French to provide garrisons for their security: for example, the Count of Hanau in March 1633, and the towns of Colmar, Thann and Selestadt, among others, in 1634. Thus, even in a time of peace, French troops were committed beyond the Rhine and were ready to intervene in the European theatre of operations.

In September 1634, the shattering victory of the imperial forces over the Swedes at Nördlingen marked a new chapter in the bloody chronicle which had commenced in 1618. Richelieu's foreign policy objective, the weakening of Habsburg power, could no longer be achieved at second-hand, by means of Dutch or Swedish allies. The phoney war was over. King and minister both knew that they had to see their policy through, and involve their country in the continental war. Since 1598, a long period of peace had prevailed along French frontiers. Thirty years had seen the damage of the Wars of Religion made good. Towns and villages had restored their fairs and their festivals. But now, in 1635, the kingdom was on the brink of a ruinous and almost interminable war. Richelieu was aware of the dangers, but believed that the stakes justified the risk and the cost.

10 France in Open War

Louis XIII and Richelieu had opted for an aggressive foreign policy, confident in the extent of the kingdom's resources yet oblivious of the delays and difficulties of mobilising those resources in support of a war which would drag on for year after year. For the cardinal minister, financial administration came down to order and thrift, and he was content to rely entirely on the prudence and integrity of the *Surintendants des finances*, from whom he required nothing but total loyalty to his cause. Michel de Marillac (during the first expeditions beyond the Alps) and then Antoine d'Effiat (during the La Rochelle affair and the crisis of 1630) had both measured up to his expectations. After the premature death of Marshal of Effiat in 1632, the superintendency passed to two wealthy magistrates, Claude Bullion and Claude Bouthillier, known for their loyalty to the cardinal. Bullion had aided Richelieu's plans in Italy, and Bouthillier had formerly managed the private property of Richelieu's family. They would remain in joint control of war finance until Bullion's death in 1640, after which Bouthillier took sole charge until 1643.

The Extraordinary Fiscal Increase

The series of spiralling financial demands began in 1626, and taxation increased by about 50 per cent during the campaigns over La Rochelle and Mantua. But it was from 1632 that the tax burden assumed unprecedented proportions, with some of the most swingeing increases in fiscal history, two- or three-fold in only a few years. This increase was met almost entirely from the *taille*, the main royal tax, which fell almost exclusively upon the peasantry because so many towns enjoyed exemption. Introducing new taxes on spending would have taken too long and would have risked causing the sort of riots in fairs and ports that had been seen over the *pancarte* in 1602 and the increase of the *traités* in 1628. As for selling another tranche of offices, the market was already saturated. The simplest and most direct solution was thus to increase the *taille*. The proportion of revenue raised through the *taille* went up from 40 to 50 per cent, reaching 54 per cent in 1639 (42 million out of a total of 79 million *livres*), and culminating in a record 62 per cent in 1648 (57 million out of 92 million *livres*).

The *Surintendants* had the power to spread the burden somewhat by means of regulations. An edict of January 1634 introduced a new code for the *taille*, replacing that promulgated by Sully in 1600. Real or supposed exemptions could be restricted through close investigation and the direct taxation of substantial contributors. Calculations regarding the allocation of the *taille* at every level from *généralités* through *élections* down to parishes could be checked, and in practice were. Other measures were introduced amid uproar in following years. In 1635 it was decreed that the fees due to financial officials by virtue of their offices would be accounted for separately rather than included in the *taille*. This thus achieved an apparent, but entirely notional, reduction in the amount of the *taille*. 1637 saw another spurious reduction when the portion of the *taille* payable by the towns was separated out and called a loan. And the *taille* was further reduced in 1639 when a substantial proportion, hypothecated towards the maintenance of troops in winter quarters, was separated out; and again in 1641 by a new levy known as the *étapes*. But none of this tinkering fooled anybody for long. In the end the burden still fell on those liable to the *taille*.

Under normal circumstances, the overall burden of the *taille* was fixed by the King's Council in July. It was shared out during autumn, and notice to pay was given to each locality at the end of the first quarter of the following year. The sums payable were brought to the receivers of the *élections* in four instalments by parish collectors. From 1636, the *taille* proved increasingly difficult to collect in many places, and the final instalments were at best only partially collected. As arrears soon mounted into years, the government had to write off the bad debts and grant the non-payers amnesties. And in fact, the huge variations in the assessment and the huge irregularities in the collection of the *taille* meant that the sums fixed by the *Surintendants* represented their hopes rather than their expectations. They never corresponded to the sums actually received by the Épargne, which were much lower, nor even to those raised in the parishes, which experienced contradictory pulls – downwards from unwillingness to pay, and upwards from the additional costs of collection itself.

The Activities of Provincial *Intendants*

The ordinary processes of collection proved manifestly inadequate to cope with these extraordinary increases. The regime had to resort to more centralised fiscal administration, dispatching *intendants* into the provinces to supervise or even replace local financial officials, and equipping them with coercive powers in order to overcome resistance to taxation.

Sending out royal commissioners to resolve local difficulties was no new thing in the administrative history of the French State. In 1598, on the return of peace, Henri IV had sent special commissioners throughout the land to make a new allocation of the *taille* and to see that the provisions of the Edict of Nantes were implemented. In 1611, at the start of the regency, such commissioners were for the first time entitled *intendants de justice*. The system of *intendants* was spread across the whole kingdom by the edict of 1634 which reorganised the *taille*. The *intendants* themselves were drawn from the junior Masters of Requests. There was one for each *généralité*, and they were furnished with wide powers to revise assessments and speed up collection. Their operations were coordinated and monitored by the new Keeper of the Seals, another trusted follower of Richelieu, Pierre Séguier (1588–1672). Séguier, scion of an old parliamentary dynasty of Paris, was a scholarly jurist who had himself been a commissioner in the provinces ten years before. Keeper of the Seals from 1633, he became Chancellor from 1635, and exercised that office, except for a period of suspension during the Fronde, until his death. Every judicial office-holder in France was thus dependent upon him for nearly forty years, which in effect meant that the entire royal administration was in his hands during that crucial and uncertain time. Overshadowed by the dominant personalities of Richelieu and Mazarin, he nevertheless played an essential part in government, lending continuity to the centralising policy which would culminate in what a later age would call absolutism. The conception of the role of the provincial *intendants* as agents of central government and all-powerful executives of the decisions of the King's Council throughout the land was clearly the creation of Séguier, not only in its origins in 1634, but also in its continuation notwithstanding the vicissitudes of events.

There was already one personal representative of the king in every province – the governor, a great magnate entrusted with political responsibility for the region, which came down to controlling the nobility and commanding the local armed forces. As these men were often obliged to be absent, either at court or on campaign, their place was taken in the province by a lieutenant-general, himself also a leading nobleman. Those governors and lieutenants-general reckoned likely to oppose Richelieu's policy were replaced after 1630, and the King's Council took a close interest in the selection of the noblemen who were to place their personal prestige and their social clientage at the service of the central administration. The *intendants*, lawyers by training and by trade, had to collaborate with them, and were meant not to supplant them, as has often been suggested, but to supplement them. The commissions which they received at their departure enumerated their tasks and powers, talking of 'justice', 'security' and 'finance'. In practice, they presided over their own courts, constituted under the terms of their commission, and could transfer cases into their own jurisdiction; and they supervised 'security' (that is, the maintenance of law and order) and 'finance', that is, the administration of the tax which was their true *raison d'être*. A Council decree of 28 September 1634 required the Treasurers of France who made up the *Bureau des finances* within each *généralité* to perform their work of tax allocation in the presence and under the supervision of the local *intendant*. In effect this was undermining ordinary local tribunals in favour of a Council representative. Fiscal institutions which had grown up over many centuries thus found themselves, at a stroke, stripped of their prerogatives and replaced by a centralised and largely arbitrary power. A further Council pronouncement of 22 August 1642 effectively suspended the Treasurers of France from the performance of their duties and made over all their powers to the *intendants*. The spirit of institutions was thus radically changed even though appearances remained largely constant. The inefficiencies or misappropriations of which the Council accused the officials of the *Bureaux des finances* and of the *élections* derived ultimately from the venality and heritability of offices. Yet here nothing changed. The *paulette* which made these offices hereditary was confirmed in 1631, and Richelieu had no intention of abolishing it. So the financial officials retained what were now in effect sinecures. The tasks they had originally performed were henceforth carried out by *intendants*.

When faced with inability or refusal to pay, the *intendants* resorted to the traditional means of coercion: distraint on the goods of the principal taxpayers of a parish in arrears, according to the principle of communal liability and parish solidarity; and the imprisonment of individual non-payers. As such proceedings, hitherto reckoned extreme, proliferated, the levy of the *taille* took on the aspect of a hidden civil war, at times requiring considerable military resources. From 1636 the *intendants* established companies of élite cavalry, known as fusiliers or carabineers of the *taille* or of the *intendant*. These troops escorted and guarded the bailiffs who carried out distraints and made arrests. They were billeted on parishes in arrears, and remained there at parochial expense until those arrears had been paid in full.

The Army of Louis XIII

The new institutional procedures bore fruit, albeit at a price, and the king was able to put considerable forces into the field.

In the 1620s, even the largest royal armies had never reached 30,000 men. But by 1634 Richelieu had already raised the effective strength of the French army to nearly 100,000, and the figure would rise to 200,000 around 1640, and nearly 250,000 at the end of the reign, in 1643. But such figures can never be precise or certain, because of the inevitable differences between the numbers recorded in the accounts of the Secretary of State for War, and the reality in the field, not to mention the perpetual fluctuations owing to losses and desertions while on campaign.

The hard core of the army was formed by the élite units of the Royal Household and the first six standing regiments, the 'old' ones: of Picardy, Champagne, Piedmont, Navarre and Normandy, along with the Marines, forces whose names referred primarily to their main theatres of operations around the kingdom. There were also five other regiments that were kept in readiness during peacetime and were better armed, trained and disciplined than the bulk of the army. They were the so-called 'little old' (the regiments of Rambures, Vaubécourt and so on). Finally, when a campaign was imminent, further regiments were recruited, and were known by their commander's name. The number of regiments (which could be over fifty), and the number of their establishment (which could be over 1,000 men) both varied considerably, as a regiment usually consisted of twenty companies whose strength could range from fifty to two hundred men. Overall, one can probably say that the demands for military manpower in France at this time amounted to about 1 per cent of the population, a figure comparable to that of modern times, about ten times more than in the sixteenth century, and ten times less than at the end of the eighteenth century. The cavalry accounted for about 15 per cent of the army. And it should be remembered that an army in the field was accompanied by large numbers of male and female camp-followers: valets, servants, cooks, prostitutes, peasants dragooned for forced labour, and so on.

Wages were handed out to the colonels according to the numbers which the commissioners for war (civil officials responsible for financial affairs, victualling, transport and lodging) found serving in their regiments at periodic reviews or parades. Richelieu was soon to replace these officials with military *inten-*

dants whose role, like that of their provincial counterparts, was to act on behalf of the central administration and make the customary channels of administration redundant. The most serious administrative problem was maintaining troops at home, in the provinces of the interior during the four months of winter, then on the roads, and finally, between April and October, on the frontiers. Only the costs of arming and paying the troops were covered in the accounts of the Secretary of State for War. The costs of lodging, feeding and supplying them, along with the costs of fortifications, fell upon the local communities who had the misfortune to lie near their quarters or their routes. As a result, even if the troops retained a modicum of discipline within the realm, the difficult business of housing them or moving them around was a frequent cause of lawsuits, riots and even popular armed resistance.

The modern reader must realise that notwithstanding the advances of State control, war remained at this time, and for long afterwards, a sort of private enterprise. Officers and men were bound by links of loyalty and common interest, while military service to the Crown was more in the nature of a contract than an obligation. Recruitment was entirely on a volunteer basis, and those setting out for war knew that their best hope of reward lay in pillage, a recognised and at times regulated business, rather than in official pay, which was seen only at the beginning and (though not always) at the end of a campaign.

One Secretary of State for War sought to regulate and rationalise the organisation of these huge forces. From 1636 to 1645 the post was held by François Sublet de Noyers, who had previously served as a commissioner for finances and a military *intendant*, and was of course a client of Richelieu.

To turn now to naval matters, the cardinal, who was familiar with the western provinces, had in 1626 secured from the king the new title of Grand Master of Shipping, followed by the governorships of two major naval bases, Le Havre (on the Channel), and Brouage (on the coast of Saintonge). He took a close interest in maritime affairs, entrusting control of them to his uncle, Amador de La Porte, a Commander of the Order of Malta, whom he made *Intendant général* of the Navy. He got results: ports were fortified, and shipyards and ordnance foundries were established, above all in southern Brittany (La Roche-Bernard). In September 1642, at the end of Richelieu's life, a concentration of naval forces at Toulon brought together twenty-two galleys and about sixty other vessels.

Expeditions beyond the sea were also encouraged, and several thousand colonists and sailors crossed to the deserted islands of the West Indies (St Christopher, Martinique, Guadeloupe and Dominica) or to Canada, where the French held the little outpost of Quebec on the enormous St Lawrence river, along with two others a little upstream, Montreal and Three Rivers. But these overseas expeditions and maritime projects were of little immediate importance. The outcomes of battles depended on great forces of infantry, as the conflict in Germany had shown. The defeat of the Swedes in 1634 meant that Louis XIII and Richelieu had their backs to the wall. The logic of their policy obliged them to intervene directly.

Open War

The decision to declare war was not the consequence of a cynical *raison d'état* divorced from all rules of common morality, according to which the end, the good of the State, justified the means. Not that such an opinion was unthinkable. The Duke of Rohan, who had passed from the head of rebels in Languedoc to the head of royal armies, expressed this point of view in his reflections on war and power, the *Discours politiques*, extracts of which were published in the *Mercure français* and would undoubtedly have won Richelieu's approval. But the cardinal's own philosophy was profoundly religious and, in intention, scrupulously Catholic. He presented its main outlines in an address to the Parlement de Paris, itself published in the *Mercure français* in 1634. The King of France, by virtue of the extent of his kingdom's resources, had not only the means but the duty to keep a balance between the powers and to bring an end to Habsburg hegemony. Nobody could deny, in the face of his military successes, that he was fulfilling a mission of divine providence. Moreover, he had no need to reject alliances with heretical powers, as such alliances were permissible in a just war, and the French king's cause was manifestly just. The Count-Duke Olivares in Madrid thought in similar terms, and had had no hesitation in supporting French Protestants against their king, or in allying himself with the King of England. It is worth noting that Richelieu never failed to insist, in his negotiations with the Swedes, the Dutch and the Lutheran princes, that Catholics be guaranteed freedom of worship in any territories they conquered. And throughout his long ministry, Richelieu always enjoyed good relations with the Barberini Pope Urban VIII, whose nuncios begged continually for a peace conference without ever calling into question the general lines of French policy. So, convinced of the justice of his cause, Louis XIII formally declared war on the Governor of the Netherlands and the King of Spain, and then, a year later, on the Emperor. A herald in a tunic of fleur-de-lys travelled to Brussels to make the declaration amid the sounding of trumpets. This chivalric ceremony represented an important principle in international relations, namely that in peace as in war they were based on the personal honour of the princes who embodied their nations.

In May 1635, 30,000 men marched in two columns into the Spanish Netherlands. The ten southern provinces which had remained Catholic and loyal to the Spanish Crown had been governed since 1600 by the Archduke Albert and his consort Isabella. Their government had coincided with the twelve-year truce in the Spanish war with the United Provinces of the north. Their reign was a period of reconstruction and renewal, and was seen as a golden age in the region's history. After Isabella's death towards the end of 1633, the government at Brussels had passed into the hands of the Cardinal Infante Don Fernando, Philip IV's brother, a talented leader of men and the victor of Nördlingen. He was assisted by another great commander, Prince Thomas of Savoy, a brother of the Duke of Piedmont who had rallied to the Habsburg cause in 1634. Relying on the dense network of fortified towns which spanned the forests and the open plains of the southern Netherlands, the Spanish forces easily held their own against the two-pronged offensive by the French and the Dutch.

Two sinister episodes in the campaign of 1635 testified to the ferocious customs of seventeenth-century warfare, but also to a nascent theory of the rights of peoples. After the sacks of Mantua and Magdeburg by imperial forces, and the terrible ravages of the Swedes, came the news of the sack of Tirlemont by the Franco-Dutch force (9 June 1635) and of the sack of Saint-Nicolas-de-Port in Lorraine (4–11 November 1635) by the forces of Bernard of Saxe-Weimar, a German mercenary commander in French service who was based in Alsace. The only real gains for France came in Italy, where Créquy got a foothold in Piedmont while Rohan reoccupied the Valtellina, to pose a double threat to Milan and Lombardy.

The campaign of 1636 farcd still worse. The initiative passed to the Spanish, who invaded Picardy in July. Prince Thomas of Savoy laid siege to Corbie and took it on 15 August. Turning south towards Paris, his advance cavalry were soon in view of Pontoise. Panic broke out in the capital. Louis XIII rode in person through the streets in order to restore morale and bolster resistance. A scratch force of 40,000 men, 12,000 of them volunteers from Paris itself, was concentrated at Senlis. The Spanish withdrew in November.

But the threat had been serious, and early in 1637 Richelieu put out feelers for peace, which Olivares saw fit to reject. The count-duke was building his hopes on a further offensive, this time in Languedoc. But the Castilian and Italian troops who concentrated in Roussillon in summer were brought to a halt at Leucate in September.

The campaign of 1638 was no better for the French. To the north they met with defeat at Thionville, while in Italy the army was for a time without a leader, as Créquy had died in 1636, and Rohan and Toiras died in quick succession in 1638. The Grisons and the Valtellina made peace with each other and with the Spanish Governor of Milan (we can note in passing that the Valtellina was reunited with Milan in 1815, and that its Italian character has never been questioned since). Piedmont found itself embroiled in a civil war between the adherents of the dowager duchess Christine (Louis XIII's sister and widow of Victor Amadeus) and her brothers-in-law Thomas and Maurice of Savoy, who had taken sides with Spain.

Richelieu gave priority in 1638 to an attack on the Basque country, where the Duke of La Valette was to try and break through Spanish lines at Fuenterrabia. The notion of invading across the plains of Navarre was pretty absurd, but Richelieu believed the region to be devoid of troops, and an initial naval victory at Guetaria (22 August 1638), where a French squadron burned a dozen large Spanish vessels caught in the roads, gave him the impression that a major victory was there for the taking. However, the impossibility of crossing the Bidassoa and the rout of several militia regiments compelled La Valette to abandon the offensive during September. A furious and disappointed cardinal sought to prosecute the duke for treason, but La Valette managed to escape to England while a special tribunal condemned him to death (the same sentence had been passed in 1636 on the commanders of strongholds which the Spaniards had seized in Picardy).

These setbacks on all fronts were exacerbated by a number of popular revolts in various parts of the kingdom.

The Age of the Great Peasants' Revolts

The extraordinary scale of fiscal demands, and the provocative and terrifying methods of recovery employed, easily explain the resistance which became evident at all levels of society and in all the provinces from a few months after the coming of open war, and which soon took the form of armed revolt. If the outbreaks were clearly connected to the overall impact of taxation, they could nevertheless be sparked off by circumstances which might appear trivial now but which then seemed monumentally scandalous in the eyes of public opinion. Thus, in May 1635, the towns of Guyenne were rocked by a series of bloody riots provoked by a fairly light tax on inn-keepers. The wave of violence swept uncontrollably and incoherently through dozens of south-western towns, in a way typical of the risings of the discontented in early modern France, and typical also of their powerlessness to change events. They brought together large numbers of people without any kind of plan or organisation, and they disappeared as readily as they sprang up, causing no lasting disquiet to local élites, and never impinging on the considerations of the politicians for more than a few months. By reason of their origin in rumour and their unpredictable spread from place to place, the urban riots of 1635 hold a place in the annals of social psychology comparable to that of the troubles at the beginning of the Fronde in 1648, or the 'Grande Peur' of July 1789.

In 1636 a series of peasant protests against taxation unfolded in Angoumois. Petitions addressed to the king were drafted at the great fairs which brought together peasants from a wide range of villages. In May 1637 the movement spread to Périgord, where, as in 1594–5, it took the form of a communal recourse to arms. There was a military structure, with companies organised and commanded on a parochial basis, and even an overall commander, the 'Colonel of the communes that have risen in Guyenne', an old squire of Périgueux named La Mothe La Forêt. Several minor country gentry agreed to serve as commanders of the peasant troops. The Croquants, as they were called, took possession of several places, among them Bergerac, before they were cut down in open country at La Sauvetat du Dropt on 1 June by a detachment of cavalry which the Duke of La Valette had hurriedly led from the frontier. More than a thousand Croquants were slaughtered that day. But on 23 June the King's Council, on the advice of La Valette and his father, the old Duke of Épernon, Governor of Guyenne, granted an amnesty, not simply suspending prosecutions but consigning the whole course of events to legal oblivion. However, the aftershocks of the May rising continued to be felt in Périgord and Quercy until 1641, in the form of riots and of sporadic gatherings of former rebels in the woods for the purposes of ambush or vengeance.

Around the regions of Astarac and Pardiac in Gascony, groups of several thousand Croquants sometimes managed to take possession of towns, such as Plaisance, and above all Mirande and Marciac (26 December 1638–7 January 1639). Tax collection in these regions was prevented from 1638 until at least 1645.

Troubles broke out in Normandy during 1639, when agents were sent to levy taxes on the parishes of *quart-bouillon*, parishes which obtained salt by boiling the salty deposits found in the bay of Mont-Saint-Michel, and for that reason had never been liable to the *gabelle*. From the Avranchin and the Cotentin, the revolt of the

Nu-pieds ('barefoot') spread throughout lower Normandy and even affected the Seine valley around Rouen. When *gabelle* officials were massacred at Rouen in August, without the Parlement or the civic militia lifting a finger to save them, Richelieu was stirred to awesome retribution. He had to wait until royal regiments could be spared from the north-eastern front, but then, on 30 November, the Nu-pieds of the *armée de souffrance* were easily shattered before the walls of Avranches. On the king's orders, Chancellor Séguier came to Rouen to supervise the subsequent prosecutions in person, staying from late December 1639 until the end of March 1640. There were several dozen executions, but there were sanctions also for the towns and local institutions which had manifested pusillanimity or even tacit support in the face of the revolt. The Parlement de Rouen was suspended for a year, while the cities of Avranches, Vire, Caen and Rouen lost their traditional rights, their walls, their fiscal privileges and their communal liberties.

Raison d'état seemed to have broken down popular resistance. The great revolts were in fact nothing more than extreme forms of a widespread refusal to pay the king's taxes. The sums outstanding from the *généralités* of the south-west in 1637 were in excess of 10 million *livres*. Like it or not, the *intendants* had to grant special reliefs in areas of vigorous resistance. And the reliefs and remissions of the *taille* served only to confirm the peasantry in their belief that the taxes were the work of 'evil councillors' and that the king himself, the incarnation of justice, could never have introduced them. Certain fiscal immunities took root across wide areas and, as a result, the sporadic phenomenon of the peasant revolt was transformed into enduring disorder. The fiscal disorder introduced since 1635 was not to be cleared up until the 1660s.

Moreover, in the successful early days of their revolts, the Croquants and the Nu-pieds had drawn up manifestos drafted by village justices, country clergy or the backwoods gentry who were often prominent in such ephemeral movements. These texts insisted that the king was unaware of the suffering of his rural subjects, and that their own demonstrations had no other objective than to enlighten him and denounce his evil councillors. But they had no clear political programme, and named neither

Richelieu nor his major princely opponents. They called for nothing more than a return to a golden age, that of Louis XII, when the king had 'lived of his own' without taxing anybody. More specific passages might go so far as to evoke the traditional Provincial Estates, to insist that taxation required consent, and to call for the abolition of such financial officers as *élus*, treasurers and *intendants*, as representatives of the peasants themselves would carry the proceeds of their voluntary taxes to the Louvre! The word which recurred again and again in these pamphlets, as in the all the French political texts of the time, was 'liberty'. The main themes were the defence of public liberty, in other words, the ending of fiscal oppression; and the maintenance of provincial liberties, in other words, respect for local privileges. The time was not yet ripe for this utopian vision, but it would see the light again ten years later, in the manifestos of the Fronde, which, in this perspective, is not so much the aberration which traditional historiography has often made of it, as the direct and unpleasant consequence of the tragic policy decisions of Richelieu and Louis XIII.

The central power looked with rather more concern on noble conspiracies, which represented a more serious political threat. Princes had the social weight necessary to turn discontent into real opposition, to rally a province (as Rohan and then Montmorency had done in Languedoc) or even the kingdom. But their platforms were little different from those of the popular manifestos. They too invoked the folk memory of a bygone monarchy in which the provinces and princes had enjoyed the peaceful and honourable exercise of their ancient liberties.

Such themes were already present in the open letter which Gaston of Orléans wrote from Nancy on 30 May 1631, and they recur in the manifesto for justice which the 'princes of peace' published in 1641 during the last great noble conspiracy of Louis XIII's reign. The plot was shortlived, but might have been spectacular. Louis II de Bourbon, Count of Soissons (1604–41), a prince of the blood from the house of Bourbon-Condé, had distinguished himself by recapturing Corbie in November 1636. Like many others, he resented the overwhelming influence of Richelieu, and he was associated with a number of noble cliques which clustered around the person of the Duke of Orleans after his return to France in 1634. Fearing for his safety, the Count of Soissons first sought asylum in the little sovereign city of Sedan, seat of the Duke of Bouillon. Sedan was a refuge for malcontents where, with the assistance of the Duke of Lorraine and the Cardinal Infante, a force of a few thousand man had organised itself early in 1641. Their entry into France was to be the signal for a revolt against Richelieu, and to show that they meant ill to him alone, they wore the white sash which symbolised the king's service. The manifesto of the 'princes of peace' called for the relief of the people and the defence of liberty. It accused Richelieu of having perverted the traditional government of the kingdom for his own private benefit: 'He has stripped all provinces and communities of their ancient liberties and privileges, and has broken the contracts they made with former kings.' The denunciation of absolutist centralisation and the appeal to mythical ancient liberties pointed towards an alternative institutional structure, in which a fragmented and aristocratic State would replace the tyranny of the cardinal.

Marshal Châtillon was sent with 10,000 men to put down the rebellion at its origin, in the Sedan corridor. The reckoning came on 9 July 1641 near a wood on the Meuse known as La Marfée. Châtillon was defeated, and the victorious forces of the Count of Soissons might have advanced into Champagne had not their leader died mysteriously in the closing stages of the battle. His strange decease, so convenient for Richelieu, led to the disintegration of the insurgent force. Imagining 'what might have been' is too risky a business for historians, and one can therefore say nothing of how Soissons and his plans might have fared under other circumstances. But the count seems to have been alone among the rebel princes of that time in pushing political reflection so far as to envisage a completely different institutional framework for France. In the opinion of ambassadors and diarists of the time, he came close to success:

There is no doubt that the death of that prince saved the State from an enormous shock, for had he lived, he could have advanced unopposed to the gates of Paris. And he would have had little difficulty in raising the people of the city and rallying to his cause a complete province.

(from a dispatch of Giustiniani, the Venetian ambassador)

The Conquests of Louis XIII's Armies

The fortunes of war were on the whole adverse to France. In his anxiety for the future, Louis XIII had decided to consecrate his kingdom to the Blessed Virgin Mary, Mother of God, and his vow was solemnly fulfilled in 1638. Marian devotion was an ancient tradition in France – witness the saying 'Regnum Galliae, regnum Mariae' ('the kingdom of France is Mary's kingdom') – and Louis had had a strong personal devotion to Our Lady since his illness of September 1630. It was the crises of 1636 that had inspired him with the idea of a solemn consecration. The text of the vow was presented to the Parlement de Paris in December 1637 so that it might be made the law of the land, and it was published on 10 February 1638 in the form of a proclamation entrusting the State to the care of the Virgin. On the following 15 August (the Feast of the Assumption of the Blessed Virgin Mary) the king, then at Abbeville with the army of Picardy, celebrated the vow for the first time.

The king's sense of the justice of his cause was confirmed by what seemed to him a sign from heaven: after twenty-two years of marriage, his wife Queen Anne had finally conceived a child. Richelieu, ever the conscientious servant of king and Crown, had played an important part in bringing the royal couple together after an estrangement of some fifteen years. The unlooked-for news of the queen's pregnancy was made public in January 1638. There was rejoicing throughout the land, for the most intimate events in the life of the royal family were a matter of enormous public concern. Against every expectation, the succession was once more secure: the Capetian miracle had been repeated yet again. The course of Queen Anne's pregnancy was followed with as much joy and anxiety as that of Marie de Medici more than thirty years before. On 5 September 1638, at the château of Saint-Germain-en-Laye, she gave birth to a son, named Louis Dieudonné

(Louis 'Gift-of-God'). Richelieu had the boy's horoscope cast by a famous Dominican visionary from Italy, Tommaso Campanella, who foretold a long and glorious reign. In Paris, the church of Saint-Germain (the parish church of the Louvre) announced the news with its bells, and peals rang out across the realm. There were lights in windows and bonfires in the streets, while wine-casks were opened in market-places and all loyal households celebrated.

Such events were crucial moments in the political psychology of the old world of monarchy. In order to understand them fully, it is necessary to set aside the systematic denigration and obliteration of the monarchical past which has been practised in France since the Revolution in two centuries of establishing contemporary ideas of political legitimacy.

The tides of war began to turn in 1640. The campaign of 1639 had brought no gains on any front, but in the following year the Spanish position started to collapse as suddenly and completely as a house of cards. At sea, the Spanish met with two major setbacks at the hands of the Dutch, losing a huge naval battle off the Pas-de-Calais on 21 October 1639, and another off the coast of Brazil early in 1640. In Italy, French forces under a new and talented leader, the Count of Harcourt, succeeded in relieving Christine, Dowager Duchess of Savoy, and in bringing her capital, Turin, firmly under her control (September 1640). In Germany, Bernard of Saxe-Weimar had died in 1639, and the French promptly bought up his entire mercenary force. His colonels, Erlach and Rosen, were happy to serve Louis XIII under the overall command of Marshal Guébriant, and were capable of advancing deep into Swabia from their Alsace bases. To the north, France gained a crucial advantage in capturing Arras, the capital of Artois. A huge offensive had been launched in May 1640, with 30,000 men besieging a city whose garrison numbered no more than 2,000, supplemented by 3,000 city militia. After a siege of two months, with no hope of relief and with breaches in the walls threatening an imminent assault, the city surrendered with honours on 9 August 1640.

The hinterland of Arras, known as 'ceded' or 'conquered' Artois, was entrusted to the rule of an *intendant*. The traditional liberties of the city were guaranteed, and only the Catholic faith was permitted. Thousands of inhabitants preferred to flee French rule and took refuge at Lille or in Flanders. The southern Netherlands had lost one of their wealthiest provinces, a city and a region on which a century of Spanish rule had stamped its mark.

Philip IV of Spain, however, faced even greater disasters. The realm and overseas empire of Portugal had been part of the King of Spain's inheritance since 1581. But the Portuguese nobility, rebelling against the foreign dynasty, maintained the rights of the Duke of Bragança, the nearest relative of the last Portuguese king, proclaiming him king as John IV (1 December 1640). France rushed to make a treaty with the new power and extend material support to this unlooked-for ally (1 June 1641).

And finally, Philip IV's principality of Catalonia had been faced with unprecedented fiscal demands as a result of the war raging in Languedoc and Roussillon. The region was shaken by riots on the streets of Barcelona and by peasant protests in the mountains. The murder of the Viceroy Santa Coloma in Barcelona on the feast of Corpus Christi 1640 gave the signal which transformed protest into secessionist revolt. French agents swiftly took advantage of this development, and an agreement was made between the Catalan Corts (the representative body of the province) and a representative of Louis XIII, Marshal Du Plessis-Besançon, on 16 December 1640. In January 1641 the spokesman of the Corts, Pau Claris, a canon of Urgel, recognised Louis XIII as sovereign Count of Barcelona, 'as in the days of King Charlemagne'. Representatives of the Corts travelled to Péronne in Picardy to commit their country to Louis, and in return, on 23 February 1642, the Marshal de Brézé, acting as the proxy of his master the Most Christian King, took an oath in Barcelona Cathedral to uphold their liberties.

The extraordinary French gains in Catalonia sealed the fate of Roussillon, to which the Spanish could now gain access only with difficulty, either across the mountains of Aragon, or by sea to Collioure. Early in 1642 an enormous French force laid siege to Salses, Collioure and Perpignan, while a naval squadron blockaded the coast. After heroic resistance which cost 2,000 lives, the garrison of Perpignan, reduced to five hundred men, opened its gates on 9 September 1642. A gentleman of Roussillon, the governor of the county, was the first to enter, taking possession in the name of the king. As in Artois, the laws and institutions of France were introduced into the conquered territory. But, also as in Artois, the loyalty of the inhabitants of Roussillon, from the nobility to the peasantry, to the change in sovereignty was less than total. Hankering after the Spanish past sparked off local but bloody risings well into the 1680s.

In the space of two years, the kingdom of France had been swollen by the conquest of two vital territories, Artois and Roussillon, which pushed out the frontiers to the north and the south and thus changed the political picture there. The acquisition of rich countryside and wealthy cities was an obvious economic advantage, but the strategic advantages were of more immediate concern to governments of that period. Ten years of fiscal terrorism and political tyranny under Louis XIII and Richelieu had borne their fruit.

The final repercussions of the relentlessness of these two statesmen were felt as yet another conspiracy was uncovered at court. A young gentleman and personal friend of the king, Henri d'Effiat (son of the late *Surintendant des finances*), Marquis of Cinq-Mars and Grand Squire of the Royal Household, had plotted with agents of Olivares. He was arrested in June 1642 with his friend François-Auguste de Thou (son of Jacques-Auguste, the famous jurist and author of a universal history). They were tried before a special tribunal staffed by magistrates who were clients of Richelieu. Both the tribunal and the accused accompanied the cardinal on his travels, with the result that it was at Lyon, on the way back from Languedoc, that the two conspirators were executed on 12 September 1642.

Richelieu scarcely outlived his victims, or his triumphs. He died after a short illness on 4 December 1642, aged fifty-seven years. He had governed the kingdom without a break for eighteen years.

The news of his death was received everywhere with relief or even joy. Even the king was hardly heartbroken. Private individuals lit bonfires throughout the land. During the days and weeks which followed, political prisoners were released from captivity, and exiles returned from the Netherlands, Lorraine and England to excuse themselves before the Parlements for contempt of court.

That these movements were under way while the king was still alive proves that the judicial terror was essentially the work of the cardinal, and suggests that a number of rebels – for example the Duke of La Valette, who became a loyal servant of Mazarin – were indeed opposed only to the person of the king's minister.

Richelieu left an enormous fortune, estimated at 20 million *livres*, but encumbered with debts of 6 million *livres*. A large part of this fortune was in cash: 4 million *livres* were hoarded in fortresses of which Richelieu was governor. Landed wealth accounted for another quarter of the total. Detailed analysis of his wealth reveals that from 1637 his income reached or exceeded 1 million *livres* a year. The most important element, though, was his income from ecclesiastical benefices. The extent and composition of his fortune are alike worth close examination. In comparing it to other notorious ministerial fortunes of that century, one is tempted to see nothing but avarice and the lust for dynastic power. A concern for the honour of his name was clearly a major part of the cardinal's motivation. The foundation in August 1631 of the new town of Richelieu, on the borders of Poitou and Touraine, in a part of the family inheritance that he had elevated to a peerduchy, was the magnificent but abortive testimony to this ambition. It has to be said that the frugal character of his personal life and tastes contrasted strikingly with his vast means, which were managed and developed by his private secretary, Michel Le Masle. In fact, the cardinal knew that the power of a minister could not be maintained in splendid isolation, and that in order to act freely and effectively it had to dispose of networks of clients, servants and above all relatives. It was therefore not only for the sake of dynastic glory but also out of political principle that he set about providing dowries for his nieces and building up the fortunes of his relations and connections both near and distant. Finally, and above all, he knew that his individual economic power had to be up to the demands for magnificence imposed by the conspicuous extravagance of the State. His wealth was the most conspicuous testimony to the power of the Crown that he served, and to the viability of the policies he wished to implement.

Historians have always been driven to express either horror or admiration at the achievements of Richelieu. Lofty disinterest has scarcely been possible in the face of moral and political stakes which have been manifest to every generation. The implacable aspects of his personality horrified Voltaire and Dumas, yet they judged his character only on the basis of accounts of the destruction of his most celebrated victims: Chalais, Montmorency and Cinq-Mars. The workings of his fiscal terrorism, which were made systematic in 1636, were entirely unknown to them.

Most historians have abandoned themselves to admiration. Anti-Catholic authors have credited him with the defeat of the *dévot* party; and nationalists with territorial expansion and with sketching the 'hexagon' – indicating the 'natural frontiers' to which France should rightly expand. The majority of historians have seen the omnipotence of the State as a historical necessity and have therefore recognised – quite rightly if one grants their premiss – the cardinal minister as a prophet and forerunner of the modern State.

In any case, it is certain that Richelieu, like all great statesmen recognised by history, was his own best propagandist. He did not leave it to posterity to evaluate his achievement, but furnished them from his own pen or through the pens of his creatures with the materials for his apotheosis. He himself dictated the history lessons of the future.

Richelieu was dominant at a crucial moment, and was responsible for momentous changes not only in the priorities of government – the option for power and expansion at the expense of reform and good housekeeping – but also in its means – arbitrary centralism at the expense of traditional regionalism. He implemented his policies with an acute intelligence and a relentless will, identifying his person and policies entirely with the interests of the State. He was unquestionably one of that small group of people who have left a distinct personal imprint on the history of France.

Louis XIII died five months later, without having altered the broad outlines of policy as laid down by the cardinal. For better or for worse, he had at least played his part. The romantic image familiar from the writings of Alfred de Vigny and Alexandre Dumas, of an impulsive king dominated by the will of his minister, is absolutely mistaken. Louis XIII wanted to see the power of the

Crown tend towards absolutism, and he wanted war to the knife. He died on 14 May 1643, in the thirty-third year of his reign.

Five days later, on 19 May 1643, a strong Spanish army which had entered the Ardennes was halted at Rocroi by a force under the young Duke of Enghien, a son of the Prince of Condé. This was not just one battle among others, but a shattering victory. The Spanish lost 8,000 dead and 7,000 prisoners. This posthumous triumph was the crowning glory of the efforts of Louis XIII and Richelieu.

11 France, the Fronde and the Ministry of Mazarin

In the last months of his life Louis XIII had abandoned the draconian methods of the late cardinal, and as a result the cardinal's clients had in their turn started to fear for their safety and to surround themselves with armed guards and friends. But the king had no intention of abandoning his warlike policy. On 20 April 1643 he summoned his brother the Duke of Orleans, with Condé, Séguier and the Secretaries of State, to his bedside at the château of Saint-Germain. He read them his will, in which he entrusted the regency to his widow and made the Duke of Orleans Lieutenant-General of the Realm, and included them all in the group of existing councillors who were to be irremovable during his son's minority. The next day he attended the ceremonial christening of his son, who had simply received emergency baptism at his birth. The godparents were the Princess of Condé and one of the leading councillors, Cardinal Mazarin, who had been conducting peace negotiations on Richelieu's instructions for three years. The king therefore died in the confident belief that he had guaranteed the continuance of his policy. His will was presented to the Parlement by the Chancellor and was duly registered.

Immediately upon the death of his father, Louis XIV became king, at the age of four years and eight months. The next day, 15 May, he left Saint-Germain with the Queen Mother and made his formal entry into Paris. The procession took several hours to get to the Louvre through the milling crowd of Parisians. On Monday

18 May his mother took the little king to the Parlement de Paris to hold a *lit de justice*. Queen Anne, finding herself in the same situation as Marie de Medici in 1610, proclaimed her reliance upon the Parlement, stated that the *lit de justice* was one of the prerogatives of the Crown, and promised that the king would on all occasions follow the advice of that assembly. The Duke of Orleans and the Prince of Condé then demanded that the Queen Mother be recognised as Regent during her son's minority. Chancellor Séguier, who a few months earlier had been a loyal servant of Richelieu, had to sing the Queen Mother's praises and call on the court to annul the king's will of 20 April. On the advice of the Advocate General, Omer Talon, the Parlement unanimously broke the late king's testament and recognised the Queen Mother as Regent with full power and authority. One should observe that in giving their opinions in their turn, Councillor Barillon and several of his colleagues from the *Chambre des enquêtes* ventured opinions verging on statements of grievances. Two days later came the news of the victory at Rocroi, and the Queen Mother made Cardinal Mazarin her chief adviser.

A mere few days had witnessed a series of contradictory decisions and ceremonies. This requires some comment. In the first place, the will of a minister and even of a deceased king had no hold over the fundamental laws and customs which put a young boy on the throne and entrusted the royal family around him with the responsibility of carrying on the government. As in 1610, the Queen Mother went to the Parlement de Paris not in search of authorisation or legal foundation for her rule, but in order to give it publicity and as it were a guarantee in the eyes of public opinion. The Parlement itself took a rather different view of the *lit de justice*. The grievances expressed by some councillors reveal that the sovereign court wanted to see in the ceremony a recognition of its own supremacy in counsel and its pre-eminence in the State, in that its consent was sought before any other act of government. Finally, to clear up a misapprehension, we should note that Queen Anne had no desire to dismiss all the late king's ministers. She took as her principal adviser the very man whom Richelieu had recommended to her before his death.

The Regency Government

Mazarin was a nobleman from a Roman family dependent on the house of Colonna. From his youth, he had won widespread regard through his diplomatic missions on behalf of the papacy, notably in 1630, when he had negotiated a resolution to the conflict over Casale Monferrato. He had subsequently found employment at Paris in 1635, among a delegation sent by pope Urban VIII to explore the prospects for a peace. There he had the good fortune to impress Richelieu with his abilities. In 1640 he chose to enter the service of France, whose power and resources had deeply impressed him. Richelieu had made use of him in the peace negotiations which were pursued somewhat desultorily and to little effect throughout the years of war. He even secured Mazarin a cardinal's hat (December 1641) when Mazarin himself had not yet been ordained priest. This was indeed an exceptional honour, as the papacy did not usually allow France more than three or four representatives in the Sacred College. It also gave a certain autonomous political status to the recipient, who henceforth enjoyed princely rank. After Richelieu's death, Louis XIII recruited Mazarin to his Council on account of his experience in European diplomacy. This agreeable and witty southerner had good looks and refined manners which immediately endeared him to Queen Anne. Alone among Richelieu's creatures (such as Séguier, whom the Queen loathed), Mazarin took the trouble to cultivate Anne of Austria. Thus it was that when the Queen Mother, though anxious to disencumber herself of the late cardinal's most compromised servants, was casting around for an adviser who could guarantee a certain political continuity, the name of Mazarin almost forced itself upon her.

Anne of Austria had at once understood the daunting burden of power, and devoted herself wholeheartedly to the interests of the French Crown and the security of her son's throne. She did not alter her former opinions, remaining anxious for peace with Spain, but in her son's interests she sought a favourable peace. The victory of Rocroi, crowning the gains of the previous three years, augured well for the fortunes of

French arms. It was hardly conceivable for her to back out of France's military commitment.

The Queen Mother was forty-two years old. To judge by contemporary observations and by the numerous portraits in which she is depicted in formal family settings with her two young sons, she was pretty and haughty. She has been called unintelligent and short-tempered. She was certainly intuitive and impulsive. Like Marie de Medici before her, she knew how to take both advice and decisions. So Mazarin, for all his undoubted influence, would not have survived in government for a moment without her confidence and support. The new regime's 'honeymoon' with public opinion lasted almost until autumn. The royal family had left Saint-Germain and taken up residence in the palace which Richelieu had built for himself beside the Louvre (to designs by the architect Lemercier). The Palais-Cardinal, which he had bequeathed to the Crown, was henceforth known as the Palais-Royal.

In order to carry on the war it was necessary to keep up the fiscal pressure. But this could not be done without provoking the indignation of the peasantry, which, while it can be safely ignored when writing history from a Parisian perspective, was something which forced itself daily upon the attention of the *intendants* in the provinces. The Council sought to reduce the burden of the *taille* by getting at people who had previously escaped that tax by virtue of privileges and exemptions. The majority of the towns were either subject only to a self-imposed levy, or else were completely exempt, like Paris, where some of the kingdom's greatest fortunes were to be found. Mazarin relied in this field on the expertise of a financial *intendant*, Michel Particelli, seigneur d'Émery, whose talents he had first recognised when he himself had been an ambassador in Piedmont. Particelli came from a wealthy banking family of Lyon, and had moved to Paris, where he held a variety of financial offices from 1617, when he was aged twenty years. He became a financial *intendant* in 1629, and was in overall charge of fiscal policy from 1643, with the office of Comptroller General, before finally becoming *Surintendant des finances* in 1647. His Italian ancestry (evident from his name) and his determination to tap the wealth of Paris earned him widespread hatred. His first move was the edict of *toisé* (March 1644), which imposed heavy taxes on built-up land in the outskirts of Paris. This aroused the indignation of the city and the implacable opposition of the Parlement, which refused to register the edict. In August 1644 a further edict introduced a tax for the well-to-do (*'taxe d'aisés'*). This struck at the wealthy merchants of Paris. The Parlement restricted the levy to those who earned interest from loans to the Crown – a wrecking amendment which meant that the edict had to be withdrawn in order to prevent damaging royal credit in the financial markets.

So once more, as ever, recourse had to be made to the *taille*. Since August 1642 the *intendants* had been in complete control of this levy. In July 1643 they had received further powers of enforcement, as refusal to pay taxes was henceforth equated with treason. The system of tax-farming, already widespread in the collection of taxes on spending, was extended wholesale to the *taille* in 1645. The anticipated receipts for the year to come were advanced to the Crown by lenders, generally acting collectively in a *traité* (company – hence the lenders were known as *traitants*). Under the supervision of the provincial *intendants*, the lenders then set about recovering their investment, employing agents and guards at their own expense. Thus the traditional apparatus of financial officialdom was made entirely redundant, and the taxpayers were confirmed in their belief that the money collected never went near the king. Mazarin's policy in managing the provinces was thus quite as indifferent and off-hand as Richelieu's. His only concern was the maintenance of credit from day to day. The regime's honeymoon with public opinion was short-lived, and opposition throughout the kingdom at every social level soon surfaced once more as under Richelieu.

The Growth of Opposition

The crowds who rejoiced at the succession of the young king had no doubt that 1643 would see an end to the war and the consequent fiscal demands: the policies were tied to the person of the late king, and should therefore disappear with him. In many provinces tax collection actually came to a halt. The Parlement de

Toulouse went so far as to promulgate a decree on 8 June 1643 announcing an end to special tribunals, such as those of the *intendants*, in a gesture reminiscent of the accession of Louis XIII in 1610, which had seen the prompt revocation of some fifty unpopular edicts. This parliamentary declaration seemed to authorise non-payment, and a new rising of Croquants broke out in Rouergue. At Villefranche, the *intendant* of Haute-Guyenne, Charreton, cornered by a force of 10,000 armed peasants, had to give public consent to a decree reducing the *taille* to the levels of Louis XIII's youth. Tours and its hinterland were likewise shaken by a long and well-organised revolt in October. Similar disturbances continued throughout the following years, breaking out sporadically over about two-thirds of France. The lot of the *intendant* was far from happy, and they would not venture into the countryside without a sizeable armed escort.

Mazarin's position at court was looking vulnerable in summer 1643. The Duke of Vendôme (an illegitimate son of Henri IV), together with his son, the Duke of Beaufort, led the faction opposed to the new cardinal minister. Their followers were arrested in September on the orders of Mazarin, who dared to have Beaufort himself committed to the Bastille. This coup demonstrated Mazarin's determination to tighten his grip on power, and gave an unmistakable sign not only of his policy and resolution, but also of the confidence which the Queen Mother had in him and of the continuity of his ministry with that of Richelieu. This little episode at court was derisively known as the 'cabale des Importants'.

The uproar which the *toisé* had provoked in Paris found an echo in the Parlement de Paris in spring 1645. Councillor Barillon and several other young parliamentarians sought to sway the court into taking antifiscal measures. There too Mazarin acted resolutely. Barillon was exiled to the provinces, notwithstanding the protests of the President, Molé and Advocate General Talon, and in the teeth of a three-month strike by the Parlement as a whole. A *lit de justice* on 7 September 1645 compelled the Parlement to register several disputed measures. On that occasion Talon dared to speak out, in his address to the Queen Mother, against the risk of devaluing royal authority through the indiscriminate use of such ceremonies, which ought to be restricted to circumstances in which the security of the State was in danger.

By 1647 the Crown was nearing the end of its resources. French troops in Italy and Catalonia were marking time or in retreat. The government had exhausted its credit not only with public opinion but also in the financial markets. Efforts to broaden the tax base to include Paris were resumed in October 1646 with a tariff edict which increased the duties on merchandise entering the capital; and there were also efforts to tax officeholders, a class which disposed if not of the greatest fortunes, then at least of the most liquid. Particelli resorted once again to creating new offices and to increasing the charges levied at each renewal of the *paulette*, which permitted offices to be inherited. Particelli and Mazarin were aware of the social and political weight of the officeholders, and of the dangers of incurring their resentment, but the regime was boxed in, and ministers felt the need for a psychological shock, a dramatic gesture in order to revive the confidence of the money-lenders in the determination and stability of the Council.

That is why a second *lit de justice* was held on 15 January 1648 in order to compel the Parlement to register a new package of fiscal measures. The expected revenue gain alone hardly seems justification for such drastic action. In his address, a masterpiece of moving eloquence, Advocate General Talon told the Queen Mother how he deplored this unnecessary use of royal authority, which had involved the unusual sight of a nine-year-old king crying as he read his text. Talon painted a gruesome picture of the country's miseries, of the thousands of wretches imprisoned for owing taxes, of the contrast between their grinding poverty and the luxurious life of the tax-farmers. His considered but passionate speech was soon in print, circulating around the provinces, where it helped stimulate resistance in other Parlements, such as Rouen and Aix, themselves alarmed at the danger of the creation of new offices within their precincts.

On 30 April Particelli published the terms on which the *paulette* would be granted that year. The Parlement de Paris received the privilege without extra charge, but the officers of the capital's other sovereign courts had to forego future salaries. Rumours of the terms were already circulating before publication, and on 29

April the magistrates of the other sovereign courts – the *Cour des aides*, the *Chambre des comptes* and the *Grand Conseil* – gathered in one of the chambers of the Palais de Justice, the Chambre Saint-Louis. The old palace, which stood at the sharp end of the city's island, housed the sovereign courts, and the gallery connecting them was filled with stalls trading in luxury goods (such as books, perfumes, engravings and refreshments), so that it was a meeting-place, a place to stop and chat, and a shopping precinct, a centre for fashion and for news. The group in the Chambre Saint-Louis was joined by some councillors from the Parlement itself, egged on by a septuagenarian councillor named Pierre Broussel, known for his integrity and his concern for the poor. The Parlement ended by joining as a body. On 13 May the Parlement issued an *arrêt d'union* authorising joint meetings of the four sovereign courts in the Chambre Saint-Louis.

The Regent formally annulled these proceedings by letters under the royal seal dated 23 May, on the grounds that 'making a fifth sovereign court out of the other four without the authority of the king and without legitimate authority is an unprecedented and unreasonable act, introducing a kind of republicanism into the monarchy, and a new power'.

The Fronde

The terms of the royal letter were entirely to the point. The assembly in the Chambre Saint-Louis was in principle revolutionary, and perhaps a comparison with the famous Tennis Court Oath of 1789 (making allowances for the inherent anachronism) best illuminates the institutional significance of these developments. Of course the magistrates of the Fronde scornfully rejected such a label. In their eyes, the *lits de justice* of 1645 and 1648 were abuses, contrary to the custom of the Crown: never before had such ceremonies been held in a royal minority. A regent had the duty to maintain the powers of the monarchy, but not the right to modify them. The Parlement's role as a source of advice and a channel for grievances ought to be more respected in such a critical period as a royal minority. The use of *lits de justice* to silence its advice was

clear proof that ministers were tyrants who had imposed upon the
trust of the young king. The magistrates of the Parlement de Paris
saw themselves as the 'fathers of the country', the guardians of the
State, the trustees of the most sacred institutions. They saw it as
their duty to denounce the tyrannical excesses of ministers and the
misappropriations of their financiers.

The parliamentarian arguments were the better received across
the kingdom in that public opinion largely reflected that of the
judicial officeholders, and that officeholders as a class had much
cause for complaint in the aggrandisement of central power. Judicial and financial administration, which amounted to almost the
whole of political life outside Paris, had until the 1630s been in the
hands of the proprietary officeholders, that is, of local worthies
who knew their own backyards and were integrated into local society. Since 1635, these officials had been systematically
superannuated, replaced by *intendants* or, even worse, by agents of
the moneylenders. They had protested peacefully, as was their
right, by way of their deputies or representatives. Since the days of
Henri IV, *trésoriers* and *élus* had been accustomed to send representatives to Paris, at their joint expense, in order to negotiate with
the Council over issues of common concern, such as wages and
transaction fees. The practice of taking up an issue with the Council and sending representatives to lobby at court was by no means
restricted to officeholders. Any interest group in the land could
have recourse to it, whether a town, a group of parishes, Protestant
churches, a guild or any other community. The 'decree of union'
and the discussions in the Chambre Saint-Louis had moreover
been prepared by the deputies and representatives who had
flocked to Paris since the start of the year. Day after day news of
developments in Paris was relayed to the provinces in letters from
activist magistrates or in flysheets printed at their instigation. The
progress of the Fronde was thus watched with equal interest as far
afield as Toulouse, Aix and Dijon. The word 'Fronde' itself was
coined in the spring, and implied that the malcontents were comparable to schoolboys playing with slings in the moats below
ramparts and then disappearing upon the arrival of the archers.

The King's Council could not ignore the institutional challenge
posed by the magistrates of the Fronde. Chancellor Séguier

pointed out that the authority of the king was indivisible, that it was undiminished during a regency, and that it was the Council's duty to abate the extravagant claims of the Parlement. Until 10 June 1648 the Council sought to secure the dispersal of the assembly in the Chambre Saint-Louis, but despite all prohibitions the meetings continued. At the end of June Mazarin and the Duke of Orleans persuaded the Regent of the need to compromise. The Chambre Saint-Louis, duly authorised, pursued its now official deliberations from 30 June to 9 July, and managed to draw up a charter of twenty-seven articles which amounted to a plan for the reform of the State. The text was soon printed and circulated throughout the realm.

The first article, agreed at the first session, stipulated that '*intendants de justice* and all other extraordinary commissions not accountable to the sovereign courts' should be revoked. The *taille* was to be reduced by a quarter, and was to be levied according to traditional practice by *élus* and their receivers (article 2). Taxation was in future to be subject to parliamentary consent, with a free vote (article 3). All tax-farming contracts were to be annulled, and the contractors were to be brought before a judicial tribunal. It was even stipulated that no subject of the king should be detained for more than a day without being brought before a judge (article 6).

This was in effect a founding charter, introducing a new style of government in which the monarch would have lost his absolute power, and would have been limited by the requirement to consult and secure the consent of the sovereign courts in matters of legislation and taxation. There was nothing far-fetched or utopian about this programme, for it commanded widespread support, and it could be paralleled in the monarchies of northern and eastern Europe, which were subjected to representative assemblies, as also in the oligarchical republics of Venice and the United Provinces.

In the short term, the regime had no option but consent. Royal proclamations of 1, 18 and 31 July ratified the majority of the articles drafted by the Chambre Saint-Louis.

On 7 July Particelli, dismissed, retired to his château of Tanlay in Burgundy. Over the next few days all *intendants* were recalled except for six based in frontier provinces, who were restricted to military functions. Throughout the land, the news from Paris had inspired enthusiasm, relief and hope. The collection of taxes came to an almost complete halt, and the month of July saw an explosion of antifiscal joy. Within a matter of days, all *intendants, taille* militiamen and agents of tax-farmers had disappeared, whether in flight, under pursuit, hunted or simply returning to Paris. Some *intendants* had tactfully approached the courts over the preceding weeks in order to arrange a dignified departure. Even the braver spirits had left their posts by 25 July. The whole of the administrative machinery established since 1635 was overthrown. The Fronde had won. France stood on the verge of a new era.

Yet here, too, a political history obsessed with the capital will not do as a history of the whole country. In confining ourselves to the accounts left by great nobles or officials, we are tempted to exaggerate the role of ministers and magistrates and to overlook the euphoria which swept the kingdom in summer 1648. The Fronde was not simply a matter of the grievances of the Parisian élite or of the pretensions of the Parlement. The attempt to introduce absolutism was producing a crisis in the body politic. All social groups and all regions played their part in the movement.

Mazarin's Civil Wars

Mazarin would not admit defeat. Throughout the five-year crisis which lay ahead, even in the blackest moments of exile, he knew that he could count on the support of the Queen Mother, who as Regent was the embodiment of legitimate authority in France. His privileged relationship with her has given rise to the notion that they were secretly married. But there is nothing in this; it is highly unlikely that their relationship was any more than one of friendship, whatever the gossip of Fronde pamphleteers. Coded letters which passed between them during the cardinal's periods of exile have survived. They reveal sentiments of tenderness and devotion, and indeed Mazarin's greatest asset was the passionate trust of the Queen Mother. The cardinal himself no more represented the

State than did any other minister, and had less claim to do so than many princes of the blood. Political legitimacy was confined to royal persons. Mazarin's sole title and claim to power lay in having won the trust of the legitimate authority. Public opinion, not without reason, was scandalised, and this indignation surfaced in a flood of ephemeral texts which are collectively known as 'mazarinades'.

Among these pamphlets was a mock life of Mazarin, published by Scarron in 1651 under the title *Mazarinade* (or 'Mazariniad', by analogy with the *Iliad*), and the word caught on. From spring 1648 to summer 1653 there were around 5,000 contributions to this polemic. The authors and printers were mostly Parisian, but the genre also flourished at Rouen, Aix and Bordeaux. The works were usually of eight pages, printed overnight in runs of 1,000 and sold the next day on the Pont-Neuf or in the streets where booksellers kept shops. The majority were in a richly burlesque vein, and almost all were opposed to the court: out of 5,000, only about 600 supported Mazarin.

We have already seen the importance of these leaflets in disseminating the news of events in 1648. Propaganda and provocative information were also conveyed by the *Courriers français*, *bordelais* and other *Nouvelles de Paris* which constantly carried the latest news of events.

In the history of public opinion, this extraordinary press explosion might seem unique and premature, but it was not in fact unprecedented. The crisis of the League had spawned thousands of comparable texts, and the troubled ministry of Concini had likewise inspired hundreds of pamphlets. Much later, the revolutionary crisis of 1789 would provoke a comparable explosion of the press. This ephemeral literature serves to prove, if proof be needed, the depths of resentment and passion and the inebriation with liberty that shook the realm and gave the period its historical importance.

Mazarin was reduced to ruses and manoeuvres, imposing his authority when he could, then getting out of the way when the torrent of events threatened to bear him down. Between 1648 and 1650 he made three attempts to halt the Fronde by force, three attempted coups which served only to embitter the situation further and to demonstrate his inability to cope with a movement which he had underestimated, much as Henri III had underestimated the League, mistaking what was in fact a nationwide movement for a mere faction of officeholders and courtiers.

On 20 August 1648, Condé won another resounding victory over Spanish arms, beneath the walls of Lens. Mazarin hoped to take advantage of this triumph by arresting Broussel and some other parliamentary leaders. The rumour in the city quarter of the aged councillor's arrest by the musketeers was the signal for three days of riots. As in 1588, the city was criss-crossed with barricades in a matter of hours, the urban militia took up arms, and chains were hung across the streets. Chancellor Séguier narrowly escaped a lynch-mob yelling 'Broussel and liberty', and it was all that 7,000 royal troops could do to hold the immediate approaches to the Louvre.

The King's Council had to set Broussel free and confirm the entire Fronde programme in a fresh proclamation (22 October). As a result, the Peace of Westphalia, signed on 24 October, went almost unnoticed by French opinion.

Mazarin made his next attempt in early 1649, hoping to take advantage of the arrival of Condé's troops in winter quarters around Paris. On the evening of 5 January 1649, on the pretext of going to celebrate the Epiphany, the Queen Mother and her son left Paris and took refuge at Saint-Germain behind lines of troops. Paris and the Parlement awoke to find the king gone, and Condé's army (about 10,000 strong) blocking every approach to the city. The kingdom was plunged into a civil war which no member of the Fronde had wanted. The defence of Paris, in revolt despite itself, was undertaken by the urban militia and various nobles who had put their swords at the service of the city, among others the Dukes of Beaufort, Bouillon and Rochefoucauld. The countryside of the Île-de-France was devastated by royal troops, and there were soon shortages in Paris itself. For its part, the court party found itself isolated as the majority of the provinces sided with the capital. Both the Council and the Parlement were obliged to negotiate, and a hasty peace was concluded at Rueil on 11 March 1649.

Over the following months, Condé, the victor of Rocroi and

Lens, and the mainstay of the court faction, laid claim to pre-eminence in the King's Council. Mazarin's third coup was against this threat from a new quarter. On 18 January 1650 he suddenly had Condé arrested together with his brother the Prince of Conti and his brother-in-law the Duke of Longueville, and threw them all into the dungeon at Vincennes. The idea was at once to secure his own grip on power and to rally the support of Paris, which still remembered the hardships of Condé's siege. Soon after this dramatic blow, the Regent and the young Louis XIV left for an armed progress through the provinces (where Condé had his clients and lands), a show of strength and an attempt to rally support for the king, along the lines of the progresses made by Charles IX in 1565 and Louis XIII in 1614. The royal train made its way uneventfully through Normandy, Berry and Burgundy between January and April.

A further royal progress towards the south-west proved necessary, and rather more dangerous. Condé's family could count on numerous allies and dependents in Guyenne, where Richelieu had favoured the previous Prince of Condé as a counterweight to the influence of the disgraced Épernon. Moreover, the Duke of Bouillon was the most powerful and most popular magnate in the region, with lands and supporters throughout the Dordogne basin. Aquitaine was therefore a stronghold of the Fronde and Condé causes. In May 1650, the Princess of Condé, having secretly travelled to the Midi, gave the signal for an armed rising. Joyous crowds greeted her triumphant progress through Bas-Limousin, Périgord and Bordelais with shouts of 'Long live the king and the princes, and screw Mazarin'.

The court and the royal army, having reached Bourg-sur-Gironde, tried to blockade Bordeaux, where resistance was led by the Princess of Condé and Pierre Lenet, a councillor in the Dijon Parlement and a faithful supporter of Condé. A compromise allowed the city gates to be opened on 5 October 1650, and the court made its way back to Paris.

The Duke of Orleans was now playing the leading role in the King's Council, pursuing a mitigated version of the Fronde programme. It looked to him as though the tranquillity of the realm need no longer be upset by the embarrassing presence of the cardinal. Mazarin, aware of the path events were taking, attempted a final blow. It failed. On 13 February 1651, he went to the citadel of Le Havre, where the captive princes had been taken in August, and released them, hoping to win their support against the Fronde. While the princes, ignoring his offers, hastened to Paris, Mazarin opted for voluntary exile at Brühl, in the territory of the Prince Bishop of Cologne. Louis XIV and the Queen Mother remained in Paris, where the Duke of Orleans dominated the King's Council. Orleans hoped to resolve the crisis by summoning the Estates General, as in 1614. And Mazarin himself had considered such a course of action in March 1649 as a means of responding to the rather confused expectations of pubic opinion and of setting up a rival to the Parlement in the form of a genuinely representative assembly.

The Year of the Estates General

In 1651 Mazarin seemed completely out of the running. Condemned not only by parliamentary decrees but even by a royal proclamation of 5 September, he was banished in perpetuity as a 'disturber of the common peace'.

A bitter power struggle was raging in the King's Council, with the Queen Mother and her supporters (such as Lionne and Servien) drawn up against Condé, Orleans and the moderate wing of the Fronde, represented by President Molé, recently appointed Keeper of the Seals.

To the country at large it seemed a suitable moment for new State legislation. The call was first voiced by informal gatherings of noblemen who had been arriving in Paris since February, even before the release of the captive princes, precisely in order to lobby to this effect. These gatherings continued after the arrival of those princes in the capital, with more and more nobles meeting at a Franciscan convent. Nearly eight hundred gentlemen from the Île-de-France and the surrounding area met for occasional discussions, sitting and speaking without hierarchy according to the conventions of noble solidarity and equality. Their main concerns were to relieve their countryside from the ravages of soldiers and to stake their claim to a political voice similar to that of the clergy in their estate assemblies, which had been held regularly since the reign of Charles IX, or to that of the magistrates (notionally that of the Third Estate). The noble assembly was viewed with some suspicion by the Parlement, which pretended, by virtue of the place it gave to peers of the realm and clerics, to represent all three orders of society. It was also suspect in the eyes of the Crown, nervous at the prospect at yet another focus of opposition. The noble assemblies gave earnest of their determination by an act of union, sought to rally the support of other provinces, and persuaded the Duke of Orleans to act as their spokesman and work for a summons of the Estates General, the ultimate forum for resolving factional and personal conflicts. The assembly broke up on 25 March after securing a promise that the Estates General would be convened at Tours on 8 September.

From June to August 1651, representatives of the three orders were selected and statements of grievances were drafted throughout the kingdom, in town halls and in parish churches 'at the ringing of the bell'. The first deputies arrived at Tours towards the end of August. Several statements of grievances have survived, for example those of the third estate from Agenais and Touraine, as well as several statements from the nobility. In these rare documents one can discern the broad outlines of a little-known Fronde ideology, quite distinct both from the juridical concerns of the Parlements and from the demands of the princes, a third Fronde, more obscure, but with deeper roots and more widely representative.

The grievances took as their starting point the principles conceded in the royal proclamations of 1648: the abolition of the *intendants* and no taxation without consent. Their particular concerns were the state of the kingdom's administration, the need for strict regulation of the billeting of troops, the rigour and efficiency of royal justice, and the reduction of the *taille* to the levels prevalent in the reign of Henri IV. They demanded that the king create no new offices and that he respect the prerogatives of traditional officers. They sought the abolition of most financial offices, as a single agent of the Provincial Estates would be enough to manage the collection and delivery of the *taille* to the royal treasury. Finally, they demanded that the Estates General, as the only institution capable of reporting the true state of affairs within the realm, be convoked on a regular basis. This last demand amounts, in effect, to the demand for a limited monarchy, accountable to the Estates and lacking a central tax machinery, with effective power devolved to local bodies – a few courts, but above all towns and the nobility.

The hope was in vain. Neither the Parlement, nor the court, nor Condé wanted to listen to the Estates. And on 7 September 1651, Louis XIV, having attained the age of thirteen years, was declared to have attained his majority. The meeting of the Estates General was postponed. It became evident that Mazarin had remained in contact with the Queen Mother throughout his exile on the Rhine, and that he had not stopped giving her his directions. Condé retired to the south-west, where he had secured the governorship of Guyenne. Mazarin, having recruited 6,000 German mercenaries, re-entered France in January 1652 and rejoined the court at Poitiers. The civil war recommenced, more bitter than ever. The court party held the central and western France, Condé held the south-west, while the capital and its environs remained in the hands of the Parlement.

The idea of convoking the Estates General did not fade away at once. The Duke of Longueville, Governor of Normandy, maintained confidence in it throughout his own region over the winter of 1651–2. In February 1652, assemblies of nobles resumed in the Île-de-France, the Orleanais and Normandy. The most active nobles were the gentry of Beauce, who elected some of their number to command them in military service to the Crown should the need arise. Such assemblies continued until July, and sought to spread the movement to other provinces around the northern cluster known as the 'United Bailiwicks'. The Duke of Orleans remained wedded to the idea of the Estates, but as always, more from laziness than cowardice, hesitated to fight his corner to the end. It was only in May 1653 that the Crown finally crushed all hope of a meeting of the Estates. There would be no further talk of recourse to this ancient institution until the end of the eighteenth century.

The War of Condé

The issue would be decided by force of arms. The final twist in the crisis was a military confrontation between Condé's faction and that of the court. Louis II de Bourbon, Prince of Condé (1621–86), an inspired general but a wilful, arrogant and implacable man, did not acknowledge his political ambitions. He had been the most effective defender of the rights of the Crown, and was driven into revolt solely by Mazarin's suspicion. He denied that his actions were seditious. Unlike the late Count of Soissons or the old Duke of Orleans, he loathed the idea of a free country under a limited monarchy. The horizons of his political imagination were bounded by the court, and he was unshakeably attached to the principles of absolutism. His military efforts were directed entirely against Mazarin. Of course the citizens of Paris or of Dijon who supported him were adherents of the Fronde, but the political outcome under a victorious Condé would certainly have disappointed them, and would in all probability have been little different from what in any case came to pass under Louis XIV. Historians have denounced Condé for his 'treasonable' negotiations with Spain in 1652, but in reality he dealt with Spain as a sovereign on equal terms, regarding himself as the trustee of legitimate political authority in France, desirous only of extricating the kingdom from the toils of Mazarin.

Condé fell back upon his heartlands in Aquitaine, but even there he was never in complete control. In 1651 the lesser office-holders of Bordeaux had formed a radical faction maintaining the liberties of the city not only against the central regime but even against the social prestige of the Guyenne Parlement. When Bordeaux and its hinterland entered a state of siege in summer 1652, this faction seized power in the city. It was known as the 'Ormée', after a street lined with elms in which the activists had held their first meetings. The 'Ormée' drove out the moderates, and passed draconian laws against the lukewarm in order to guard the city against surprise attack. Some scholars have seen in this a revolutionary programme, but in fact it merely reflected the parlous situation in which Bordeaux, rather like Paris that same summer, found itself. Each city was blockaded by royal troops, and in each the fear and sense of isolation begotten of a siege spawned faction and suspicion. The Condéans of Paris and the Ormists of Bordeaux were simply taking the usual, if drastic, precautions of cities under siege.

Inside Paris, many citizens and parliamentarians were getting tired of civil war, while outside the gates was the threat of a royal army commanded by another victorious general, the Viscount of Turenne (1611–75).

Condé, determined to rely only on himself, secretly left the Midi and took command of the Parisian forces. He managed to halt the royal force at Bléneau on 7 April 1652. But the experienced royal troops made their superiority felt in a bloody campaign around Paris, notably in an engagement in the Faubourg Saint-Antoine (2 July).

On 4 July a group of Parisian citizens was meeting in the Hôtel de Ville, with a view to opening peace negotiations, when it came under attack from a mob of popular Fronde supporters and Condé's soldiers. More than two hundred citizens were killed. Condé's position in the city could not survive this atrocity. Victory slipped away from him, and his old supporters were overcome by weariness. With consummate skill, Mazarin made himself scarce in August, withdrawing once more into voluntary exile, this time at Bouillon, in the Ardennes. Condé left Paris on 14 October and headed for the Spanish Netherlands. On 21 October, the young Louis XIV returned in triumph to his capital. And on 3 February 1653, even Mazarin was applauded as he re-entered the city.

The Fronde held out in the south-west. It took several months of fighting and a difficult siege before the 'Ormée' and the Condéan faction lost their credit in Bordeaux, and the Prince of Conti finally agreed to throw open the gates on 31 July 1653. The last Fronde stronghold to surrender was Villeneuve-sur-Lot, on 13 August.

The Defeat of the Fronde

How is it that the Fronde, which was triumphant throughout almost all France in summer 1648, and again in summer 1651, was unable to impose lasting change? The Queen Mother's support for Mazarin, and Mazarin's own skill, undoubtedly played a part, but it was above all the weaknesses of the Fronde itself, which was internally divided and unable to find and unite around a single leader, that account for its failure. The Duke of Orleans lacked the character to take control, and Condé lacked the desire. The Parlement de Paris itself was far from united: its more radical measures were passed only by qualified majorities. The legal proceedings instituted against tax-farmers and particularly vicious *intendants* were never seen through to completion, because the new fiscal system had already struck roots deep enough to implicate a large part of society in the profits it offered. Many parliamentarians had shares in loans and advances to the royal treasury, and did not wish to see proceedings pursued too zealously.

The search for simple social explanations of the factional divisions is fraught with error and confusion. It has been found that in each camp there were representatives of each social order, of each interest group, even of each family. The most one can say is that among Mazarin's supporters one finds rather more financial officials and shareholders in tax-farms, while the peasantry and the urban mobs, when not overwhelmed by dearth or fear, generally rallied to the Fronde. The taking of sides, and the divisions which emerged in provinces, towns and families more often reflected links of clientage and loyalty, with provincial gentry rallying to their governor, and peasants lining up behind their lords. Provincial governors were the major players, aligning the bulk of the local gentry and of the civic magistracies behind causes which they themselves had chosen for reasons of family ties or friendship.

In many towns, the outcome hung in the balance. Civic assemblies were never so well attended as in those years, swollen by craftsmen and tradesmen whose unaccustomed affluence threatened to disturb the traditional oligarchies. Governors, *intendants* and generals sometimes held assemblies which brought together all the bodies and communities within a town, as was done in 1652 by the *intendant* Heere at Angers, or the Count of Harcourt at Agen. Traditional local divisions were often deepened by a tax, a shortage or a disputed civic election, and could escalate into little civic wars between feuding families. National factions supervened upon and complicated or realigned local divisions. Thus, at Angers, Saint-Maixent and Carcassonne, local factions opposed to the officeholders sided with the court, while the merchant oligarchy sided with the Fronde. In the greater cities, the seats of sovereign courts such as Toulouse, Bordeaux, Rouen and Aix, divisions opened between the clients and the supporters of the magistracies. Generally, quarrels broke out over the arbitrary replacement of aldermen or consuls, or the replacement of civic tribunals and councils by extraordinary commissions, much like councils of war, which fixed prices, expelled dissidents and took drastic security measures. The divisions which opened in these years of crisis would endure long after the disappearance of the Fronde itself. While a single family might find itself now supporting the Fronde and now Mazarin, these vicissitudes were soon forgotten. But social conflict continued at Aix, Angers, Sarlat and elsewhere, often for many decades.

Between 1649 and 1652, the majority of towns were committed to neither camp. As at Paris, the weight of street mobs and client networks could shift the local balance one way or the other. Thus in 1652, at Orleans, Nevers and Moulins, support for the court combined with demands for Mazarin's dismissal. Agen and Limoges shut their gates to royal and Condéan forces alike. Larger villages made agreements with regiments and alliances with each other, and put their support on the market. Each walled village played an independent part, giving the kingdom the appearance of a mosaic of local and civic loyalties, a complex web of corporations and communities, of kinship and client networks.

When peace returned in 1653, local autonomy was unacceptable to the restored central power. The King's Council increased the influence of agents of central government, cutting civic privileges, controlling or even confiscating the revenues of town councils, and restricting urban electorates. Between 1653 and 1657, elections at Angers were annulled three times, while civic corporations were slimmed down at Béziers, Dijon, Limoges, Aix, Marseille and elsewhere. And although without great success as yet, the King's Council also clearly and resolutely set about reducing traditional provincial liberties.

The struggle for a utopian vision of a limited monarchy presiding over countless autonomous localities had ended, ironically, in the triumph of the very absolutism and centralisation against which it had been directed. There was an important but frequently overlooked psychological contribution to this outcome. In 1649, the English Civil War had culminated in the execution of Charles I. This unbelievable news stuck horror into the profoundly legitimist hearts of the French, and the Fronde, obliged to defend itself against the analogy with the English Parliamentarians, became prey to self-doubt. The ebbing of the parliamentary tide in 1651 and 1652 was undoubtedly in part a consequence of the news from England.

Mazarin had managed to identify himself consistently with the cause of legitimacy. He knew that he was indispensable to the impulsive Anne of Austria, isolated as she was on a Council which was rent by divisions and impotent in the provinces. Mazarin wagered on a cause which had a long past and a glorious future: the power of the French State. His calculations were convincing enough for the Swiss regiments who, though unpaid, remained loyal to the young Louis XIV. They knew that legitimate political authority was inseparable from the royal person, and that victory would come in the end to those who remained obstinately and unfailingly loyal to him.

Mazarin and the Aftermath of the Fronde

Although the king had reached his majority in 1651, he had not yet been crowned. There was no particular schedule for this ceremony according to the traditions of the French monarchy, so it seemed as though the coronation might be a suitable way to mark the restoration of domestic peace. Louis XIV was therefore anointed and crowned at Reims on 4 June 1654 with not a cloud in the political sky. This lull lasted for some two years. A royal proclamation of 22 October 1652 had restored the administrative status quo, obliterating at a stroke the proclamations of July 1648 and September 1651. *Intendants* had started to return to their provinces since 1650, and by the end of 1653 they were all back in post. Their title was changed as a precaution, and they were now called 'delegated commissioners'. The traditional financial officials, treasurers and *élus*, were given back their former responsibilities, but were to fulfil them under the strict supervision of the *intendants*. The costs of war had returned to their former levels, with the Council's expenditure reaching 113 million *livres* in 1653, and 154 million in 1657. Under these conditions, fiscal pressure also resumed, and the *intendants* once more waged unscrupulous petty wars against tax-payers with the aid of their tax militias.

In February 1653 Mazarin entrusted the superintendency of finances to two men, an old diplomat named Abel Servien, and a rising official called Nicolas Fouquet, who took sole charge after Servien's death in February 1659. Fouquet (1615–80) came from a wealthy parliamentarian family, and had been made a Master of Requests at the age of twenty years. He had been noticed by Mazarin, and in 1650 he obtained the post of Procurator General in the Parlement de Paris, in which capacity he made himself very useful to the cardinal. Brilliant, likeable and a tasteful patron, *Surintendant* Fouquet sought to rebuild financial confidence in the government. Circumstances were favourable, as the restoration of peace had stimulated commercial activity. Fouquet's policy was to resume payments on old Épargne bills in order to ensure that future issues would find a ready market. As a result, credit was easy until summer 1656.

The setbacks suffered by French forces in the Netherlands in 1656 and 1657 revived the revolutionary conditions of 1648. The *intendants* and their militia, Mazarin and the tax-farmers, all operated more rigorously than ever, and peace never seemed a step nearer. Popular risings and noble assemblies began to appear all over the country. As usual, the south-west experienced the worst popular unrest, with outbreaks in Chalosse, Astarac, Médoc, Libournais, Saintonge, the Auvergne and elsewhere. The lesser gentry of Beauce, who had been so active in 1651–52, resumed their agitations and inspired similar movements in the Orleanais, Berry, Perche and Lower Normandy (where there were more than a dozen clandestine gatherings in a few months). One of the largest gatherings took place in the forest of Conches, while another, held at Peray in the Vendôme region, brought together deputies from fourteen provinces. Discontented nobles once more clamoured for a convocation of the Estates General, peace and an end to fiscal terrorism.

In Berry, noble discontent grafted itself promptly onto peasant unrest. The region had been flooded with copper currency, *liards*, which had been minted on the orders of the *surintendants* in order to lubricate small transactions, but whose grievous inflationary effects served to discredit them entirely. As a result, collectors of the *taille* refused to accept payment in *liards*, which ended up in the pockets of peasants who could not get rid of them. A peasant revolt broke out in Sologne in April 1658, known as the war of the 'Sabotiers' (or 'saboteurs', literally 'clog-men'). The King's Council was seriously worried. A Council of War was set up in summer 1658, and troops were sent to Berry. The old Duke of Orleans was begged to intervene one last time, and about thirty gentlemen were gaoled – though only one was executed, Gabriel de Jarcourt, Marquis of Bonnesson (on 13 December 1659). Municipal conflicts which broke out at that moment in Marseille were suppressed with unaccustomed brutality: the town had its privileges reduced, and 6,000 troops were billeted there in January 1660.

It was at this point that Spain finally gave up hope of securing a more favourable peace. The dispersal of the peasant forces within France and Turenne's victory at Dunes, near Dunkirk (14 June 1658) forced Spain to open negotiations. The Peace of the Pyrenees, and Louis XIV's concomitant marriage to Maria-Teresa, daughter of the King of Spain, were announced to the country by royal circular in February 1660. The royal progress from the Basque country to Paris was an occasion for unbounded political rejoicing. It was widely imagined, as in 1610 and again in 1643, that peace would mean an end to the extraordinary fiscal impositions which, according to the the terms of the edicts themselves, were justified only by the demands of war, and should therefore terminate with it.

Further measures confirmed these expectations. Arrears of the *taille* for the years 1647–56 were written off, and those for the years 1657–9 were subjected to a discount, while a reduction in the *taille* was announced for 1661. Mazarin's death (9 March 1661),

Louis XIV's decision to take personal control and the arrest of Fouquet (5 September 1661) raised hopes still more.

Nobody can put a precise figure on the staggering fortune accumulated by Mazarin and managed for him by his *Intendant général*, Colbert. His known possessions in France alone have been valued at about 38 million *livres*. Amid the general enthusiasm for the revival of the monarchy, the terrible years of war were forgotten and and unrest subsided. The young Louis XIV understood the need to live up to the high expectations. The spectacular disgrace of his *Surintendant des finances* and the establishment of a special tribunal to deal with tax-farmers were thoughtful and successful bids for popular approval. Fouquet was made the scapegoat for Mazarin's arrogance, for the endless oppression of tax-payers, and for the shabby treatment of the lesser provincial gentry. His trial, held in 1664, ended in a sentence of life imprisonment. The injustice was blatant, but well received by public opinion. The loathsome ghost of Mazarin was exorcised by this travesty of justice.

At the institutional level, no risks were taken. It was quite proper for a young king to play to public opinion, convening solemn tribunals in the Parlements in order to make royal justice effective even in the darkest corners of the land, consolidating and clarifying legislation in great reforming ordinances as in the days of Marillac, and trying to shift the burden of taxation from the peasantry to taxes on consumption. Colbert set about all this with his usual efficiency. One might perhaps have expected a summons of the Estates General, a restoration of the status of officeholders, the suppression of the market in offices promised since 1615, and a reduction in the powers of the *intendants*. There was not in fact the slightest question of any of this, although nobody at the time could have predicted it one way or the other. France still had the machinery to follow an alternative constitutional path, that of a limited monarchy along the lines of Poland, Sweden or even England, where Charles II had just regained his throne. But it was not to be. The rising generation opted for absolutism. Louis XIV's contemporaries, those aged about twenty years in 1658, feared civil war like the plague, and repudiated the conspiracies and risings of their forefathers. Not for them the futile and violent disorder which had plagued the realm, off and on, for a century, since the outbreak of the Wars of Religion. They hankered after a centralised kingdom, with an all-powerful and absolute monarch ruling according to the dictates of reason. This generation finally implemented the absolutist programme laid out in the articles proposed by the Third Estate in the Estates General of 1614. Louis XIV was the most outstanding representative of that new generation.

12 The New Balance of Power in Europe

After entering the European war in 1635, the kingdom of France had found itself engaged upon four fronts: Catalonia, where French troops were garrisoned from 1641; in northern Italy, where they were trying to advance beyond Pinerolo and Casale; in the southern Netherlands, where each spring brought a fresh round of siege operations against minor fortresses; and finally in Germany, where operations were launched into Swabia and Bavaria from bases in Alsace and the bridgehead at Breisach. More than 200,000 men had to be kept on a war footing, at home in winter quarters, or in the field during the campaigning season, which began in March, when troops headed for the frontiers in accordance with the strategy chosen by the King's Council that year. Once there, the generals for the most part avoided great pitched battles, preferring instead to seize towns in order to secure lines of communication and ensure against attack from the rear, and seeking to occupy territory to use as a bargaining counter in eventual peace negotiations. Autumn was the time to consolidate any gains or to withdraw once more to winter quarters in France. The plains of the southern Netherlands and northern Italy were the two principal theatres of operations. They presented similar tactical problems: flat, fertile and densely populated countryside, dotted with fortified cities that could be taken only by substantial forces equipped with plentiful artillery. In the meantime, enemy forces continually offered resistance and mounted diversions, harassing foragers and rear-guards. The war dragged on interminably from one campaign to the next, draining the resources of the combatants to little or no effect.

Mazarin not only directed French strategy but also drew up plans for peace, tinkering merrily with the map of Europe. He had after all been trained as a papal diplomat. He has often been credited, according to the racial stereotype, with Italian subtlety. It would be more accurate to speak of his skills as a typical papal negotiator: a man of peace, prudent yet stubborn, relying more on the power of discussions than on the fortunes of war.

French Offensives Beyond the frontiers

Offensives in northern Italy had ground to a halt in 1636, 1640 and 1646, yet the cardinal never accepted his inability to exercise any significant influence upon affairs in his native Italy. The election of a new pope, Innocent X, in September 1644, was a disaster for France. Innocent soon revealed his Spanish sympathies, refusing to recognise the secession of Portugal and Catalonia, and refusing to appoint bishops there without the consent of Madrid. Mazarin hoped to scare the pope by bringing off a bold coup in the Mediterranean. His plan was to launch a naval expedition against Spanish bases on the coast of Tuscany. There were several fortresses garrisoned by Spanish troops along the Gulf of Genoa, protecting that stage of the 'Spanish Road'. In May 1646, all the ships that Provence could furnish gathered to transport 6,000 men under Marshal de Brézé and Prince Thomas of Savoy (who had now joined the French) to attack the Orbetello peninsula. The first assault was a failure, and Marshal de Brézé lost his life in the engagement. A second assault in October succeeded in taking possession of the island of Elba, which Provençale privateers then used as a base from which to prey upon the shipping of the western Mediterranean.

In spring 1647, the French were presented with another opportunity. Popular riots against taxation had broken out in the Spanish territories of southern Italy, in Palermo and the major towns of Sicily (May 1647), and then at Naples itself (7 July). The Neapolitan riot, led by a fishing-boat owner named Masaniello, grew during summer into a full-scale revolt. The Viceroy and his Spanish troops were trapped in their fortresses, so that authority in the streets of Naples and the surrounding provinces fell into the hands of anyone who could grab it. In October 1647 the worthies of Naples recalled the ancient liberty of their city and its tradition as a maritime republic. French interest was shown by the discreet arrival in November of Henri, Duke of Guise (grandson of the head of the Catholic League), distantly related to the Angevin kings of Naples who had ruled southern Italy before the kings of Spain. Guise was proclaimed duke of the new republic in the cathedral of Naples on 24 December 1647, endowed with powers similar to those of the House of Orange as Stadtholders in Holland. But the adventure did not last long. Starved of support by Mazarin, Guise was betrayed by local factions and handed over to the Spanish, who had returned in force in April 1648. Thomas of Savoy's fleet attempted a raid on Salerno during the summer, but without success.

In northern Italy, Marshal Du Plessis-Praslin brought huge numbers of troops together from June to October 1648 for the siege of Cremona. Cremona commanded southern Lombardy, and its capture would have been a devastating blow to Spanish interests there. But disease and the attacks of local troops forced the French to abandon the siege and retreat westwards. The Fronde crisis cut off the supply of reinforcements, and the strongholds on the Tuscan coast taken by the French fell back into Spanish hands between May and August 1650. In the absence of relief from Toulon, the Swiss garrisons surrendered on dates stipulated by the besiegers, following their rule of never prolonging resistance beyond a reasonable point. To crown their misfortunes, the French had to evacuate Casale Monferrato in October 1652, which left the garrison at Pinerolo as the sole relic of French ambitions beyond the Alps, where Richelieu had first looked for territorial gains. Mazarin's policy towards the land of his birth had been a series of costly disappointments.

It was in Germany that the enormous military potential of France earned its greatest reward in the 1640s. The French could hope to affect the course of the war beyond the Rhine either by means of their Swedish allies, or more directly by the use of the mercenary regiments inherited from Bernard of Saxe-Weimar, based in Upper Alsace, which could cross the Rhine at Breisach, and from 1638 could reach eastwards throughout Breisgau. The theatre of operations shifted southwards, threatening the Catholic regions of southern Germany, notably the powerful reserve of men constituted by the Duchy of Bavaria. Duke Maximilian, who reigned at Munich from 1596 to 1651, and was Emperor Ferdinand II's son-in-law from 1626, had once been viewed by Richelieu as a potential ally. But after the French decision to enter the war openly, he had committed himself wholeheartedly to the imperial cause.

From 1644, the campaigns of Turenne and Condé took the war into Swabia and the Black Forest, on the borders of Bavaria. Each summer they engaged the enemy in bloody if indecisive battles, around Freiburg-im-Breisgau in August 1644, and at Nördlingen in August 1645. From summer 1646 they combined their operations with those of Swedish forces under Marshal Wrangel. The decisive offensive came in early 1648. Turenne and Wrangel, acting together, compelled the imperial army under Montecuccoli to retreat after the Battle of Zusmarshausen (17 May 1648), and shortly afterwards occupied Munich itself. They even advanced towards Vienna in Austria. Emperor Ferdinand III (1608–57), who had hitherto hoped that peace would involve little in the way of territorial adjustment, was obliged to speed up the peace process.

The Negotiations and Treaties of Westphalia

The need to restore peace to central Europe had long been evident. The ravages of war had wiped out the wealth and prosperity which Germany had enjoyed at the start of the century. Initial discussions had begun as early as 1638, and formal talks opened in the free city of Hamburg in 1643. The papacy, fulfilling the Holy See's traditional role, and the Republic of Venice, which hoped that peace in Europe would pave the way for opposition to the Ottoman threat in the Mediterranean, had offered to act as mediators.

It was decided after lengthy bickering over conventions and proceedings that the Catholic combatants should hold talks among themselves at Münster under the auspices of the papal nuncio Fabio Chigi (later Pope Alexander VII), while the Protestant powers should treat with imperial ambassadors at Osnabrück under the auspices of the Venetian Contarini. For four years these two cities in Westphalia were rendered neutral ground, and hosted continuous gatherings of diplomats. It was in effect a continental congress, akin to the Diet of Regensburg which had met in 1630. The negotiations dragged on from August 1643 to October 1648. For the French side, Abel Servien, Marquis of Sablé, and Claude de Mesmes, Count of Avaux, had full powers to negotiate, and were assisted by teams of secretaries, clerks, guards and servants.

The objective was to establish a lasting European order by settling once and for all the often age-old conflicts between nations. And this order had to have the consent even of the smallest powers. The map of the Holy Roman Empire, a complex of sovereignties, religious confessions and political prerogatives, was on the table, as were the territorial losses and gains of the combatants, be they German princes or outsiders like the kings of France and Sweden.

Spain, represented by the Count of Peñaranda, took part in the negotiations. Spanish policy was divided over peace priorities, with some ministers preferring peace with the United Provinces, others peace with France. Exchanges of prisoners were agreed with France in 1645 and with the United Provinces in 1647. The Dutch for their part were henceforth more concerned with the maritime power of Portugal and their powerful neighbour France than with their ancient sovereign, Spain. Following the proverb 'Gallus amicus sed non vicinus' ('Let France be a friend, but not too close'), the Dutch preferred to see French troops busy elsewhere. So a separate peace was concluded between Spain and the United Provinces in January 1648, much to the annoyance of the French. After eighty years of war, Spain had finally recognised the independence of the northern Netherlands.

The outbreak of civil unrest in France in July 1648 combined with hopes of military advances in Catalonia to dissuade the Spanish from participating in the general treaties agreed in October that year. As a result, hostilities between the two great Catholic powers continued for many more years.

The two treaties of Westphalia signed simultaneously on 24 October 1648 led to a complete restructuring of institutions and territories within the Empire. In effect they laid down a new constitution, replacing the conventions agreed in 1555 in the days of Charles V. It has even been called the *Constitutio Westfalica*, an essential element of European public law which would survive for one hundred and fifty years. The three hundred and fifty or so states of the Empire henceforth enjoyed full sovereignty (known in German as 'Landeshoheit'), giving them the right to make treaties and maintain armed forces on condition that they should not do so against the Emperor or the Empire.

Princes who had fared badly in the wars, such as the Duke of Württemberg and the Elector Palatine, regained all their lands. The German peace was really intended to repair the terrible devastation wrought by thirty years of merciless conflict. Some regions were not to recover their pre-war population levels until the end of the century.

One might think that after 1648 the Empire was nothing but an empty title. And it is true that Habsburg hopes of transforming Germany into a unitary state were utterly dashed. But the power of the House of Austria within its ancestral territories was fully imposed, and it completed within those domains the work of the Counter-Reformation begun at the start of the century. Moreover, the status of the Emperor was in a paradoxical way reinforced. He was no longer a dangerous rival, but the bulwark of the German nation against the Ottoman threat from the east and perhaps also the French threat from the west. The early death of Ferdinand III in 1657 confirmed this development. The succession of his young son Leopold had not been arranged in advance, and the occasion might therefore have arisen under the new regime of Westphalia for a change in the succession – French diplomacy, indeed, actively canvassed Louis XIV as a possible successor. But despite all this, Archduke Leopold (1640–1705) was in due course raised to the imperial throne, once again confirming the hereditary Habsburg stranglehold on this theoretically elective position.

France and Sweden each received their rewards. Sweden acquired western Pomerania, a duchy on the left bank of the Oder. This Swedish colony on the southern shores of the Baltic gave the Swedish kings the privileges and status of a prince of the Empire. It also gave them a decisive advantage in their age-old rivalry with the other Baltic power, the kingdom of Denmark, which now began an inevitable decline.

France was granted the rights of the Emperor and the House of Austria in Upper and Lower Alsace, a somewhat ambiguous concession. To the French it was regarded as a territorial gain pure and simple, but to the imperialists it was seen as a bundle of feudal prerogatives. In fact, France clearly gained the fortress of Breisach, Sundgau, the district of Ensisheim, and the 'prefecture of the Decapolis' (ten cities, including Hagenau, Colmar and Selestadt), besides various vague rights in other cities, towns and regions. But the free city of Strasbourg and the republic of Mulhouse remained completely outside French control. As in all the areas they conquered, the French introduced their administrative institutions into Alsace: a governor, an *intendant* (Colbert de Croissy in 1655) and the fiscal machinery (in 1661 Alsace was annexed to the *Bureau des finances* of Metz). This policy of patient, effective and authoritarian Gallicisation was brought to completion in 1681 with the military occupation and annexation of Strasbourg itself.

The two treaties also settled some long-disputed issues. The Swiss Cantons were finally recognised as a fully autonomous sovereign body entirely outside the Empire, and French sovereignty over the Three Bishoprics – Metz, Toul and Verdun – held since 1552 was also conceded.

The treaties of Westphalia were of an evident importance which historians have quite properly emphasised. They fixed the constitution of the German lands for a century and a half. They marked the emergence among the statesmen and people of Europe of a sense of European public law, a sense of responsibility for the peace and harmony of Europe shared among the community of nations. This sense of public law replaced the medieval concepts of imperial or papal tutelage which had already had their day many years before, and were from this time clearly regarded as obsolete.

The Continuation of the War Between France and Spain

From 1650 the internal problems in France began to have an impact on military operations abroad. It was in 1650 that the captured bases in Tuscany had to surrender for lack of relief. The offensive in Flanders could no longer be maintained, and the provisioning of troops in Catalonia was becoming ever more difficult. The scales tipped heavily towards Spain in 1652, when Dunkirk, held by the French since 1646, was retaken. In northern Italy, the Governor of Milan (the Marquis of Caracena) took possession of Casale Monferrato. Finally, the French garrison in Barcelona, the Catalan capital, had to capitulate to Don John of Austria (the illegitimate son of Philip IV) on 13 October, after a fourteen-month siege. Hopes were high in Madrid that the series of Spanish disasters had at last come to an end, and that Philip IV's 1648 gamble of rejecting Mazarin's peace terms in favour of fighting on would be vindicated. However grave the exhaustion of Spain, the disorder prevalent in France was at least as bad, and new conflicts were brewing in Europe, such as the Anglo-Dutch war of 1652–4, which could alter the balance still further. Don John of Austria was appointed Governor of the Spanish Netherlands, and halted French offensives at Valenciennes in 1656 and Cambrai in 1657. Discontent broke out once more in France, and a third Fronde movement seemed to be on the cards.

Franco-Spanish rivalry had once more come to a sort of stalemate in mutual exhaustion. Victory would go to the superior diplomats, to the side which could entice some third power into the fray, such as England, which under the Protestant regicide Cromwell had just emerged from the civil war that had kept it out of European politics for a decade. In October 1655 Cromwell opted for an alliance with France, on largely naval grounds: it would be relatively easy to pick up scraps of the Spanish possessions in America, and the price of an English alliance was French help against Dunkirk, from which Catholic pirates preyed upon English shipping. The alliance soon delivered results at sea. And in spring 1658 a joint Anglo-French offensive was launched against Dunkirk. Turenne led the attack against a roughly equal force commanded by Don John and Condé. But the Spanish were almost without artillery, and were heavily defeated in the Battle of the Dunes (14 June). Dunkirk itself fell on 23 June, to be followed later in the summer by a series of other places, ending with Ypres. At the end of the year Philip IV agreed to open negotiations for peace.

Convincing the Spanish to negotiate was Mazarin's final coup, and although it belongs to the microhistory of diplomacy, it is worthy of special consideration. Louis XIV was now twenty years old, and it had long been expected that he might marry a Spanish princess. A royal marriage would have been a symbolic sealing of the peace between the two kingdoms. In order to hurry things along, the French therefore made as though to pursue another matrimonial alliance, opening negotiations for the hand of a princess of Savoy, a cousin of Louis. The French court moved by stages from Paris to Lyon, and the Spanish court took the bait, urgently sending a special ambassador there (November 1658). In May 1659, Louis XIV's decision in favour of a Spanish match was announced, and the peace conference opened in August that same year.

The Treaty of the Pyrenees

The place chosen for the conduct of negotiations was itself a sign of reconciliation: the island of Faisans in the middle of the Bidassoa river, which marked the frontier between the two kingdoms and had often witnessed exchanges of royal brides. Pavilions were once again set up on either side of an imaginary line which notionally marked the precise border, and talks lasted from August until 7 November 1659.

Spain abandoned to France three provinces which had been in French hands since 1640 or 1642. On the southern borders of the Netherlands, a number of small strongholds stretching between Luxembourg and Flanders were left in French hands, such as Thionville, Montmédy, Avesnes, Le Quesnoy, Landrecies and, further to the north, Gravelines and Bourbourg. Dunkirk was handed over to England. In exchange, Spain secured the return of all other strongholds seized by the French in their 1658 offensive. They also secured Condé full pardon and the restoration of his lands and dignities. Duke Charles IV of Lorraine was given back his domains, which had been under French occupation since 1634. The separate Treaty of Vincennes settled affairs between France and Lorraine in February 1661.

The royal marriage between Louis XIV and his cousin Maria-Teresa (daughter of Philip IV and Elizabeth of France), which sealed Franco-Spanish *rapprochement*, was solemnised on 9 June 1660 at Saint-Jean-de-Luz. The royal couple's return through the south-western and western provinces culminated in a triumphal entry to Paris, amid general rejoicing, on 26 August.

Mazarin's diplomatic triumph was complete. A group of German princes had put themselves under French protection in the 'League of the Rhine', a treaty made in June 1658 at Frankfurt. The kingdoms of the Baltic, which had been at war for many years, sought French arbitration. The Peace of Oliva (the name of an abbey near Danzig), which restored peace between Sweden, Denmark, Poland and Prussia in June 1660, was a tribute to French prestige in Europe.

The greatest satisfactions of the cardinal minister's latter days were to have established himself as the arbiter of Europe, and to see his young godson, the king, firmly established at the head of the most powerful kingdom in Europe.

Nothing had been lost, despite 1648, when all France had combined to execrate the Italian usurper; despite 1652, when all Richelieu's gains seemed doomed; despite even 1657, when the last offensives had ground to a halt in the Netherlands. Largely because of Mazarin, France had undergone five years of disorder and civil war. The fiscal terrorism introduced by Richelieu had been prolonged fifteen years beyond his death. But success had finally come at the negotiating table, the only success which Mazarin really cared about. Mazarin's greatest good fortune was without doubt to have been the witness and the beneficiary of the sudden decline of Spanish power, of which he harvested the first fruits. But whether by good luck or by good judgement, in 1660 Mazarin had certainly emerged as the winner.

13 Hopes and Beliefs

The label 'baroque' has often been rather loosely applied to the early seventeenth century. Several aspects of the culture of that age can properly be so described, for example the paintings of Simon Vouet, with their intricate composition and sharp tonal contrasts, or the emergent opera, the new musical drama born in Italy. But the soothing harmonies of Poussin and the classicising tendencies in architecture can hardly be called baroque. It can indeed be tempting to map the totality of artistic development on a single curve, but closer observation invariably reveals a whole range of currents and cross-currents cutting across this generation in the life of the mind, in social life, and in the life of the regions. If there is any underlying unity in what we call an age or an epoch, it is perhaps more obvious to posterity than to contemporaries. In the early decades of the seventeenth century such unity lies in a distinctiveness from the ages of humanism and Reformation which had gone before, and from those of absolutism and classicism which were to follow. If I had to sum up the character of that period in a few words, I would call it the age of the picaresque or comic novel, that new cultural form which rose and fell with the early seventeenth century and so closely reflected its tensions. It was in 1605 that Cervantes published the first part of *Don Quijote*, and his *Novelas ejemplares* were translated into French in 1615. The picaresque genre appealed to some bent in French taste, and Charles Sorel took it up in his *Histoire comique de Francion* (1623). Other landmarks in this genre, with its combination of realism, comedy, adventure, the burlesque and the picturesque, were Tristan l'Hermite's *Le page disgracié* (1642) and Scarron's *Le roman comique* (1651). The setting of ideals of honour and liberty in the midst of knavery and absurdity was certainly true to the vicissitudes of the age. And the picaresque novel is a fitting introduction to a consideration of the hopes and beliefs of the subjects of Henri IV and Louis XIII.

Such consideration must cover the faith of the huge Catholic majority, conceptions and representations of the world, the rhythms of life, and conceptions of society, and must seek to discover what changed with the years, what remained constant, and what was purely ephemeral or transitory.

The Catholic Faith

The first half of the seventeenth century witnessed one of the greatest flowerings of religious faith in French history. The age of the Wars of Religion had been typified by fervour, heroism and fanaticism. The succeeding generations professed a faith matured in adversity, more reflective and serene, fostered, at least for Catholics, by the great movement of renewal and reform which the Council of Trent had brought about within the Catholic Church.

Mysticism, the direct personal experience of the divine though prayer and contemplation, characterised the piety of this age. A mystical spirituality of southern, predominantly Spanish, origin coloured the decades of the League and the peaceful years of Henri IV. The classic of the new spirituality, printed dozens of times, was the *Introduction à la vie dévote* (known in English as the *Introduction to the Devout Life*) by St François de Sales (1567–1622). This first appeared at Lyon in 1609, and enjoyed immediate success. The reflections of the holy bishop of Annecy and Geneva were explicitly addressed 'to such as live in towns, in households, or in courts'. The strongest personality in the French church was Cardinal Pierre de Bérulle (1575–1629), one of the king's almoners, whose influence with the Crown secured royal authorisation for the introduction of new religious orders such as the Discalced

Carmelites (founded by St Teresa of Avila) in 1604 and the French Oratory in 1611.

New forms of devotion flourished in all areas and at every level of society. They were often introduced by the Jesuits. Despite their exclusion from northern France (the jurisdiction of the Parlement de Paris) between 1594 and 1603, the Jesuits had retained their houses in the parliamentary jurisdictions of southern France. Enjoying the support first of Henri IV and later of Richelieu, they founded colleges across the land (forty by 1610, and eighty by 1650). These innovative, dynamic and free centres of education, which trained their pupils for life, played an essential part in the formation of the élites of early modern society.

Municipal intervention was indispensable in new religious foundations, be they colleges or nunneries. It was because civic élites wanted to provide for the education and future of their children that municipal authorities would grant land or buildings, with privileges and endowments, for the establishment and development of some new religious house. Within a few decades, even quite small towns might see three or four new or reformed religious houses founded within their walls. The Carmelites, for example, opened about sixty convents in this period. The Ursulines, whose special vocation was the education of girls, were established at Paris in 1612, and numbered some four hundred houses by the end of the century, while the Order of the Visitation, founded by St Jeanne de Chantal in Savoy in 1610, opened more than one hundred houses in France in half a century. Not until the nineteenth century would such a flood of religious vocations once again be seen in France.

Among the anonymous mass of the faithful, the same period witnessed an enormous vogue for pilgrimages, processions, penitential or professional confraternities and devotion to Our Lady and the saints – all specifically Catholic devotional modes. The expectations of the faithful were reflected in the numbers of miracles recorded and duly verified by the clergy at traditional pilgrimage sites, which attracted thousands of visitors when times were good. Crowds of unprecedented size were drawn to such sites as Sainte-Anne-d'Auray (a miraculous sanctuary from the 1620s), Notre-Dame-des-Ardilliers in Saumur, and Notre-Dame-de-

Verdelais near Bordeaux. Chartres and Liesse in northern France, and Rocamadour, Fourvière and Notre-Dame-de-la-Garde, three ancient pilgrimage centres in the south, also benefited from the resurgence of piety.

The recitation of the rosary (a series of Hail Maries said with the aid of beads) became widespread from the 1620s, and was one of the most popular manifestations of the intense popular devotion to Our Lady. Catholic military victories from Lepanto to La Rochelle were occasions for outbursts of fervour in Marian confraternities throughout the land.

The canons of the Council of Trent were slowly but steadily implemented throughout the Catholic world. The French bishops and clergy had resolved upon strict implementation during the Estates General of 1614. Episcopal residence within the diocese, regular diocesan visitations, the drafting of catechisms, and a concern for the moral standing of the clergy were among the most dramatic requirements, and those most likely to make an impact among the faithful at large. The requirement that a seminary be established in every diocese was only in fact implemented in a handful of dioceses (such as Reims, Bordeaux and Toulouse) at the start of the seventeenth century. But a succession of foundations, some eighty in about twenty years, began in the 1640s. Moreover, the ideal of the formation of model clergy was sustained in many of the new companies of priests, such as the Jesuits, the Oratorians or the Sulpicians (a group founded in 1641 by Jean-Jacques Olier, parish priest of Saint-Sulpice, a new and rapidly growing suburb to the south-west of Paris), whose establishments provided models for the new seminaries. Many religious orders held preaching missions in rural France. A group of priests would spend a week or two in isolated villages, preaching, hearing confessions, instructing and edifying the peasants. Such were the activities of the Priests of the Mission, or 'Lazarists' as they were known from their origin in the priory of Saint Lazare in Paris, founded in 1625; or of the Eudistes, founded by St Jean Eudes in Normandy in 1643.

The fruits of this huge programme of Christian instruction and formation were felt for generations afterwards. An analysis of criminal proceedings under Henri IV and Louis XIII shows that there were still clerical scandals (drunkenness, misconduct and so on), in marked contrast to the image of the good priest which prevailed a century later. But the period was scarred by conflict and shaken by violent change and controversy. The new devotional currents were by no means accepted without protest.

The major tendencies of the Counter-Reformation provoked a sharply Gallican reaction, especially among lawyers, who were uneasy about Ultramontanism, fearful of the political influence of the Jesuits, and suspicious of innovations coming from Rome. Thus the Parlement de Paris evinced bitter opposition to the Jesuits and to the unpatriotic tenets of Ultramontane political theology throughout the reign of Henri IV and the youth of Louis XIII.

There was also a reaction against the triumphalist and optimistic humanism of the Counter-Reformation. This new tendency, which emerged in the 1640s, was known as Jansenism, after Cornelius Jansen, Bishop of Ypres in the Netherlands. His theology was pessimistic about the weakness of human nature, relying entirely upon the grace of God for salvation, and basing itself upon the more extreme aspects of St Augustine's refusal to exalt human liberty and merit. This body of thought attracted a substantial following among Parisian officeholders, whose Gallican opinions and austere personal tastes and habits predisposed them to it. It enjoyed a particular vogue in the Reformed Benedictine convent of Port-Royal, in the country a little south of Paris, which for a while housed the young Blaise Pascal (1623–62), whose apologetic and polemical writings had a widespread impact. A papal warning about Jansenism in 1653 marked the start of a protracted theological struggle. At the time, however, nobody would have imagined just how long that struggle would be, or how widespread and deep would be its impact in the field of political ideas.

Works of Charity

1630 saw the return of years of wretchedness and high mortality. History and legend recall the work of St Vincent de Paul (1581–1660), a priest of modest background from Landes, an eloquent, warm-hearted and inventive man, able to devise new and effective responses to the rising tide of distress. Thanks to the patronage of the Gondi family, Vincent de Paul became Almoner of the Galleys in 1619, and all his life he took on heavy responsibilities in the religious life of the kingdom. In 1625 he founded a group of priests, the Priests of the Mission, whose task was to open seminaries and encourage the founding of charitable confraternities. The crisis of the 1630s had a decisive effect on the development of these foundations. Thus 1633 saw the foundation of the 'Charity of the servants of the poor and sick', better known as the Daughters of Charity, devoted to the care of the sick and the relief of the indigent as well as (from 1638) the upbringing of orphan children, another manifestation of the demographic scourges of the age. They were also known as the 'Grey Sisters' from their modest style of dress. The prestige of Vincent de Paul illuminated the entire social order. His example and his influence also led the way in another development typical of the ideas of the age, the Company of the Blessed Sacrament.

Worthy layfolk, concerned to put their faith into practice, combined in societies dedicated to the exercise of a social apostolate. The title Company of the Blessed Sacrament appeared in 1630, bringing together many prominent figures at court or in the Parlements. Vincent de Paul supported it all his life. The Company acting secretly for greater effectiveness, worked against social evils like prostitution and violence. It seems that, among other achievements, the Company managed to wean the youthful nobility off the murderous fashion for duelling. Royal edicts against duelling had been issued repeatedly to little or no effect, and duelling accounted for hundreds of young lives each year. The patient labours of the Company among the aristocracy achieved genuine results in the private forum of conscience. But the secretive nature of its operations brought down suspicion upon the Company, earning it the label of a 'cabal of *dévots*' taken up by anti-Roman historians. From the 1660s, the State of Louis XIV was no longer prepared to tolerate the exercise of significant social influence by bodies independent of royal authority, and meetings of the Company were therefore banned.

The effects of Vincentian spirituality and the influence of the Company of the Blessed Sacrament can also be detected in another field of great social importance. An edict of April 1656 announced the establishment of a general hospital intended to house the poor of the streets of Paris. The buildings were to go up in an area known as the Salpêtrière, named after a disused arsenal to the south-east of Paris, not far from the Seine. Since the days of François I there had been a *Bureau des pauvres* in Paris, which dealt with the influx of the destitute in years of scarcity. Most of the larger cities of Europe were equipped with such institutions early in the sixteenth century. But the deficiencies of Parisian poor relief were glaring: the Hôpital de la Pitié, founded by Marie de Medici in 1612, offered fewer than a hundred places. From the 1660s the Salpêtrière was able to offer shelter to nearly 6,000 people. A certain historiographical fashion has taken to referring to such enterprises as the 'great enclosure'. Repudiating the conventions of hagiography, this label assimilates such charitable endeavours to repressive institutions and instruments of social control. Now it is true that the members of the Company of the Blessed Sacrament, such as the advocate Duplessis-Montbard, the chairman of the board of the general hospital, lamented in 1656 that relief was undertaken 'as a police measure, and not solely out of compassion and hardly at all out of charity and the love of Jesus Christ'. But the Salpêtrière was certainly not a prison. Inmates were free to leave, but it was hard to gain admittance. More than half the inmates were aged or infirm, and the rest were orphans or poor women with children. This is a far cry from the forcible imprisonment of beggars that became a reality only in the later eighteenth or even the nineteenth century. The scandal against which the good people of the early modern age struggled was not the oppression of the poor, but the complete indifference of society towards them. The poor were not a source of fear: they were held to be the images of Christ in suffering. The greatness of a person and the standard of living of their house were measured in terms of the number of the poor who crowded at the gates to receive alms. The reputation for abject poverty which clung to Paris at that time was a consequence of the city's sheer size. It had more than 400,000 inhabitants by 1650, but most of the greater cities of France had comparable problems of sanitation and poverty. It was in 1667 that Colbert established a lieutenant for police in Paris, and only in the 1680s that provincial cities saw general hospitals and police lieutenancies introduced along the same lines. Vincent de Paul died in 1660 at the end of the period of wretchedness which had served both as the cause and the stage for his charitable inventiveness.

The half-century which divided the Wars of Religion from the age of Louis XIV saw profound changes in Catholic France. The religious life of Henri IV's days thereafter seemed simple, patchy and disorganised. The faithful were now heading towards a more rational and internalised piety. But that destination was still some way ahead. Only the first fruits of that development had been harvested by 1660.

The Conception of Time

Time is the greatest resource of the poor, who have more of it than they know what to do with. Judicial records frequently show the accused justifying an hour of leisure that had ended in crime or drunkenness in terms of the need to pass the time. The pre-industrial world was not attuned to the rhythm of passing hours, and left whole days for leisure or boredom. Time was measured in seasons or stages of life. Liturgical, agrarian and political calendars came together in these changeless structures, adding their own particular rhythms to them. The life of the country was unchanging, repeating itself from year to year as regularly and predictably as the conventional scenes which represented the months in old calendars. The agrarian year began in October, with the sowing of corn, and that month also saw hunting, the pressing of grapes for wine, the harvesting of apples, and the fattening of pigs on acorns in the forests. November saw the slaughter of the pig, and the first of the new wine. Winter was a time of long evenings, spent in patient fireside labours: cracking nuts, peeling chestnuts, spinning hemp, linen or wool. Christmas and the New Year came when the cellars and storehouses were full and when the weather enforced the greatest amount of leisure upon the peasants and rural labourers. The free time extended into February or even March. This was the time of year for marriages and family celebrations, and included here or there the more or less prolonged and boisterous festivities of Carnival. March brought the sowing of the spring cereals (oats and barley), the weeding of the winter crop and the pruning of the vines. The most important time of year for cereal-growing regions (and most of the villages of France, whatever the quality of the soil, depended on their grain) was the harvest – July and August. Harvesting was done with a sickle. Farms on the great cereal plains employed seasonal labour, often from far away, for the harvest. Once the last sheaves had been gathered in, the fields were left to be gleaned by the poor, who could not afford to lose so much as a single precious grain among the straw. Harvest was followed by threshing, carried out by a stone roller on a patch of dry flat ground in sunnier places, or by a flail inside a barn in most of France, a procedure which allowed the work to be spread over a longer period and protected from summer storms. Better farms marked the completion of the harvest with a great feast. Hay-making, aftercrops and the harvesting of spring crops came at varying points through the rest of the summer, as the troops of seasonal labourers filled the roads. At the end of the season they would return home with a little money, or with a sack of corn on their back.

The end of September brought the vintage. The cultivation of the vine was more widespread then than today, because towns had to be supplied, and the price of wine was not high enough to justify carrying it far to sell. Wine was not aged, and local vineyards had little in the way of reputation. Parisian innkeepers had casks brought from Burgundy along the Yonne and the Seine, and from Champagne along the Marne. The judicious selection of wine and the distinction of good vintages were still fifty years in the future.

In upland regions, autumn was the time when flocks were brought down from their high summer pastures. The great fairs coincided with this, and were the primary markets for cheeses and summer meats (veal and lamb). Autumn was everywhere a season for getting together, a time for striking agricultural deals, fixing leases and making sharecropping arrangements. It was the time for hiring labour for the year to come, farmhands and domestic servants, apprentices and journeymen. Those in search of a master paraded in the traditional hiring fairs with a ribbon in their hat or pinned to their tunic. Then October was back, with the sowing of the winter corn, and so it went on.

Ecclesiastical Time

In the early centuries, the Church inscribed the liturgical festivals of its year into the agrarian calendar. So each year the story of human salvation came around with the seasons, staring with Advent, which prepared the way for the coming of the Messiah at Christmas. Lent recalled Christ's sojourn in the desert in preparation for the sacrifice of Holy Week. Advent and Lent were seasons of special recollection in which the faithful of the cities could listen to the sermons of some talented preacher, brought in by the cathedral chapter, a confraternity or even the municipal authorities to deliver a course of sermons.

The celebration of the Resurrection at Easter, which, calculated according the lunar calendar, might fall anywhere between 22 March and 25 April, was the greatest Christian feast, and gave the signal for the most general rejoicing of the year. Easter Monday and the following Sundays were taken up with fair-weather games like ninepins, bowls or quintain. Some places had more elaborate celebrations, with junketing, jousting or mock combats in boats, tilting at the ring or at the *faquin* (a wooden man which had to be knocked over), climbing a greasy pole, or shooting-matches with longbows, crossbows or even muskets. In regions of northern and eastern France, such customs have sometimes been preserved to this day, but in the early seventeenth century there were confraternities of archers almost everywhere. The essentials of the competitions were constant, even though the target, the prize and the title of the victor ('king of the bird', 'popinjay' and so on) might vary from place to place.

Ascension and Pentecost brought Eastertide to an end some time in May or early June. The Monday, Tuesday and Wednesday before Ascension had been appointed by the Church as Rogation Days, an essential part of peasant religion. The Rogation Days were days of prayer and processions which called down the blessing and protection of Heaven upon the harvest of corn then ripening in the fields. Processions were held along the parish boundaries, with regular stops for prayer. The villagers thus trod out the limits of their communal horizon – the edge of the forest or the border with the neighbouring community – in a rite which marked out the extent and limits of their territory, and the nature and fragility of their communal solidarity.

The feast of St John the Baptist, on the longest day of the year (24 June), was hardly religious in anything but name. Coming on the eve of the harvest labours, it was the last outburst of the cycle of youthful rejoicing that had begun on the night of 1 May. Those two nights in May and June saw crowds of young unmarried men rampaging through the village setting up 'mays', that is, garlands of flowers, before the houses of those whom they wished to honour – the lord, for example, or the local judge, or more agreeably, the pretty girls. These happy lads, who were no longer children but not yet married men, chose one of their number to preside as the 'king', 'duke', 'abbot' or 'prince' of youth. He had to be wealthy enough to pay for the drinks, and was regarded as the organiser of his group's festivities, which could include dances, farces and vengeful tricks. Thus they would inflict practical jokes or charivaris upon those who had earned the disapproval of the community: a remarried widow, a young married man from outside the village, or some old miser though to be hand in glove with the *taille* officials. Such nocturnal juvenile rituals always had much the same purposes, whether they took place at Carnival, on May Day or at Midsummer: to encompass, accompany and control courtship and marriage, and thus assure the survival of the community. They almost always took much the same form as well. Youths braved the dark with great torches, and danced around the village. It was as though fire burned up bad luck and charmed away misfortune in order to help the forthcoming harvest. Youths dominated nature, silence and the night with the noise of their songs and the light of their flames.

The interconnection of the agrarian and the religious calendars was made even more obvious by the traditional manner of dating memorable events and accounting days according to the saint's day. 'Towards St Martin's Day (11 November) the river burst its banks'. Or again, 'on St John's Day (24 June) soldiers came to be billeted in the village'. St George's Day (23 April) was the usual date for business transaction in spring, and Michaelmas (29 September) was the usual term for leases, although the feasts of St Mary Magdalene (22 July) and St Luke (18 October) were also used. St Urban's Day (25 May) usually marked the departure for high summer pastures, and Michaelmas saw the flocks start to descend again. The fattening of pigs on acorns was customarily confined to the days between Michaelmas and St Andrew's Day (30 November). One can actually chart the progress of the Reformation in some parts of Languedoc by the substitution of numerical dating for traditional dating in notarised rural contracts. Numerical dating had long prevailed in the commercial world, but the measurement of time in terms of the liturgical calendar remained predominant in everything which concerned the household and the family.

Historical Time

The powers-that-be in any given place took part in local festivities, or more often stamped their authority upon them by giving permission for them or decking them out in their own colours. The permission of the town hall, the lord or the royal judge had to be obtained before anyone could beat a drum through the streets to attract punters and show a bear or a wirewalker, or to set up a stage so that pipers could provide dancing music for the local youth. Each city had its own calendar of festivities which the civic magistrates would mark with fine hats and scarlet hoods: a dozen or so days, two or three of which would involve a grand procession in which all the social groups within the community would make their way from the town hall to one of the principal churches. This parade of local society brought together the trade guilds and the corporations of officials with their fine costumes and banners, in an order of precedence sanctioned by tradition. The loyal sons of the town (that is, the urban militia) turned out and fired volleys into the air. Some of the festivals involved the figure of a dragon or a giant, recalling some legendary moment in the local past when an imminent peril was averted by a holy bishop or a heroic knight. Thus at Tarascon they paraded the 'Tarasque', at Metz the 'Graouilly', at Reims the 'Kraulla', or at Douai the 'Gayant'. Other festivals might celebrate more recent events, such as the departure of the English at the end of the Hundred Years War, or the raising of a siege during the Wars of Religion, or deliverance from the plague during the epidemic of 1626–32.

Nor did royal power hold itself aloof. Youthful kings often took part in the Carnival or Midsummer festivities in Paris. And the key moments in the life of the king, from the birth of a prince to a victory over enemies, were occasions of universal rejoicing, with Te Deums in the churches, thanksgiving processions, bonfires and drinking.

Sometimes the idioms of the festival were annexed and distorted for political ends. Thus an effigy of Concini was mocked as King of Mardi Gras at Amiens in 1614, as was an effigy of Mazarin at Bordeaux in 1651. There were many burlesques between 1648 and 1651 in which a straw Mazarin was arraigned for his crimes and packed off to Hell. But such episodes were exceptions, not the rule, and it would be anachronistic to imagine that, in the way of contemporary ideological manifestations, there was frequent interaction between these very different cultural domains.

The day was coming, however, when central government would grow jealous of civic privileges and of the independence manifested during the years of the Fronde, and would therefore confiscate municipal revenues on the pretext of liquidating civic debts, abolish the military responsibilities of urban militias, and also start attacking the particularism of local festivities. A chance accident during some spectacle or tilting match, or youthful excesses during a public dance, might equally offer an excuse for denouncing them as occasions of licentiousness and idleness, and thus for suppressing them by judicial decree. This development became more obvious after 1660.

Rather stronger opposition to traditional festivities derived from the reformed churches, whether Calvinist or Tridentine Catholic, which distrusted the pastimes of leisure hours, which they sought to make more morally profitable. Many youthful festivals or confraternity celebrations were moderated through the influence of the clergy, or even came to be confined to the world of children. The aspiration towards a purified religion free from material attachments and from liturgies too dependent upon externals led some priests and bishops to protest that the excessive number of liturgical feasts represented a threat to public morality. The papal constitution *Universa* of 1627 sought to restrict the number of holidays of obligation in any given diocese to twenty-five (together, of course, with the fifty-two Sundays). But it was not until the time of Colbert that treating certain traditional feasts as holidays was to be effectively prohibited. The first effective measure in this regard was a decree issued by the tribunal of the Grands Jours of Auvergne in 1667.

Notwithstanding the fancies of nineteenth-century folklorists, these customs were neither timeless nor changeless. Periods of distress and crisis caused long breaks in these popular traditions, or even brought them to a close. When scarcity or infection reared their heads, or when war or taxation overwhelmed a community, then public festivities were set aside. As a result, the crisis of the 1630s marked the end of the good times that had prevailed since the Edict of Nantes.

Conceptions of Society

Each period has its own system of values and social ideals, and these systems define patterns of behaviour, methods of social advancement, and lifestyle. The ultimate social ideal of early seventeenth-century France was that of the gentleman. Everyone aspired to identify themselves with the special trappings of nobility. The wealthiest could actually acquire titles and invest in the land and country property that would enable them to pursue the truly noble way of life. Even the poorest would strive in their dress, their speech and their deportment to imitate the real or presumed manners of the gentry, setting a feather in their hats, bearing arms and sorting out their affairs noisily. Nobody questioned the pre-eminence of the nobility in the life of society, even if the nobility itself granted precedence in church to the clergy for the honour of God, or in court to judges who wore the royal livery out of respect for the king. The social hierarchy was not merely implicit, but was expressed in myriad everyday actions, from dress to the way one walked. One could quite easily reconstruct the social order from a close examination of rules of precedence and sumptuary laws.

Rules of precedence defined the place of the individual not only in political or liturgical ceremonies, but also in everyday situations. To hold the inside of a pavement, to be first across a threshold, to speak first, to keep one's hat on, to remain seated in public, all these were the prerogatives of persons of quality, who would themselves give way, rise or uncover their heads in the presence of someone of still higher rank. In a municipal procession, or at mass in a major church, it was important to know who should go first. Should officials of the *élection* give way to those of the *présidiaux*? Did the carpenters' guild take precedence over the bakers? Such doubts were resolved by reference to tradition, or by consulting the oldest inhabitants, or by examining the records in the town hall. Scuffles could break out over precedence, and servants might be summoned to help: such quarrels could end in pitched battles. Such disputes have seemed petty and ridiculous to later historians who have failed to appreciate what lay behind them. Ceremonial precedence was an index of political influence. Giving way in a procession could mortgage the future by creating a precedent, or could compromise a position taken over some burning political issue. Every corporation or society was therefore obliged to defend a legacy of privilege and precedence which made plain to everybody its place in the city.

In accordance with a long legislative tradition, sumptuary edicts sought to regulate luxury in dress, adornment and retinues. The primary motives for such legislation were economic. Ostentation in dress required silk, lace and cloth of gold or silver, stuffs which were not produced at home and had to be imported from Italy. Because of the mercantilist obsession with the flight of bullion abroad, which was thought to be a drain on the nation's meagre money supply, efforts were made to prevent such expensive imports. But the motives could also be ethical – there were denunciations of the moral degradation and the waste of inherited wealth which occurred among better families as a result of a foolish vanity in dress – and social – it was thought proper that an individual's social status be reflected in their attire. In the words

of the proverb, it was the habit that made the monk. A notorious
edict of November 1633 forbade the use of cloth of gold, and
another of 1656 sought to regulate the appearance of carriages
and coaches. Such measures were invariably dead letters, but they
reflected accurately enough the widely shared notion that the
quality and colour of materials, the use of furs, lace and ribbons,
the wearing of hats and the bearing of arms should correspond to
an individual's place in the social order and to the conventions
appropriate to each station in life.

The true mirror of social hierarchies in any society, especially
one founded on respect for tradition, is marriage. One would only
give one's daughter's hand to an equal or a superior. Marriage
joined together not two individuals, but two families, and the
selection of a spouse was a matter for parents. This is not to say
that love had no place in marriage, rather that it was expected
to arise afterwards, in the context of life together as man and
wife. Marriage could provide a route to social advancement, and
could form part of a family strategy patiently pursued across
generations. The conventional equality of partners always accommodated itself to a slight social ascent by the wife. One sees also in
the seventeenth century a young wife bringing both her pretty eyes
and (or) her dowry. The notarised marriage contract, common
enough even among the worse off, laid down the contributions of
the respective parties, fixing the woman's dowry and trousseau,
and the husband's contribution. The importance attached to
financial considerations could make it almost credible that marriage was a purely a matter of the market. The magistrate and witty
humorist Furetière published in 1666 a work entitled *Le roman
bourgeois*, in which he presented an imaginary table or tariff for
dowries showing what a reasonably endowed woman could hope
to get for any given price. A dowry of between 6,000 and 12,000
livres should secure a Parisian merchant, a procurator in the
Châtelet or the secretary of some great lord, and so on. In fact,
though, the nature of the dowry (in land, or goods, or whatever),
the antiquity of the family, position at court or in the city, dignities
(such as noble titles, court appointments, or judicial offices), and
the honour of the name (that is, the overall reputation of the family), could all affect the equation, and show that it was not a simple

matter of accountancy. Certain wealthy trades, for example, did not command proportionate social status, and found themselves therefore without social position and almost doomed to endogamy. For all her money, the daughter of a wealthy market-town butcher with his own stock-farm would be unlikely to marry anyone other than the son of another master butcher. On the other hand, an impoverished gentlemen with a military reputation could bring honour rather than wealth to a match. Social esteem was thus the product of a complex equation, with many variables of rank, honour, merit and wealth. But it clearly placed a titled nobleman above a mere squire; a royal office-holder, however modest, higher than a merchant; a master of a trade above a journeyman; and a journeyman above a simple labourer.

The Logic of the Social Order

The strict and precise social ranking of individuals found a rationale in a number of analogies and metaphors which emphasised the need for stability in all things for the sake of harmony in the world and individual contentment.

The world order consisted in the interdependence of its elements in an ordering laid down by providence. The activities of those who sought to alter that ordering were therefore not only shocking and sinful, but senseless and suicidal. Many images illuminated this reasoning. The world was compared to an immense chain of living beings or to an enormous pyramid. To break a link in the chain or to shake loose a block in the pyramid was to imperil the entire structure. An anthropomorphic metaphor likened society to a human body in which the head was the king, and in which each subject had a special function, like the various limbs and organs. Or there were fables, like that of the serpent whose tail wanted to be in front, and which therefore tore itself to pieces on sharp stones; or that of the feet which wished to wear hats like the head; or of the limbs which were jealous because the mouth got all the food. This last gem was derived from an episode in Roman history (from the sixth century BC) in which a plebeian mob rioting on the Avelline hill was made to see reason by the consul

Menenius Agrippa, who used the fable to show the absurdity of having the various elements of single body fight each other in rebellion or civil war.

Nature itself furnished many examples of order: the sun ruled the courses of the stars; the lion was king of the beasts; the eagle was sovereign among birds; the diamond outshone other stones; and the lily was supreme among flowers. To aspire to a dignity one did not have, to strive to play another role than one's own was a sin against the order of nature, comparable to that of Satan in wishing to be equal to God. Thus, observed Ambroise Paré, it was shocking to see a monkey imitate a man, and was amusing only to little children who had no concept of the monkey's fault in so doing. Another justification for the ideal of stability was found in the image of the world as stage, found for example in the writings of the Venetian essayist Zuccolo (1624): each person should play the part assigned to them, and the best actors were those who stuck to their allotted role, while the worst were those who spoiled their part in the effort to appear more important.

The ideal of social stability also sought historical justification. Thus the nobility were taken to be the descendants of ancient conquerors, be they Gaulish chiefs, Romans or Franks. There were thus supposed to be racial explanations for social hierarchy. The inheritance of rank also found expression in the concepts of blood and lineage which underlay dynastic legitimacy.

Finally, as in every age, a moral justification for social fixity was sought in notions of the superiority of traditional wisdom, in the benefits of prudence, and in the virtues of modesty, resignation and obedience.

The idealisation of an immutable social hierarchy had number of important social consequences. The first was the utter condemnation of revolt and rebellion, something which tormented the consciences of English Catholics opposed to Elizabeth, French Protestants taking arms against their kings, Croquants or Frondeurs. Moreover, social mobility as such was regarded as a sin. This prejudice was among the most widely held commonplaces of the time, and was enshrined in many proverbs and sayings: the barrel always stinks of fish, there's none so conceited as a louse on a velvet tunic, and so on. Sooner or later, social climbers were bound to show the baseness of their soul, and thus remind everyone of the baseness of their birth. The inflammatory theme of the flunkey turned financier by means of exploiting poor taxpayers was a commonplace of peasant revolts. Concini and Mazarin embodied this loathsome creature. Nor was this creature entirely a figment of the imagination. In the king's service, the best posts went to the highest bidders, and in two or three generations a family could rise, though financial operations, from provincial obscurity to the highest royal offices.

It remains true, of course, that conservatism was the most prudent attitude in a society in which change was slow and structures seemed well-nigh immutable. In a demographic context in which life expectancy was short, the father often died before his children were old enough to work. It was essential to pass on one's fields, one's workshop or one's skills quickly. There was no time for a protracted adolescence or for leisurely studies. One had to follow almost immediately in the footsteps of predecessors with whom one often shared even the forename. The knowledge of the elderly was rare and consequently precious, for they alone knew how things should be, and how they had been in the past. The younger a society, the more dependent it is on custom, and the more suspicious of innovation.

This brief survey of beliefs and prejudices must not be taken too univocally. Commonplaces did not stop malcontents from rebelling, even if they rebelled not against the king but against his evil counsellors. They did not stop people trying to better themselves and improve their children: the social climber was always someone who had outdistanced you. Nor did they prevent technical or intellectual innovations arising from the collapse of traditional wisdoms, which were continually called into question, and from the exploration of new worlds beyond the seas.

It is generally recognised that individualism was a fruit of the industrial and urban revolutions, and that the pre-modern societies of orders wrapped people in complex networks of solidarity. One did not live alone: one belonged, like most peasants, to a family and to a parish, and perhaps also to a trade guild, a confraternity, to a civic community, to an extended family which included distant cousins, to a clientage, to a corporation or a company, to a province, to an order. Each of these social ties affected one's precise status, entailing rights and responsibilities, defining one's precise position in society and the kingdom.

No society is completely without mobility. Change can result from the arrival of newcomers, or from the natural renewal which sees the constant disappearance of family names through marriage, disinheritance or ruin. Social mobility works downwards as well as upwards, but shame, wretchedness, silence and oblivion enshroud the fate of fallen noble families, returned to the bosom of the peasantry. Upward mobility is always easier to spot. In predominantly rural France, social ascent always began with a family diversifying its activities. A well-off labourer would one day set about selling grain himself, acting as both carrier and merchant, lending to his neighbours, taking out leases of more land, managing the affairs of a local landowner, or going into business with people in a nearby town. The merchant labourer would send his son to college, to train as a notary or an advocate. The grandson might purchase a royal office, and his son in turn might aspire to an office which conferred nobility. The daughters would marry gentlemen, of the 'sword' or the 'robe', the first born sons would inherit the land, and the younger sons would serve in the wars or enter the Church. College education and the purchase of office played a good part in the process, but so too did lifestyle and social esteem. That was the way of the world.

The Work and Influence of Descartes

The life of Descartes spans almost exactly the period under consideration here, and his work in a sense sums up the ambitions and achievements of his age, marking an epoch in the history of thought.

René Descartes was born in 1596 on the borders of Touraine and Poitou, the son of a councillor in the Parlement de Rennes. He was educated at the Jesuit college of La Flèche, which had just opened. After studying law, he spent two years as a gentleman volunteer in foreign armies, first that of the United Provinces, then that of the Empire. He travelled throughout Europe before settling in the Netherlands to pursue a life of scholarship.

The old system of knowledge based on Aristotle was already tottering, shaken by a wave of new discoveries. The later generations of humanists, including in their respective fields figures such as Jean Bodin and Ambroise Paré, understood that Aristotelianism had had its day, and appreciated the need for reflection on the very nature of knowledge itself. In astronomy and physiology, as in all fields of science, experimental methods and new discoveries were calling into question the old certainties of the medieval schools. Francis Bacon, the Lord Chancellor of England, rejected all appeal to tradition and authority in his *Novum Organum* (1620), recommending instead doubt, observation, experimentation and induction. The work of Descartes belongs in this new context of European philosophy. While scholarly contemporaries like Peiresc and the Dupuy brothers restricted themselves to exchanging questions and amassing collections of curiosities, the young Descartes dedicated himself obstinately and obsessively to laying down a new logical foundation for the pursuit and justification of scientific knowledge. He drew up treatises on 'The Rules for the Guidance of the Spirit' (1628), on the world and on man (1633), though without publishing them. Finally, at Leiden in the United Provinces, he published in French his *Discours de la méthode* (1637), which was presented as an introduction to three essays, 'Dioptrique', 'Météores', and 'Géometrie', which were simple applications of his method. In 1644 he published his Latin *Principia philosophiae*, which aimed to establish a single and coherent system of knowledge. The system was deduced from first causes or principles, which were the matter of 'first philosophy' or metaphysics, and constituted the roots of the tree of knowledge. Physics, in other words natural science, was 'second philosophy', the trunk of the tree. Mathematics did not figure in this system, as it was seen as a mere preparatory exercise, a purely abstract method lacking proper subject matter of its own. Descartes died prematurely in February 1650 at Stockholm, where he was a guest of Queen Christina of Sweden.

Descartes's work enjoyed immediate success in France. Although some of his works had been published in the Netherlands in order to escape the censorship of the Sorbonne, a French translation of his *Principia* appeared at Paris in 1647, and that same year he was granted a royal pension. His *Passions de l'âme* appeared simultaneously in Paris and Amsterdam in 1649. His works subsequently ran into dozens of editions in France. In the 1660s, treatises on physics and medicine were published in Paris, claiming to be based upon the 'principles of nature and methods expounded by M. Descartes'. Great figures such as the Duke of Luynes, the Duke of La Rochefoucauld and the Prince of Condé studied his thought, and held conferences in their houses to explain and comment upon his work. The reservations and censures of the still profoundly Aristotelian Sorbonne were of no avail in the eyes of the huge audience won by 'Cartesianism', which was immediately taken up by the authors who wrote for the *Journal des savants*.

The scepticism of Descartes, his repudiation of tradition whatever its source, his subordination of all phenomena to the rules of reason, and his concern to construct a rational metaphysics were the foundations of the philosophy of the age of classicism.

14   Artistic Life

The history of art is also the history of taste and of the priority which a given age attaches to different art forms – not only of the taste of professional artists, but also of the perception of art in society as a whole. Frescos, paintings, panels and hangings were among the more or less lasting works of art which were exposed to general view in everyday life, whether in the decoration of churches or town halls, or in the apparatus of public spectacles and festivals. These places and occasions were opportunities for artists to earn their keep and for the public to participate in art.

The Painter's Trade

Painting for a living was a regular trade with a structure of sworn guilds with apprentices, journeymen and masters. Most painters were born to the trade. Even the modestly gifted sons of master painters would soon be busy in the workshop, and would later be sent on their travels to discover new masters and new styles, as well as to visit Roman monuments and collections of antiquities, and to examine, study and copy the works of modern masters in the churches and palaces where they were to be found. The aims were to collect sketches and models, to recognise genres and to find their own style. The voyage above all others was of course the tour of Italy, where one discovered the shades of light, the Mediterranean landscape and the ancient monuments. There one could learn from the great masters: from the Venetians of the sixteenth century (Titian, Veronese and Tintoretto); from the strict classicism of the Carracci brothers of Bologna; or from the marked contrasts of light and shade mastered by that tempestuous, fashionable, but short-lived genius Caravaggio.

Among the Italian genres, the sun-drenched and desolate landscapes of the Roman countryside offered the most suitable settings for scenes taken from classical mythology or fable. Scenes of crowded streets and inns, bustling with soldiers, beggars, scoundrels and prostitutes were known as 'bambochades' after the Flemish painter Van Laer, called Il Bamboccio ('the midget'). Some visitors, such as Gellée and Poussin, settled down for a long period at Rome, but most spent only a few seasons there.

On returning to France, these young artists could find a variety of work open to them. Some became more or less itinerant, seeking orders from town halls which wanted portraits of their aldermen or consuls, or from the convents or churches which were so busy building at that time. They had to find favour with the church's committee of works or with the wealthy confraternity that was putting up the money in order to win the contract for decorating a vault, or for painting an altarpiece. A classic example of religious patronage can be found in the paintings offered to the cathedral of Notre-Dame de Paris every May by the guild of goldsmiths, which were commissioned from La Hyre between 1635 and 1637, and from Sébastien Bourdon in 1643.

Solid citizens furnished a constant demand for portraits. With the rise of a commercial bourgeoisie, rich *arrivistes* loved to see themselves immortalised in oils, surrounded by the trappings of their trade or their loving families. This genre had been pioneered among the wealthy businessmen and ship-owners of the Netherlands. It was introduced to France by two artists of Flemish origin, Franz Pourbus of Antwerp, who moved to Paris in 1610, and above all Philippe de Champaigne, whose portrait of Louis XIII consecrating his realm to Our Lady made him for twenty years one of the most sought-after painters in Paris.

Bourgeois taste also extended to genre painting, to lively street scenes in the Italian or Flemish styles, picturesque or burlesque scenes, and even to military subjects, such as scenes of battles or of soldiers, all of which amused, astonished or bewildered them. Feminine tastes leaned towards floral compositions, to 'vanities' (moralised still-life paintings which spoke of the fragility and brevity of human life), and to subjects from chivalric romances, which were especially fashionable around the time of the Fronde.

In order to meet the huge variety of commissions, artists betook themselves to iconographical handbooks which explained the symbolic vocabulary of pagan and Christian allegory. The oldest example of this genre was the *Emblematum liber* of Andrea Alciato, but the most up-to-date and useful was Cesare Ripa's *Iconologia* (Rome, 1593), although this would later be superseded by the efforts of the Jesuit Claude Ménestrier (1631–1705). Such lore might today seem esoteric and a trifle affected, but the grammar and vocabulary of symbolism were everyday matters for the artists and indeed the educated public of the time.

The most prestigious commissions were those from the king and the court. The works undertaken by Marie de Medici in the Palais du Luxembourg called upon some of the outstanding talents of the day. It was Rubens himself who, between 1622 and 1625, decorated the first-floor gallery with twenty-one paintings depicting the life of the Queen Mother. Louis XIII's commissions for the Louvre, and those of Richelieu and Mazarin for their various residences, offered further work to artists. The comings and goings of artists all over Europe fostered a rapid circulation of styles and fashions. Thus the Parisian visits of Romano Romanelli, a decorative painter hired by Mazarin at various times between 1645 and 1655, introduced or rather encouraged the new classicising vein in French taste.

The artists who received these courtly commissions were themselves men of some social standing. Painters like Rubens and Van Dyck were the dinner guests of princes. Their workshops employed dozens of assistants, from close relatives, through temporary colleagues and journeymen, to apprentices and pupils. Larger commissions or cycles were parcelled out among the workshop's specialists, with one painting the draperies, another the landscapes and so on. It often happened that one particular work would prove highly popular, in which case the workshop would be flooded with demands for similar works, and would churn out copies or variants almost on a production line.

The day came when the fashionable artists of Paris grew tired of being classed with the ruck of jobbing painters who provided frescos for confraternity chapels or paintings for bourgeois hearths. Those who received royal warrants and commercial privileges soon found themselves involved in litigation with the Parisian company of master painters. In 1648 a group of fashionable painters, including Champaigne and the Le Nain brothers, founded the Académie de peinture (Academy of Painting), an association of gentlemen along Italian lines, in effect a claim to be pursuing 'liberal arts' rather than practising the 'mechanical arts' of the sworn guilds. Under the auspices of Chancellor Séguier, the Académie was based at the Louvre. But it did not attain its full status until 1663, when Le Brun secured the automatic admission of all painters who received a warrant from the king.

Other developments in the painter's trade arose from new methods of reproducing paintings. Tapestries, a traditional way of decorating walls with images, were based on cartoons which the weavers used as models. In order to ensure that tapestry copies were faithful reproductions, artists took to designing the cartoons themselves. Rubens and Jordaens took the trouble to do this. Moreover, tapestries were not the exclusive preserve of the very rich. Even merchants' houses would be decorated with the simple leaf or flower patterns of Bergamo or Brussels tapestries. Henri IV enticed Flemish tapestry weavers to France, establishing them first in the Faubourg Saint-Antoine and then in the Louvre itself, as well as in the Faubourg Saint-Marcel at the place known as Les Gobelins. In 1622 Louis XIII commissioned Rubens to produce original cartoons for a cycle on the life of the Emperor Constantine, and in 1627 he charged Simon Vouet with the task of designing cartoons for the royal workshops, and a number of other artists received similar commissions.

Engraving was another means of reproducing works of art, and of doing so in bulk for a large market. The sixteenth century had seen the arts of incising and of etching become widespread. Etching involved cutting the design into a layer of wax or varnish on a metal plate, which was then dipped in acid in order to deepen the lines. The ability to vary the depth of the cut or the strength of the acid allowed nuances of line and shade which could give an idea of the colours and tones of a painting. One editor of engravings, Hieronymus Cock of Antwerp, made a fortune in the later sixteenth century by publishing the works of the Flemish painters. Many artists, such as Rubens, Vouet, Van Dyck and Rembrandt, produced engravings of their own works in order to profit directly from this new commercial opportunity. Yet others, such as Jacques Callot (1592–1635) of Lorraine and Abraham Bosse (1602–76) of Paris, actually specialised in producing original engravings.

The diffusion of engravings increased the painter's repertoire, by making distant models available to all. For example, La Hyre and Champaigne never made the journey to Rome, but discovered the Italian masters by means of engravings. Above all, the emergence of a large market for pictorial images changed the nature of domestic decoration. Engravings of pious scenes or saints and portraits of the king could be bought from tradesmen at fairs or markets, and even the households of simple craftsmen and labourers could have one hanging above the bed or over the threshold.

Some Great Painters

For the first time in the history of painting, French artists gained a reputation that extended beyond the confines of the Parisian market and the frontiers of the realm. The young French artists who had grown up amid the Wars of Religion had, with the return of peace, set out southwards to discover the artistic riches of Italy. Simon Vouet (1590-1649) was perhaps the most typical figure of this generation. Like all French artists, he began by discovering in his youth the frescos of the château of Fontainebleau. Travelling to Venice and then Rome in 1613, he had been dazzled by the style of Caravaggio, had entirely assimilated it, and had forced himself upon the attention of cultured Roman society. In 1627 Louis XIII summoned him back to royal service in Paris. Vouet was the undisputed master of the age, and was commissioned to decorate a number of noble residences in Paris and châteaux in the Île-de-France. His workshop was crowded with journeymen and pupils.

In all his works he combined sumptuous colour with original and inventive composition, making the baroque style triumphant.

Georges de La Tour (1593–1652) was one of several artists who came from the little Duchy of Lorraine. He began his career at Lunéville under the patronage of Duke Charles IV. Displaced by the war, he came to Paris and received a royal warrant in 1639. His depictions of nocturnal scenes were influenced by the style of Caravaggio, with picaresque Roman figures looming amid strong contrasts. His combination of picturesque themes with simple forms has won him much appreciation today.

The works of Claude Vignon (1593–1670) and Jacques Blanchard (1600–38) are typical of the fashion for the picaresque.

Nicolas Poussin (1594–1665) followed the usual itinerary in his youth, but stopped at Rome and spent the rest of his life there, with only a brief return to Paris in 1641-2. Poussin was a scholarly and cultured artist, widely respected by Roman connoisseurs, and his allegorical and historical scenes baffle facile stylistic classification. His landscapes harmonise subtly with the mythological scenes for which they are the stage, inviting the viewer to meditate and dream.

Laurent de La Hyre (1606–56), a painter of compositions remarkable for their clever perspective and often striking colour, was a herald of the new wave of French taste which, towards 1650, renounced the affectations of mannerism and opted instead for simpler forms and colours.

Claude Gellée (1600–82), known as 'le Lorrain' (the Lorrainer), pursued his career at Rome, like Poussin, and did a lot of work for popes as well as for King Philip IV of Spain. The almost ethereal quality of his imaginary scenes of twilit ports made his works especially popular among English collectors of the eighteenth century and among their Romantic successors.

The three Le Nain brothers, Antoine and Louis (*ca.* 1600–48) and Mathieu (*ca.* 1600–77), came from Laon but soon moved to Paris. Of all their enormous output, which included portraits and religious scenes, posterity has bestowed the most esteem upon their realistic depictions of peasant life and of the little world of foundling children. It is worth noting that their country scenes present not unmitigated misery, as is often suggested, but the daily life of the arable-farming villages of their region, the area around Soissons.

Sébastien Bourdon (1616–71) was a Calvinist from Montpellier who also made the tour of Italy before establishing himself at Paris (1637). He also worked at Stockholm, whither he was summoned by Queen Christina in 1652, and in Languedoc. His best work is seen in portraits, street scenes and decorative paintings such as those in the Hôtel de Bretonvilliers in the Île Saint-Louis.

Philippe de Champagne (1602–74) came to Paris from Brussels, working in the Palais du Luxembourg from 1625, and then collaborating with Vouet in the Palais-Cardinal. In the 1640s he enjoyed an enormous reputation as a portrait painter. His religious tastes were of the school of Port-Royal, which one of his daughters entered in 1656, and he brought a new vein of classicism into devotional painting.

Charles Le Brun (1619–90) developed along similar lines, typifying the tastes of a new generation. In his early days at Rome he too was influenced by Caravaggio, and in the 1650s he made a name as a fashionable decorative artist, working at the Hôtel Lambert and the Château de Vaux (1658). The turning-point for both his fortunes and his taste came in 1660, when he produced in the king's presence a painting entitled *The Queens of Persia at the Feet of Alexander*. This eloquent and learned piece provoked discussion in and won admiration from the Académie, and became a model of classical style for succeeding generations of artists and connoisseurs.

Environment and Buildings

Each age lives in the environment and the surroundings bequeathed to it by its predecessors. The landscape is not composed of innovations and alterations, which arise only in a limited number of locations, tied to great power or wealth, but of the more or less glorious or mediocre remains of preceding ages. The cityscape of the seventeenth century, with its forms and balances, ought therefore to be called medieval, although even this label is somewhat misleading, dependent as it is upon the conventions of a stylistic vocabulary defined in the nineteenth century. In fact this complex of appearances and constraints was simply the product of the development of cities during the fifteenth and sixteenth centuries. We should never read history backwards. And although this is a counsel of perfection, given that we cannot actually watch the past in the process of unfolding, it is only by striving for the proper perspective that we can measure, weigh and evaluate the accumulation of minute changes in the everyday environment and way of life.

The majority of peasant dwellings consisted of a single room with a single chimney and a single window, furnished with a large bed, a chest and a table. There might also be outbuildings – barns, stables, chicken coops and runs – but the whole family would eat and sleep in the one room. Among wealthier labourers and on lands farmed by an extended family, there might be larger buildings, solid houses capable of being defended against attack, and proudly bearing the family name. But even at this level the norm of one room for each nuclear family still prevailed, together with the almost complete absence of furniture. The parents slept in the bed, behind a screen or curtain, the children had mattresses on the floor, and the servants slept in the barn.

Towns and cities, which are rather better known thanks to the old pictures often found in modern guidebooks, retained their 'medieval' appearance. Protective walls were still maintained for security reasons. Not only towns, but even quite small villages were densely built-up within their surrounding ramparts. A small number of gates opened onto the suburbs, which fanned out along the roads leading from the towns. The streets were narrow and winding, following the contours, and the squares were few, irregularly shaped and lacking design. The houses were on restricted sites, which they often overflowed with stalls and overhanging upper floors. Larger houses and religious institutions might have courtyard gardens, but you had to be up the bell-tower to see these between the roofs.

The urban environment would have its outstanding features, a few well-built houses for tradesmen who owned workshops. But crowding and discomfort were the rule. Wood was the chief construction material, evident in timber or half-timber frames, wooden laths and panels, overhangs, galleries and stairs. Cut stone was used only in doorsteps or window frames, with rubble used in the structural walls, and mud or plaster in dividing walls. The few openings were enclosed in cut stone arches with wooden shutters, now that people wanted windows which could let in a little light. There were more rooms, with a large entrance hall, which housed the servants, and then, at least among people of some standing, a variety of more or less spacious chambers and antechambers in which the lady of the house might receive her fashionable guests and visitors. Dense building with shoddy materials was a recipe for frequent fires, which often destroyed entire streets and quarters before they could be brought under control. Entire villages could be destroyed by fire in a single night, leaving the villagers destitute: such folk were known as *quêteurs de brûlé*, or 'burnt beggars'. There were, among many others, famous fires at Montauban in 1614 and 1643, Nérac in 1611 and Bolbec in 1656.

More grandiose residences also reflected the influence of the past. The châteaux of the nobility were still fortified dwellings. With the advent of domestic peace and a new sense of security, the ancient fortified look became softened, by pulling down a surrounding wall, and building on a 'U' plan, with an open courtyard flanked by the old defensive towers, and new windows in the walls to let in more sun.

In accordance with the proposals of the Assemblies of Notables between 1596 and 1626, many fortifications were dismantled, especially in the 1620s. Strong castles were lowered or even flattened, and civic ramparts were knocked down. But important as these efforts were (and a single province might contain hundreds of demolition sites), they nevertheless left in place the vast majority of the kingdom's many thousand fortifications. A further campaign of destruction would be waged against civic defences in the second half of the century.

Even churches had often been fortified during the Wars of Religion, at least in rural areas; and many of them had been destroyed or damaged. The early seventeenth century saw an intensive programme of church reconstruction, even in the smallest villages. Village masons built in the traditional fashion, with Gothic vaults and windows, and what were called 'Roman' porches and walls. Even in the great cities, traditional styles prevailed for the reconstruction or completion of older buildings. The cathedral of Orleans, largely rebuilt between 1611 and 1636, was roofed with ogival vaults, and the great parish church of Saint-Eustache near Les Halles in Paris, begun in 1623, was covered in 1650 with a lofty ribbed vault.

Like all mechanical arts, those of the architect and the master mason were organised as sworn guilds. Just as apothecaries distinguished themselves from grocers, and surgeons from barbers, so too architects, designers with a fund of bookish learning, sought from the sixteenth century to distinguish themselves from run-of-the-mill masons, mere practitioners. There were about one hundred and fifty master masons in Paris, but by no means all of them would have thought of themselves as architects, as the lines of demarcation were unclear. They had learned their trade not only from their fathers or as apprentices, but also thanks to the publication of architectural treatises. The works of Italian theoreticians of the sixteenth century, such as Serlio, Vignola and Palladio, circulated in translations or adaptations. And the booksellers also offered handbooks of models such as Pierre Le Muet's *La manière de bien bâtir pour toutes sortes de personnes* (1623), or the collections of doorways, ceilings, chimneys and so on published from 1647 by the engraver Jean Marot.

Some New Buildings

The new generation wished to open up the medieval built environment, and introduce light, space, perspective and something of the monumental. Henri IV personally fostered several projects for his capital. In 1598 he set about completing the Pont-Neuf, the first bridge entirely free from houses, and equipped with an imposing pump surmounted by a statue of the Samaritan woman at the well. In the developing quarter of the Marais he laid out the Place Royale (today's Place des Vosges) in front of the old Tournelles. This took from 1605 until 1612, while from 1607 to 1615 he laid out the Place Dauphine in front of the Palais de Justice on the Île de la Cité. The Place Royale, undoubtedly designed by the architect Louis Métezeau (1559–1615), was surrounded by individual houses built to a single design which embodied all that was dear to French taste at that time: steep, pitched roofs tiled in slate and interrupted by stone dormer windows, and brick and stone courses on the façades. Another square, almost identical and also designed by Métezeau, was built between 1606 and 1627 for Charles de Gonzague (Governor of Champagne, and a major land-owner in the Mézières region) on the border with the bishopric of Liège, in a little sovereign territory henceforth known as Char-leville. The duke's square was completed by Clément Métezeau (1581–1652), a younger brother of Louis, and famous chiefly for having constructed the great earthwork during the siege of La Rochelle to cut off the harbour from the sea.

Other examples of conscious urbanisation can be found in Sully's creation of a new town at Henrichemont in Berry (1608), or in the city of Richelieu founded by the cardinal minister in 1631. These two artificial foundations soon foundered. Richelieu had entrusted the task of creating the new town and a château to the architect Lemercier (1585–1654), who collaborated on the sites with Salomon de Brosse. The château, of which little now remains, was then the largest in France. It comprised a great courtyard sur-rounded on three sides by buildings, and on the fourth by a huge monumental entrance. It might have served as model for the château at Versailles.

In Paris, building fever was at its height. Stone was a highly profitable commodity. The level of rents tripled between 1600 and 1650. New quarters rose up: the Île Saint-Louis was parcelled out in 1614, and was built up from 1627; the quarter of Saint-Sulpice was an extension of the settlement surrounding the abbey of Saint-Germain-des-Prés; and the quarter of Palais-Royal arose between the Louvre and the north-western walls. It has been said that 2,000 separate *hôtels* were built during this boom. The figure is doubt-less exaggerated, but reflects the distinctive status of Paris accurately enough. The contrast with the problems of the peas-antry provides ample confirmation that the resources of the kingdom were being diverted to the capital. The *hôtels*, or noble town houses, were mostly organised around an entrance court. The main body of the residence contained halls and monumental staircases which led up to great chambers with decorated ceilings, while the domestic offices were relegated to the wings.

The provinces did not affect the same fashions, and thanks to local architects the buildings might follow either traditional models, as in the town hall of La Rochelle (renovated in 1606), or more Italianate models, as in the town halls of Lyon (begun in 1645) or Salon-de-Provence (1655). The greatest provincial public building was the Parlement at Rennes, designed by Salomon de Brosse in 1618. Many town councils were still based in medieval fortified houses, with a great hall and public weighing scales added on the ground floor, and a city clock aloft as the only concession to modernity. The law courts, with poky courtrooms above dirty and overcrowded prisons, fared scarcely better. There would be no great change for many decades.

The magnificence of the palazzi of Italy was surpassed early in the century in the construction of the Palais du Luxembourg (1614–26), which Marie de Medici modelled on the Palazzo Pitti of Florence. Few examples now survive of perhaps the most productive architect of the time, François Mansart (1598–1666): the Château de Balleroy in Lower Normandy (1631), the improvements to the Château de Blois carried out for the Duke of Orleans (1635–8), and the Château de Maisons (Maisons-Lafite), built between 1642 and 1651 for the President de Longueil.

Church building timidly and laggardly followed Roman models. The now disappeared church of the Feuillants (1601) was the first church in Paris to embody the prescription of the Council of Trent for a single nave without aisles. It was based on the Jesuit church of the Gesù (1568–75), designed by Vignola. The influence of the simple and functional Roman style owed much to Father Martellange (1569–1641), the architect-in-chief of the Society of Jesus. The church of the professed house of Paris, Saint-Louis, completed between 1627 and 1641, had the capital's first great dome. Other domes soon followed, on the chapel of the Sorbonne (1635–42) and the church of Val-de-Grâce (1645–62).

The changes to the French built environment during this period were distributed very unevenly. They were massively obvious in Paris, where new buildings reflected an increasingly original French taste which no longer simply followed southern models from afar. But the provinces remained predominantly Gothic or Italianate in their architectural proclivities. However, the impression of unevenness may have been distorted by the greater attention that has been accorded to the buildings of the capital. The châteaux of the Duke of Lesdiguières (Governor of the Dauphiné) at Vizille, of the Duke of Épernon (Governor of Guyenne) at Cadillac, of the Prince of Condé at Chantilly and Montrond, as well as the residences of members of the Parlements in Aix, Toulouse, Bordeaux, Rennes, Rouen, Dijon and Grenoble show even today that many provincial cities were autonomous and vibrant cultural centres.

The Music Trade

In the rustic dances and youthful festivals that took place each year in May and June, shawms (ancestors of the modern oboe) and bagpipes entertained the villagers. But little is known of the traditional tunes and songs, which were often embellished with snatches of more courtly fashions derived from the passage of some nobleman's entourage or a royal visit to a province.

> It is a curious and wonderful thing to see how rich is the region of Limousin, in particular the Basse-Marche area, in shawm-players and pipers, and in dances. There is scarcely a well-off household or a village without someone who can play. Although they may be peasants or labourers who have no formal knowledge of music, indeed who can neither read nor write, they nevertheless play all sorts of styles, new as well as old.
> (excerpt from the journal of Pierre Robert, Lieutenant-General of Le Dorat, 1630)

Each province and region had its local dances in a distinctive style, as well as rustic musicians, trumpeters, pipers and flautists who, perched on barrels, ribbons in their hats, backed by fifes and drums, accompanied the rejoicings of the summer months.

In towns, municipal festivals likewise filled the streets with trumpets, fifes and hunting-horns, the instruments which traditionally belonged to the civic treasury. A young townsman could hire a string-band to perform an *aubade* for his beloved. The characteristics of the violin were largely fixed by the end of the sixteenth century, and it was highly favoured by musicians of all provinces. It was reckoned the most appropriate instrument for dance music, and was henceforth to be found alongside the shawms in open-air festivals. Lutes, spinets and harpsichords were too expensive, and guitars too foreign, so were not much in evidence. Such instruments, which might be seen in bands at fashionable events, were the prerogative of a refined élite, notably at Paris towards 1640, and at the royal court.

The musician's trade was regulated in Paris, and in some other major cities, by a sworn guild of instrumentalists. The royal musicians attached to the Chapel, the Chamber or the Stables managed to have their privileges recognised by the guild in 1658. They thus detached themselves definitively from the ruck of small-timers who had to tout for clients and patrons. The celebrated musical dynasty of the Couperins was descended from a labouring family in a village of Brie. The talents of the three brothers were spotted when they performed an *aubade* during a summer festival at a château in the Île-de-France around 1650. Louis Couperin was the first of them to make his name in Paris, obtaining the post of organist at Saint-Gervais in 1653.

Many musicians were itinerant. There was a cant term, *vicarier* (going from house to house, as we might say in England 'knocking'), for travelling the kingdom in search of work. The humblest musicians played to attract custom to the market-stalls of pedlars. The more fortunate gave music or dancing lessons in well-off households. The church offered many opportunities for choristers, cantors, organists and choirmasters. A musician had to turn his hand to many things: arranging compositions for choirs of nuns, training children in plain-chant, and composing anything from motets and Christmas carols to settings of Tenebrae for rich benefactors, be they cathedral chapters, bishops or great noblemen.

Not only cathedrals but even collegiate or wealthy parish churches worked hard to keep up a choral tradition or to construct a fine organ. The installation and maintenance of organs was a major financial commitment and an opportunity for patronage. Some local notable or a civic corporation might organise a subscription to purchase an organ for their parish. Even smaller towns, such as Rodez in the south-west, or Salon in Provence, would often pride themselves on their reputation for church music. An organ was commissioned from the organ-builder of Rodez Cathedral for the celebration of Louis XIV's marriage in the church of Saint-Jean-de-Luz. He built it in little more than a year, at a cost of only 1,800 *livres*. This was a real stroke of luck for the little Basque town. The expense of building and decorating temporary structures for royal pageants in a Parisian parish, such as Saint-Étienne-du-Mont or Saint-Louis-des-Jésuites, could be ten times as much.

As in painting and architecture, so too in music, innovation came from Italy. The Counter-Reformation Church had called forth new genres and encouraged compositions for liturgical purposes: oratorio (religious opera performed in churches), countless motets (usually settings of texts from the Psalms) and church sonatas. Developments in secular music came above all from Venice. Here, the most original new genre was opera, musical drama. It was born at Venice and Florence in the 1590s, derived yet distinct from the *intermezzi* performed during intervals, which were akin to other kinds of contemporary court spectacle such as the English masque or the French ballet. Perhaps the first true opera was Monteverdi's *Orfeo*, staged before Vincenzo Gonzaga, Duke of Mantua, at Mardi Gras in 1607. Mazarin, an ambassador of Italian culture in France, paid huge sums to bring troops of Italian singers, actors and stage-hands to Paris. Parisians were greatly impressed by Luigi Rossi's *Orfeo*, which was performed in the Salle du Petit-Bourbon in 1647. It lasted six hours and was sumptuously staged with magnificent special effects. But it would be several decades before the new genre accommodated itself successfully to French conventions and taste.

In music, as in the other arts, there was a gulf between the fashions of Paris and the customs of the provinces. Only in Paris could one find learned music, an instrument-making trade, a large and wealthy public, regular theatrical performances, and the potential for major patronage. If the southern provinces of Provence and Languedoc were sometimes exposed to new fashions and talents from across the Alps before Paris, the bulk of central and western France remained locked in its rustic musical traditions.

15 Material Life

There can be no economic vitality, no production, no invention and no mercantile fortunes without networks of trade and transport. Yet knowledge of the vast spaces of France was still rather vague. The discovery of the extent of the provinces and the exploration of their potential for trade or travel can be seen in the first printed route guides and travel narratives. The first guide to France was Charles Estienne's *Grande guide des chemins de France*, which appeared in 1552. It was followed in 1591 by Mayerne-Turquet's *Description de France*, which included an appendix detailing routes and posts. Louis Coulon's *Ulysse français* appeared in 1643, and there were half a dozen more such publications in the seventeenth century. It was as yet neither easy nor pleasant to tread the rough and endless roads of the more isolated provinces.

Routes, Fairs, Ports and Waterways

The vast bulk of France, landlocked and often mountainous, was not obviously well endowed with communications, although even the most insignificant waterways were busy, when the weather permitted, with boats, rafts and all kinds of river traffic. The Seine, the Loire, the Garonne, the Saône and the Rhône carried passenger traffic and barges loaded with heavy goods such as timber, iron and coal. Their banks were dotted with villages in retreat from flood zones and with landing-stages on sites and routes of which not a trace survives today. The sea coasts were likewise strewn with hundreds of tiny ports devoted to fishing and coastal trade. Most of them were little more than beaches sheltered from storms. Only a few ports boasted stone quays or wooden pontoons. The vast majority of boats never exceeded 20 or 30 tonnes capacity, though this did not deter their sailors from daring the ocean in their trips from port to port, or even as far afield as England and Spain. In fact, most of the major maritime trade of the French ports – the trade in wine and grain with the countries of northern Europe – was carried in English and Dutch vessels (Dutch ships could be between 200 and 300 tonnes) which came south by the hundred in the early months of the year in order to buy the new wine. With ships of 50–100 tonnes, French fishermen could range as far as the Newfoundland banks in search of cod. The most important fishing ports, with fleets of at least fifty ships each, were Les Sables-d'Olonne, Saint-Malo and Le Havre. The skippers made two trips to Newfoundland each year, bringing back green cod, either salted or dried on the American shore, for sale in Portugal, Spain and the ports of the Mediterranean. The Basque fishermen would go after whales in the cold seas of the north. Other popular catches were sardines, taken by almost all the Atlantic ports, tuna around Brittany and herring in the North Sea. Salted or smoked fish, which kept well and could be easily transported, played an essential role in feeding the towns. Amid the fragility of a largely agrarian economy, coastal regions enjoyed a relatively privileged position, with lower prices and less risk of dearth.

During the ministry of Sully, who from 1599 bore the title of Grand Voyer (the official responsible for roads and bridges) of France, there was an attempt to develop the routes of France. But it was shortlived, and under Louis XIII the tax revenues of bridges and toll-roads were generally diverted to financing the war effort. The costs of maintaining roads otherwise fell entirely upon the towns, with the result that most roads were only paved on the approaches to towns. Routes therefore varied. In winter it was worth taking the longer way round to stay on high ground, but in summer it was easier to take the shorter routes in the valleys. A map of roads showing the posts which provided teams of fresh horses was drawn up by Samson d'Abboville in 1632. It is confined almost wholly to routes radiating from Paris. The two exceptions are the routes from Lyon to Clermont, and from Nîmes to Toulouse. From Paris, roads left direct for Amiens, Brussels and Nancy. The road for Dijon opened the way to the Saône valley, the road to Moulins led to that of the Allier, and that to Orleans opened the way to the Loire. There were few routes to the west. Normandy was reached by way of the Seine, and Brittany by way of the Loire, while the south-west was reached by the great road from Blois to Poitiers and then Bordeaux. The carriage of heavy goods by road was therefore very restricted. Heavy four-wheeled carts with a pivoting front axle, capable of carrying about fifteen hundredweight, could hardly do better than 20 or 30 kilometres in a day, and might spend weeks on the road in a long journey. This placed serious restrictions not only upon commercial traffic but also upon troop movements, whose strategic capabilities were therefore much reduced. Postmasters, equipped invariably with stables and usually also with an inn and a forge, were established along the king's highways. Protected by royal edicts, and well placed for profitable trading, the postmasters were often substantial figures in their area. It was possible to entrust letter to the royal messengers who regularly travelled between the principal towns and cities, but those who could afford it (such as city councils, wealthy merchants and great lords) usually employed their own couriers and messengers. The speed of circulation of information was quite simply the speed of a man on horseback. The news of Henri IV's death, which occurred in the afternoon of 14 May 1610, reached La Rochelle on 17 May, and Pau late on 19 May.

Merchants and pedlars, with their heavily laden mules, crowded the great fairs, such as those of Paris of course, at Saint-Germain-des-Prés and Lendit (Saint-Denis), but also those of Caen and Guibray (near Falaise) in the west, Amiens in the north, and Niort and Fontenay in Poitou. The four great free fairs of Bordeaux attracted hundreds of ships to the port, and the four great fairs of Lyon, each lasting a fortnight, attracted traders from Germany and Italy. The fairs of Beaucaire were the most famous of the south-east, and each year the shores of the Rhône there were lined with hundreds of tents and booths at the end of July.

Moreover, every little town had its own market, so there were thousands of places across the kingdom where peasants of the surrounding area could come to sell their vegetables, herbs, poultry and dairy goods to the townsfolk. And they would often find there pedlars of hardware and haberdashery from whom they could purchase knick-knacks or tools before finishing their day out in the local taverns.

Certain fairs and local markets specialised in livestock trading. Stock-raising for commercial purposes was undertaken mostly with a view to supplying either towns or troops. There were stock-traders and master butchers in the towns of central and western France, of Normandy, Limousin and the Auvergne, who combined to send flocks of animals on the hoof to the Paris market or to the royal armies in the east. There were fairs throughout the country specialising in horses, which were the main means of ordinary transport as well as valuable draught animals and beasts of burden. It was said that France did not have enough good horses of its own, and had to import them at great cost from Germany. The Boulogne region, Perche, Limousin and some areas of the Auvergne and the Pyrenees already enjoyed an enviable reputation for breeding and selecting horses. We have little idea what these animals looked like, though they were probably short and squat, a far cry from the image of regional breeds that we know today, whose characteristics were in fact fixed only in the last century. Even so, the value of horses was enough to sustain an illicit trade in animals stolen from meadows, disguised and resold far away. This may well have been the first form of organised crime in France.

From towards the end of our period we have the valuable evidence of the merchant of Nantes, Jean Éon, whose *Le commerce honorable* (1646) describes the conditions and the constraints of the movement of trade across the realm. The greatest quantities of both goods and money were found in the textile trades, above all in the linens of western France, with the wine trade coming a distant second. Towards 1650 England emerged from its civil war, and the United Provinces ended their protracted conflict with Spain. These two maritime powers, whose rivalry sparked off three wars in twenty years, immediately increased their activities along the American trade routes, especially in the West Indies, islands which, still uninhabited around 1630, were now beginning to reveal their potential for tropical agriculture. Richelieu, who was a native of Poitou, and subsequently Fouquet, who had commercial interests in Brittany (at Concarneau, Yeu and Belle-Île), can be credited with having appreciated the significance of these new regions. But the first fruits were harvested only under the personal rule of Louis XIV, and French ports only began seriously looking towards the West Indies in the 1680s.

Under these conditions, the economic life of the age was largely a matter of a national self-sufficiency based on grain crops, with each area producing roughly what it consumed, untouched by the movements of trade and sometimes even by the circulation of money.

Agriculture and Peasants

The vast majority of the French peasantry had long been tenant farmers who succeeded their fathers in the occupation of lands which they looked on as their own and over which they indeed exercised almost all the rights of ownership. The framework of lordship which governed the countryside was very uneven in its distribution but was little disputed. Lordship was of little importance in the Midi, although in other regions – for example, the Breton interior, Burgundy, Berry and the Auvergne – it had a regulatory role and sometimes weighed heavily upon peasant incomes.

The regulatory role of lordship consisted in the right to dispense justice. There were tens of thousands of lords (*seigneurs*) who took cognisance of agrarian disputes and exercised much the same powers as those that would later be carried out by justices of the peace. Wealthier plaintiffs or defendants might well prefer the greater reliability and efficiency of the king's courts, but peasants still flocked willingly to seigniorial tribunals.

Most of those who worked land held it from a lord and therefore paid him a *cens* (rent in cash or kind), usually trivial enough. But

the lord's rights to levy fees on both buyer and seller in land transactions were more significant, and could amount to a twelfth of
the price. Seigniorial rights were little discussed because they were
generally a part of immemorial tradition and seemed a fair price
for the very real services rendered by the gentleman who was the
local lord. In the early decades of the seventeenth century there
was still considerable value in being able to bring one's family,
cattle and possessions inside the château for protection in times of
danger. The peasant therefore belonged to the clientage of his
lord, who provided him in exchange with protection, sometimes
military protection, perhaps against the billeting of soldiers, and
also with social and institutional support in litigation or in the ups
and downs of daily life.

To judge by the quantity of litigation, two seigniorial rights were
contested. First were the *banalités*, which, where they existed,
obliged peasants to perform burdensome labour services at their
lord's communal mill or oven. It was not uncommon for entire
rural communities to plead in a body against their lord over such
matters. The other fiercely contested area involved hunting rights,
by which peasants saw themselves denied the chance of trapping
game on their own lands. As the bearing of arms was still widespread, peasants continued to hunt almost without restriction
throughout the first half of the seventeenth century.

An average landholding covered between 10 and 30 hectares.
However, like all averages, this can be misleading. As at all times,
so too in the seventeenth century it is important to distinguish
land tenure from land use. Granting that the peasantry owned
around half of the land, we must note that the proportion varied
with the location. They owned less around towns, because of
creeping expropriation by townsfolk, and rather more on poorer
soils or in isolated areas, and above all in the mountains. A peasant's landholding might include lands he owned outright, lands
held from his lord and subject to the *cens*, and lands he held as a
cash tenant or by a sharecropping contract. In the Île-de-France
there were large farms of 100 or 200 hectares, with half a dozen
horses in the stables and dozens of men working in the fields. On
the other hand, in the so-called *bocage* regions (thinly populated
areas where land was fenced in by hedges), there were many hold-

ings of less than 10 hectares, barely enough to support a family. Even further down the social scale came the farmhands and day-labourers who had nothing but a wretched hovel to their names and subsisted on seasonal labour. There were some well-trodden migration routes, of folk from Brittany and Le Mans to labour in the Île-de-France, of masons from Limousin and Marche to work in Paris, and of highlanders from the Alps in search of casual employment in the capital as sweeps, bricklayers or tinkers. From Poitou and Normandy a few hundred people headed for the New World. The largest migration was from the Auvergne, Limousin and the Pyrenees into the great towns of Spain, where there was plenty of work with good pay. Tens of thousands of French crafts-men found work in Barcelona, Madrid or Zaragoza. They would stay five years or so, and then head home with a money-belt full of silver. This human traffic stayed constant despite the wars between the two countries.

It is reckoned that a fifth of the country was still forest. Irrespec-tive of ownership, these areas offered rich pickings to those who lived nearby, in the form of fruit-picking, hunting or poaching, as well as *affouage*, the gathering of sticks for firewood. There were very few enclosed forests, and they were exploited for the most part on a communal basis, not without conflict and litigation. Wastelands, heaths and marshes offered other resources, which might seem trivial today, such as the gathering of reeds and osier, the digging of peat and clay, fishing, bee-keeping, duck-hunting, and so on. But their importance for countryfolk of the time can be seen in the opposition manifested to marsh-drainage projects, which were encouraged by Sully and later Richelieu.

Corn was, always and everywhere, the predominant crop. Even on poor soil the peasants stubbornly cultivated grain. In the dry and sun-baked south, land was left fallow every other year, in what is called two-yearly rotation. On the richer and damper soils of the northern provinces, a year of spring cereals (barley or oats) was introduced between the year of winter corn and the fallow year. Thus the land available for grazing sheep consisted of the fallow fields together with those awaiting a spring sowing after the har-vest of winter corn in July. In the villages of the great northern plains which practised this three-yearly rotation, the land was divided into three parts, and farmers co-operated in organising a crop rotation which left a third of it completely free for common grazing. Customary law devoted a great deal of attention to ensuring that a proper balance was maintained between the interests of common grazing and the protection of the crops in the fields.

Crop yields are measured in terms of quantities harvested over quantities sown. Thus a yield of about four or five to one means that for every 150 litres of grain sown per hectare, something between 400 and 800 litres would be harvested nine or ten months later. Allowing for the yield of gleaning and the use of animal fertiliser, a yield of between 1,500 and 2,000 kilograms per hectare might be expected. But this would apply only in the best years and on the best soils. Bad weather and crop disease could reduce these figures considerably.

The fear of dearth or of reaching the spring months with nothing left to sow led to every available patch of soil being sown with grain. Rather than sowing pure wheat, people sowed a mixture or *méteil* of wheat and rye, and perhaps buckwheat, in order to reduce the risk of a bad harvest. A portion of the harvest was set aside for sowing the following year, so that a given piece of land always produced the same kind of grain, and one could tell from its appearance precisely where any given sack of corn had come from.

Hillsides which were open to the sun and not too far from towns were given over to vines, so the Seine valley, for example, had plenty of wine-producing villages. In an effort to free more land for grain and to improve the quality of the wine sold in Paris, the Parlement de Paris issued a decree in 1577 forbidding Parisian innkeepers to buy wine from less than 20 leagues (about 80 km) away. This measure was good for the sales of wine from the regions of Auxerre (Chablis), Orleans, Champagne and even Beaujolais (Brouilly), from which last area the wine came along the Loire, a journey that was improved in 1642 by the opening of the Briare canal, which facilitated access to Paris. But while there was a marked increase in wine consumption among the humbler townsfolk, and the growth in the number of taverns to be found beside main roads, in suburbs and around market squares was alarming to respectable folk, the wine-growers' profits remained modest. In the absence of any means of guaranteeing ageing and transport, the differentials of price and reputation between the wines of different regions remained vague. The only significant changes were in the production of the spirits sold to the maritime nations of the north. The medieval privileges of Bordeaux prevented wines from the highlands coming to the market before the those of the Bordeaux region itself had been sold. Dutch merchants who purchased the inferior upland wines had the idea of improving them, and the art of distilling was introduced in the Cognac and Armagnac regions in the 1620s. In Languedoc, where vines had hitherto been confined to patches of land on stony hillsides, distilling was introduced in the 1660s.

Little gardens beside the cottages were devoted to growing vegetables, cabbages, coleseed, salad stuffs, and even hemp and flax. This labour-intensive but small-scale agriculture was entrusted to the women. All the effort came to down to them: sowing, tending, harvesting, preparing, carding, spinning and weaving the textile crops in order to produce clothes for the whole family on the basis of domestic self-sufficiency. The peasants who lived near the great textile centres (such as Amiens, Beauvais, Vitré, Alençon and Le Mans) sometimes did weaving for the cloth trade. A merchant from town would put out work among the countryfolk, and in the winter months the women's manual labour played an important part in balancing the family budget.

There was little scope for innovation. Maize, which the Spaniards had brought back from Mexico, had reached the Basque country by about 1600, and spread throughout the Aquitaine basin between the 1620s and the 1650s. Maize was a vigorous and productive crop which offered useful insurance against grain shortages. However, maize flour and cakes were not highly regarded, and the plant was unable to flourish north of Saintonge.

Sweet chestnuts were ground into flour, and were baked to produce *pain d'arbre* (or 'tree-bread'). They thus provided a nutritious dietary supplement in areas such as Limousin and the Auvergne where corn was hard to grow, and were even cultivated systematically. As a result, large areas of the Massif Central, a consistent exporter of surplus population of Paris or Spain, nevertheless succeeded in maintaining a high levels of population in poor places which would later be deserted during the nineteenth-century flight from the countryside.

However, agricultural innovations with a great future were already appearing even under Louis XIII in the hinterland of Paris, stimulated by the enormous market which the capital constituted. These included the introduction of fodder crops (clover, sainfoin and lucerne) into the three-year rotation, which enriched the soil and provided better grazing. There were other fertile innovations elsewhere. The Vivarais saw the spread of mulberry trees for the encouragement of silkworms and thus the production of silk, while there was a more intensive plantation of olive groves for the production of oil. But such changes were sporadic and often unremarked. It has taken the patient research of many historians among notarial archives, terriers and account-books to uncover and chart their gradual progress.

Crafts, Trades, and Industry

The practice of a trade began early, because in an age when life expectancy was short, a son might have to succeed to his father very soon, and also because the craft guilds were for the most part strictly regulated. Take, for example, the case of the son of a master carpenter in a wealthy town with several sworn trade guilds. During his adolescence he would be sent by his father to serve an apprenticeship to another master carpenter. There would be a notarised contract stipulating the respective obligations of master and apprentice. The apprentice received food and lodging in his master's family in lieu of wages, and was initiated into all the skills and secrets of the carpenter's trade. After an apprenticeship of between three and eight years (depending upon the nature of the trade), an apprentice would become a journeyman, that is, a paid employee of the master. In many trades it was common for a journeyman to move from one master to another, even travelling around the country to do so, in order to widen his experience and gain acquaintance with the latest developments. Such practices are difficult to date, but seem to have been in place at the start of the seventeenth century.

The journeymen of certain trades combined for purposes of self-help in discreet or even secret associations. These associations offered a welcome to travelling journeymen, and protected salaries and employment by means of strikes and boycotts. Bloody affrays could break out between rival associations, as in the case of the joiners, who were divided into the *gavots* and the *devoirants*. Such disorders were frowned upon, and in 1655, after appeals by religious authorities, the Parlement de Paris issued a decree banning such associations of journeymen. But such measures were largely unenforceable, and the associations retained their independence chiefly thanks to their secrecy.

Most craftsmen remained journeymen all their lives. The better-off among them, usually themselves the sons of masters, could produce a 'masterpiece' as defined by the guild regulations, purchase letters of mastery and thus ascend to the rank of master of their craft. They then belonged to a sworn association which was recognised by the civic authorities and perhaps also by royal warrant, and might be known as a *jurande*, *métier* (or craft), *serment* (oath) or *guilde* (guild). The association's statutes or regulations were registered with the town council and laid down how the trade should be conducted. The association exercised a monopoly on the practice of the trade within the town, limited the number of masters (in the interests of those already established), and fixed standards of work (in the interests of the consumer). The power of policing the trade, and the right of representing its interests, were entrusted to an elected official known as a warden, *jurat*, *syndic* or *prud'homme* (councillor). The guild performed works of piety, charity and mutual assistance through a devotional confraternity dedicated to the patron saint of their profession.

There were more than a hundred trade guilds in Paris, but the most important were six that had existed since the fifteenth century: the drapers (who were the richest), the grocers, the mercers (easily the biggest guild, with over 2,000 members), the skinners (who numbered about five hundred), the hatters and the goldsmiths (the most specialised). These six guilds took the places of honour in civic ceremonies and exercised very real powers in economic regulation.

The rigid structures of the guilds impeded competition, protected families already established in the trade, and slowed the pace of innovation. But many highly specialised or unimportant trades escaped guild control. Moreover, the regulations, which varied from place to place, could only be enforced adequately in the major cities. Workers in the black economy, who worked at home (hence the name *chambreland*), ignored the regulations. Above all, certain towns, some entire provinces (such as Béarn), and all villages and hamlets were without a guild system. The vast majority of craftsmen established outside guild cities had no interest in protectionism or guild regulations.

The textile industry, which was established in almost all towns and villages, employed the most workers, and produced the most goods, had long been far the most important industry. The major cloth-producing cities had since the Middle Ages been concentrated in north-eastern France, above all in Picardy (which contained Amiens and Beauvais). However, sheep-raising and the cultivation of linen and hemp were both widespread and relatively easy, which meant that cloth production could be carried on almost anywhere. There were thousands of textile workers in Normandy and Champagne, as well as in Languedoc (especially at Montpellier and Carcassonne). Lace was produced at Troyes, Angers, Puy-en-Velay, and above all at Alençon and in the villages of the surrounding region of Perche. Linen cloth was woven in Maine and Brittany, for use not only in clothing but also in sails for ships.

The iron industry was also widespread, as it needed only a little outcrop of iron ore and a nearby forest to provide all that was needed to set up ironworks. The industry could be found in Brittany, Périgord, Angoumois, the Pays de Foix (the valley of the Ariège) and the Ardennes (the valley of the Meuse). As a result, clusters of small workshops of nailers, cutlers, braziers, iron-mongers, blacksmiths and armourers could give a reputation for technical excellence to areas that have since lost all trace of a metal-working tradition.

Large concentrations of labour, perhaps dozens or even hundreds of men, were to be found in cannon foundries, shipyards and certain factories producing rare goods such as rope, tapestry and glass. But there were no establishments in France to rival the arsenal of Venice or its Dutch equivalent, the Zaandam.

The Monetary Situation

The modest scale and wide diffusion of economic enterprises, and their close dependence on local resources, give some idea of the limitations of the money supply in the France of Louis XIII. The early seventeenth century was a period of recession and deflation throughout Europe. Precious metals had been flooding into Europe from the New World since the 1560s at a rate of about 300 tonnes a year. The balance of trade, together with migrant labour from the Auvergne, had brought American silver into France, and the coins minted along the Atlantic coast show how important this import was. But in the early seventeenth century this strong inflationary trend halted. An unfortunate edict of December 1614 had overvalued gold against silver, which led to the rapid flight of Spanish *pistoles* ('pieces of eight', i.e. worth eight *reals*) to foreign countries where they could buy more gold. Then in 1618 war broke out in Germany, and there was an immediate and lasting collapse in trade with this region, noticeable even in Venice, which functioned as Germany's Mediterranean port. Finally, the war between Spain and the Netherlands resumed in 1621. Spain's transatlantic convoys proved unable to maintain the flow of American silver at its hitherto remarkable levels. Even though imports of Mexican silver recovered in the 1660s, the economic impact was catastrophic in the meantime. France, which had never managed to lay its hands on more than a modest share of this bullion, found itself in a real cash shortage around 1630, at the very moment when the State was striving through increased taxes to raise more revenue than ever before.

We should recall at this point that specie, actual coins, did not have a stable value. Their value was fixed by edict in terms of a currency of account (the *livre*, divided into 20 *sous*, with each *sou* divided into 12 *deniers*).

Monetary stagnation aggravated the effects of economic autarky. The rare silver coins in circulation, French *écus* or Spanish *pistoles*, were kept under the carpet, or appeared only in clipped or debased forms. Good coin of true weight was therefore overvalued and hoarded, while carefully clipped coin filled the pockets of those, such as peasants, who were in no position to refuse it.

This monetary dislocation was partly resolved by a programme of reform embodied in two edicts, of March 1640 and September 1641. With the aid of technical innovations, chiefly more accurate scales and the milling of coins, the king introduced two new coins with a great future: the golden *louis*, of 22 carats, valued at 10 *livres*; and the silver louis, 26 grams of silver, valued at 3 *livres* (one *écu*).

The reforms of 1640–1 restored the true market equivalence of gold and silver, putting an end to the ridiculous flight of silver occasioned by the 1614 edict. But money remained short, thanks to the continuing war and the consequent poor relations with Spain. In order to facilitate the petty transactions of everyday economic life, the provincial Estates had since the later sixteenth century taken to minting copper coins, *billon* currency, which rusted black in use, and were known according to their value as *liards*, 'dozen *deniers*' or 'double *deniers*'. The King's Council, seeking quick profits, soon succumbed to the temptation of inflating the value of these coins, with the effect that, in some months or years, their usefulness in transaction was limited, and in the end they were devalued. Peasant riots sometimes broke out when they found their copper coin was not welcome, for example in 1643 and 1645. The most dramatic case was the revolt of the 'Sabotiers' of Sologne in 1658. But from the 1670s the monetary situation improved, and such outbursts were forgotten.

During the monetary disruption between 1630 and 1660, silver coin was hardly to be seen in the countryside. A notary or a village merchant would play the money-lender, providing the inevitable advances for paying the *taille* or purchasing animals. But a labourer or a servant would never see the colour of real money except at the expiry of a lease or the end of a term of service. Most of the time people got by thanks to self-sufficiency, eating their own bread and their own vegetables. Family agreements, bits of notarised paper and complex chains of compensation – the thousand and one forms of barter – made up the economic life of the peasantry. But this subterranean economy was of course almost

devoid of written record, and can only be guessed at through notarial documents and narrative sources.

Difficult and dangerous travel, agrarian self-sufficiency, craft
industry, monetary shortage and barter, such were the obscure
realities of economic life in early modern France. But the resources of the kingdom, although largely untapped by big
business, were nevertheless vast. The French were slowly discovering the extraordinary potential of their country. It is reckoned that
the population of France at the beginning of the seventeenth
century was between 18 and 20 million. Even if it was less, the
kingdom of Henri IV and Louis XIII was still by far the leading
European power, hardly shaken by the crisis of 1630, the demands
of a continental war and the trials of civil war. This is the true
secret of the glorious policies which were to lead France to a
position of European dominance under Louis XIV.

Chronology

Politics

13 April 1598	Edict of Nantes
13 May 1598	Treaty of Vervins
17 December 1600	Henri IV's marriage to Marie de Medici
17 January 1601	Treaty of Lyon
27 December 1601	Birth of the Dauphin, later Louis XIII
31 July 1602	Execution of Biron
April 1606	The Sedan expedition
14 May 1610	Assassination of Henri IV
17 October 1610	Coronation of Louis XIII
25 August 1612	Contracts for the Spanish marriages
June 1614	Summons of the Estates General
October 1614–February 1615	Sessions of the Estates General
June 1615	Condé withdraws from Court
25 November 1615	Louis XIII's marriage to Anne, at Bordeaux
3 May 1616	Peace of Loudun
1 September 1616	Arrest of Condé
24 April 1617	Murder of Concini
February–April 1619	First 'War between Mother and Son'
7 August 1620	Battle of Ponts-de-Cé
20 October 1630	Louis XIII's formal entry at Pau
December 1620	Rebellious assembly at La Rochelle
25 June 1621	Capture of Saint-Jean-d'Angély
10 November 1621	Raising of the siege of Montauban
16 April 1622	Battle of the Rié marshes
18 October 1622	Peace of Montpellier
April 1624	Richelieu admitted to the King's Council

August 1624	Richelieu becomes chief minister
November 1624	The Valtellina expedition
11 May 1625	Charles I of England marries Henrietta-Maria
18 September 1625	Naval defeat of the La Rochelle forces off Ré
12 October 1627	Commencement of the siege of La Rochelle
8 November 1627	English forces evacuate Ré
29 October 1629	Capitulation of La Rochelle
February 1629	French forces enter Piedmont
26 May 1629	Capture of Privas
28 June 1629	Edict of grace of Alès
18 July 1630	Fall of Mantua
10 November 1630	Day of the Dupes
March 1631	Treaty of Cherasco
May 1631	Treaty of Bärwald
31 May 1631	Manifesto of the Duke of Orléans
1 September 1632	Battle of Castelnaudary
Autumn 1633	Occupation of Lorraine
Spring 1634	General introduction of *intendants*
May 1635	Commencement of open war
May–June 1635	Urban revolt in Guyenne
15 August 1636	Fall of Corbie
1 June 1637	Rout of the Croquants at La Sauvetat
5 September 1638	Birth of the Dauphin, later Louis XIV
30 November 1639	Rout of the Nu-pieds at Avranches
9 August 1640	Capture of Arras
16 December 1640	Alliance with the Catalan rebels
9 July 1641	Death in battle of the Count of Soissons at La Marfée
9 September 1641	Capture of Perpignan
4 December 1642	Death of Richelieu
14 May 1643	Death of Louis XIII
19 May 1643	Condé's victory at Rocroi
July 1643	Revolt of the Croquants in Rouergue
September 1643	Cabal of the 'Importants'
March 1644	Edict of *toisé*
August 1644	Tax on the *aisés* (or well-off)
7 September 1645	*Lit de justice*
October 1646	Tariff edict
November 1647–April 1648	The Duke of Guise's expedition to Naples
15 January 1648	*Lit de justice*
29 April–9 July 1648	Assemblies in the Chambre Saint-Louis
17 May 1648	French victory at Zusmarshausen
18 July 1648	Royal proclamation recalling the *intendants*

20 August 1648	Condé's victory at Lens
26-27 August 1648	Barricades up in Paris
22 October 1648	Royal proclamation confirming the July proclamation
24 October 1648	Peace of Westphalia
5 January 1649	Court flees to Saint-Germain
11 March 1649	Peace of Rueil
18 January 1650	Arrest of Condé.
5 October 1650	Peace of Bordeaux
13 February 1651	Release of Condé
March 1651	Summons of the Estates General
7 September 1651	Louis XIV attains his majority
7 April 1652	Condé's victory at Bléneau
4 July 1652	Massacre at the Paris Hôtel de Ville
14 October 1652	Condé chooses exile
October 1652	Capitulation of Barcelona
21 October 1652	Louis XIV's return to Paris
31 July 1653	Capitulation of Bordeaux, the last Fronde stronghold
4 June 1654	Coronation of Louis XIV
Spring 1658	Revolt of the 'Sabotiers' of Sologne
14 June 1658	Battle of the Dunes
August–November 1659	Franco-Spanish talks at Fuentarrabia
7 November 1659	Treaty of the Pyrenees
9 June 1660	Louis XIV's marriage to Maria-Teresa at Saint-Jean-de-Luz
9 March 1661	Death of Mazarin
5 September 1661	Arrest of Fouquet

Intellectual and Artistic Life

1604	Completion of the Pont-Neuf
1605	Publication of *Don Quijote* by Cervantes
1607	Honoré d'Urfé writes *L'astrée*
1612	Completion of the Place Royale (later the Place des Vosges)
1620	Francis Bacon's *Novum Organum*
1622	Marie de Medici commissions Rubens to decorate the Palais du Luxembourg
1623	Sorel publishes the *Histoire comique de Francion*

1627	Completion of the Place Ducale at Charleville Simon Vouet is recalled from Rome to Paris by Louis XIII
1632	Callot engraves *Les grandes* and *Les petites misères de la guerre*
February 1635	Foundation of the Académie française
November 1636	Corneille completes *Le Cid*
1637	Descartes publishes the *Discours de la méthode*
1642	Completion of the chapel of the Sorbonne
1643	Molière founds the Illustre-Théâtre
1647	First opera performed in Paris (Luigi Rossi's *Orfeo*)
1648	Foundation of the Académie de peinture
1651	Scarron publishes *Le roman comique*
1652	Completion of the Church of Val-de-Grâce
January 1656	Pascal begins publishing the *Lettres provinciales*
1658	Construction and decoration of the Château de Vaux Privileges granted to the King's Musicians
1659	Molière produces *Les précieuses ridicules*
1660	Boileau's first satire
1666	Furet publishes *Le roman bourgeois*

Religion

1604	Establishment of the Discalced Carmelites in France
1609	François de Sales publishes *L'introduction à la vie dévote*
1611	Establishment of the French Oratory
1612	Establishment of the Ursulines in France
1620	The miracle of Notre-Dame-d'Auray
1625	Foundation of the Priests of the Mission (or Lazarists)
1627	The papal bull *Universa* reduces the number of feast days
1633	Foundation of the Daughters of Charity
1638	Louis XIII's vow (10 January)
1642	Foundation of the Congregation of Saint-Sulpice
1653	Papal warning against Jansenist doctrine
1660	Death of Vincent de Paul

Economy and Society

1599	Sully appointed Grand Voyer de France
1600	Edict conerning the *taille*
	Olivier de Serres publishes his *Théâtre d'agriculture*
December 1604	Introduction of the *paulette*
December 1614	Edict revaluing gold against silver
December 1617–January 1618	Assembly of Notables at Rouen
1620	Richelieu appointed Grand Maître de la Navigation
November 1616–January 1627	Assembly of Notables at Paris
15 February 1629	*Lit de justice* imposing the 'code Michaud'
Spring 1630	Peak of the plague epidemic (1626–1632)
November 1633	Sumptuary edict regulating dress
February 1634	New *taille* code
November 1638	Establishment of the charity for bringing up orphans
March 1640–September 1641	Monetary reform
1642	Opening of the Briare canal
1646	Jean Éon publishes *Le commerce honorable*
April 1656	Opening of the General Hospital of Paris
1658	Fouquet's improvements to the Atlantic ports

Bibliography

Aumale, Henri d', *Histoire des princes de Condé* (Paris, 1863–96) vols 3–5.
Avenel, Georges d', *Richelieu et la monarchie absolue* (4 vols, Paris, 1895).
Aristide, Isabelle, *Le fortune de Sully* (Paris, 1989).
Babelon, Jean-Pierre, *Henri IV* (Paris, 1982).
Barbiche, Bernard, *Sully* (Paris, 1978).
Batiffol, Louis, *Autour de Richelieu: sa fortune, ses gardes et mousquetaires, la Sorbonne, le château de Richelieu* (Paris, 1937).
Batiffol, Louis, *La Duchesse de Chevreuse: une vie d'aventures et d'intrigues sous Louis XIII* (Paris, 1913).
Batiffol, Louis, *La vie intime d'une reine de France au XVII siècle: Marie de Médicis, 1600–1617* (2 vols, Paris, 1906).
Baxter, Douglas Clark, *Servants of the Sword: French Intendants of the Army, 1630–1670* (Urbana, Ill., 1976).
Bayard, François, *Le monde des financiers au XVII siècle* (Paris, 1988).
Beik, William H., *Absolutism and Society in Seventeenth-century France: State Power and Provincial Aristocracy in Languedoc* (Cambridge, 1985).
Bercé, Yves-Marie, *Croquants et Nu-pieds* (Paris, 1974).
Bercé, Yves-Marie, *Fête et révolte: des mentalités populaires du XVI au XVII siècle* (Paris, 1976).
Bercé, Yves-Marie, *Histoire des Croquants: étude des soulèvements populaires au XVII siècle dans le sud-ouest de la France* (2 vols, Genève, 1974; abridged edn Paris, 1986).
Bérenger, Jean, *Turenne* (Paris, 1987).
Bergin, Joseph, *Cardinal Richelieu: Power and the Pursuit of Wealth* (New Haven, Conn., 1985).
Bergin, Joseph, *Cardinal de La Rochefoucauld: Leadership and Reform in the French Church* (London, 1987).
Bergin, Joseph, *The Rise of Richelieu* (London, 1991).
Bertière, Simon, *Le vie du Cardinal de Retz* (Paris, 1990)

Billacois, François, *Le duel dans la société française des XVI–XVII siècles: essai de psychosociologie historique* (Paris, 1986).

Biraben, J.-N., *Les hommes et la peste en France* (2 vols, Paris, 1975).

Bluche, François, *Louis XIV* (Paris, 1986).

Bluche, François, *Dictionnaire du Grand Siècle* (Paris, 1990).

Bonney, Richard, *L'absolutisme* (Paris, 1990).

Bonney, Richard, *Political Change in France under Richelieu and Mazarin, 1624–1661* (Oxford, 1978).

Bonney, Richard, *The King's Debts: Finance and Politics in France, 1589–1661* (Oxford, 1981).

Bosher, J. F., 'Chambres de justice in French monarchy', in *French Government and Society, 1500–1850: Essays in Memory of Alfred Cobban*, ed. J. F. Bosher (London 1973) pp. 19–40.

Bourgeon, Jean-Louis, *Les Colbert avant Colbert* (Paris, 1973).

Buisseret, David, *Henri IV* (London, 1984).

Carmona, Michel, *La France de Richelieu* (Paris, 1984).

Carmona, Michel, *Marie de Médicis* (Paris, 1981).

Carmona, Michel, *Richelieu: l'ambition et le pouvoir* (Paris, 1983).

Carrier, Hubert, *Le presse et la Fronde, 1648–1653: les mazarinades* (2 vols, Genève, 1989).

Chartier, Roger *et al.*, *L'éducation en France du XVI au XVII siècle* (Paris, 1976).

Chartier, Roger and Richet, Denis, *Représentations et vouloirs politiques autour des États généraux de 1614* (Paris, 1982).

Chevallier, Pierre, *Louis XIII* (Paris, 1979).

Chevallier, Pierre, *Les régicides* (Paris, 1989).

Clarke, Jack Alden, *Huguenot Warrior: The Life and Times of Henry de Rohan, 1579-1638* (La Haye, 1966).

Collins, James B., *Direct Taxation in Early Seventeenth-century France* (Berkeley, Calif., 1988).

Constant, Jean-Marie, *Les conjurateurs: le premier libéralisme politique sous Richelieu* (Paris, 1987).

Dessert, Daniel, *Argent, pouvoir et société au Grand Siècle* (Paris, 1984).

Dessert, Daniel, *Fouquet* (Paris, 1987.)

Dethan, Georges, *Gaston d'Orléans: conspirateur et prince charmant* (Paris, 1959).

Dethan, Georges, *Mazarin: un homme de la paix à l'âge baroque, 1602–1661* (Paris, 1981).

Deyon, Pierre, *Amiens, capitale provinciale: étude sur la société urbaine au XVII siècle* (repr. Amiens, 1986).

Dix-septième siècle, no. 185 (1984), 'retour à la Fronde'.

Dodin, A., *La légende et l'histoire: de Monsieur Depaul à Saint Vincent de Paul* (Paris, 1985).

Doolin, Paul R., *The Fronde* (Cambridge, Mass., 1935).

Duccini, Hélène, *Concini* (Paris, 1991).

Dulong, Claude, *Anne d'Autriche, mère de Louis XIV* (Paris, 1980).

Dulong, Claude, *La fortune de Mazarin* (Paris, 1991).

Dulong, Claude, *Le mariage du Roi-Soleil* (Paris, 1986).

Dupaquier, Jacques, *La population française des XVII et XVIII siècles* (Paris, 1979).

Elliott, John H., *Richelieu and Olivares* (Cambridge, 1984).

Elliott, John H., *The Count-Duke of Olivares: The Statesman in an Age of Decline* (New Haven, Conn., 1986).

Elliott, John H., *The Revolt of the Catalans* (Cambridge, 1963).

L'État baroque, 1610–1652 (Paris, 1985).

Foisil, Madeleine, *La révolte des Nu-pieds* (Paris, 1970).

La Fronde en questions (Marseille, 1989).

Fumaroli, Marc, *Rhétorique et dramaturgie cornéliennes* (Genève, 1990).

Garrisson, Janine, *Henry IV* (Paris, 1984).

Giesey, Ralph E., *The Juristic Basis of Dynastic Right to the French Throne* (Philadelphia, Penn., 1961)

Giesey, Ralph E., *The Royal Funeral Ceremony in Renaissance France* (Genève, 1960).

Golden, Richard, *The Godly Rebellion: Parisian curés and the religious Fronde, 1652–1662* (Chapel Hill, NC, 1981).

Goubert, Pierre, *Beauvais et le Beauvaisis de 1600 à 1730* (Paris, 1983).

Goubert, Pierre, *Les français et l'Ancien Régime* (Paris, 1984).

Goubert, Pierre, *Mazarin* (Paris, 1990).

Gutton, Jean-Pierre, *La société et les pauvres: l'exemple de la généralité de Lyon, 1534–1789* (Lyon, 1971).

Gutton, Jean-Pierre, *La sociabilité villageoise dans l'ancienne France: solidarités et voisinages du XV au XVIII siècle* (Paris, 1979).

Hanley, Sarah, *The Lit de Justice of the Kings of France: Constitutional Ideology in Legend, Ritual and Discourse* (Princeton, NJ, 1983).

Harding, Robert R., *Anatomy of a Power Elite: The Provincial Governors in Early Modern France* (New Haven, Conn., 1978).

Hayden, J. Michael, *France and the Estates General of 1614* (Cambridge, Mass., 1974).

Héroard, Jean, *Journal*, ed. M. Foisil (2 vols, Paris, 1990).

Hickey, David, *The Coming of French Absolutism: The Struggle for Tax Reform in the Province of Dauphiné, 1540–1640* (Toronto, 1986).

Hildesheimer, Françoise, *Richelieu: une certaine idée de l'État* (Paris, 1985).

Jackson, Richard, *Vivat rex: histoire des sacres et couronnements en France* (Strasbourg, 1984).

Jacquart, Jean, *La crise rurale en Ile-de-France, 1550–1670* (Paris, 1974).

Jansen, Paule, *Le Cardinal Mazarin et le mouvement janséniste français* (Paris, 1967).

Jouanna, Arlette, *Le devoir de révolte: la noblesse française et la gestation de l'État moderne, 1559–1660* (Paris, 1989).

Kermina, Françoise, *Marie de Médicis: reine, régente et rebelle* (Paris, 1979).

Kettering, Sharon, *Judicial Politics and Urban Revolt in Seventeenth-century France: the Parlement of Aix, 1625–1659* (Princeton, NJ, 1978).

Kettering, Sharon, *Patrons, Brokers, and Clients in Seventeenth-century France* (Oxford, 1986).

Kleinman, Ruth, *Anne of Austria: Queen of France* (Columbus, Ohio, 1985).

Knecht, Robert, *Richelieu* (London, 1991).

Kossmann, Ernst H., *La Fronde* (Leyde, 1954).

Labatut, Jean-Pierre, *Les ducs et pairs de France au XVII siècle* (Paris, 1972).

Lebrun, François, *Les hommes et la mort en Anjou aux XVII et XVIII siècles* (Paris, 1975).

Ligou, D., *Le protestantisme en France de 1598 à 1715* (Paris, 1968).

Livet, Georges, *La Guerre de Trente Ans* (Paris, 1963).

Lottin, Alain, *Lille, citadelle de la Contre-Réforme, 1598–1660* (Lille, 1984).

Major, J. Russell, *Representative Government in Early Modern France* (New Haven, Conn., 1980).

Martin, Henri-Jean, *Livre, pouvoirs et société à Paris au XVII siècle, 1598–1701* (2 vols, Genève, 1969).

Mastellone, Salvatore, *La reggenza di Maria de' Medici* (Firenze, 1962).

Méthivier, Albert, *La Fronde* (Paris, 1984).

Méthivier, Albert, *Le siècle de Louis XIII* (Paris, 1964).

Meyer, Jean, *Colbert* (Paris, 1981).

Meyer, Jean, *La naissance de Louis XIV* (Bruxelles, 1989).

Mongrédien, Georges, *10 novembre 1630: la journée des dupes* (Paris, 1961).

Mongrédien, Georges, *Léonora Galigaï: un procès de sorcellerie sous Louis XIII* (Paris, 1968).

Moote, Lloyd, *The Revolt of the Judges: the Parlement of Paris and the Fronde* (Princeton, NJ, 1971).

Moote, Lloyd, *Louis XIII, the Just* (London, 1989).

Morineau, Michel, *Incroyables gazettes et fabuleux métaux* (Paris, 1985)

Mousnier, Roland, *L'assassinat d'Henri IV* (Paris, 1964).

Mousnier, Roland, *Les institutions de la France sous la monarchie absolue* (2 vols, Paris, 1980).

Mousnier, Roland, *Paris capitale au temps de Richelieu et Mazarin* (Paris, 1978).

Mousnier, Roland, *La plume, la faucille et le marteau* (Paris, 1970).

Mousnier, Roland, *La vénalité des offices sous Henri IV et Louis XIII* (Rouen, 1945; Paris, 1971).

Muchembled, Robert, *L'invention de l'homme moderne* (Paris, 1988).

Murat, Inès, *Colbert* (Paris, 1980).

Pagès, Georges, 'Autour du "grand orage": Richelieu et Marillac, deux politiques', *Révue historique*, vol. 179 (1937) 63–97.

Parker, David, *La Rochelle and the French Monarchy: Conflict and Order in Seventeenth-century France* (London, 1980).

Parker, David, *The Making of French Absolutism* (London, 1983).

Parker, Geoffrey, *The Army of Flanders and the Spanish Road, 1567-1659* (Cambridge, 1972).

Parker, Geoffrey, *The Thirty Years War* (London, 1984).

Parker, Geoffrey, and Smith, Leslie (eds), *The General Crisis of the Seventeenth Century* (London, 1978).

Pérouse de Montclos, Jean-Marie, *Histoire de l'architecture française* (Paris, 1989).

Petit, Jeanne, *L'assemblée des notables de 1626-1627* (Paris, 1936).

Picot, Georges, *Cardin Le Bret (1558-1655) et la doctrine de la souveraineté* (Nancy, 1948).

Pillorget, René, *Les mouvements insurrectionnels de Provence entre 1596 et 1715* (Paris, 1975).

Pintard, René, *Le libertinage érudit dans la pr.emière moitié du XVII siècle* (Paris, 1988).

Porchnev, Boris, *Les soulèvements populaires en France de 1623 à 1648* (Paris, 1963).

Ranum, Orest, *Les créatures de Richelieu* (Paris, 1966).

Ranum, Orest, *The Fronde: A French Revolution, 1648-1652* (New York and London, 1993).

Richet, Denis, *La France moderne: l'esprit des institutions* (Paris, 1973).

Salmon, John H. M., *Renaissance and Revolt: Essays in the Intellectual and Social History of Early Modern France* (Cambridge, 1987).

Schalk, Ellery, *From Valor to Pedigree: Ideas of Nobility in France in the Sixteenth and Seventeenth Centuries* (Princeton, NJ, 1986).

Solnon, Jean-François, *La cour de France* (Paris, 1987).

Tallon, Alain, *La Compagnie du Saint-Sacrement* (Paris, 1990).

Tapié, Victor-Lucien, *Baroque et Classicisme* (Paris, 1957; repr. 1980).

Tapié, Victor-Lucien, *La France de Louis XIII et de Richelieu* (Paris, 1980).

Tapié, Victor-Lucien, *La Guerre de Trente Ans* (Paris, 1965; repr. 1989).

Taveneaux, René, *Le catholicisme dans la France classique, 1610-1715* (2 vols, Paris, 1980).

Thuau, Étienne, *Raisons d'État et pensée politique à l'époque de Richelieu* (Paris, 1966).

Thuillier, Jacques, *Nicolas Poussin* (Paris, 1988).

Vaissière, Pierre de, *Un grand procès sous Richelieu: l'affaire du maréchal de Marillac, 1630-1632* (Paris, 1924).

Vassal-Reig, Charles, *La prise de Perpignan* (Paris, 1939).

Vincent, Jean-Antoine, *Relations militaires des années 1634 et 1635*, ed. M. Huisman, J. Dhondt and L. Van Meerbeck (Bruxelles, 1958).

Index